# ARES&APHRODITE

*love wars*

AN ONI PRESS PUBLICATION

# ARES&AP

# HRODITE

*written by* **Jamie S. Rich**
*illustrated & colored by* **Megan Levens**

*lettered by* **Crank!**

*edited by* **Jill Beaton & Robin Herrera**
*designed by* **Hilary Thompson**

*published by* Oni Press, Inc.
*publisher* Joe Nozemack
*editor in chief* James Lucas Jones
*v.p. of business development* Tim Wiesch
*director of sales* Cheyenne Allott
*editor* Charlie Chu
*associate editor* Robin Herrera
*production manager* Troy Look
*graphic designer* Hilary Thompson
*production assistant* Jared Jones
*administrative assistant* Ari Yarwood
*inventory coordinator* Brad Rooks
*office assistant* Jung Lee

1305 SE Martin Luther King Jr. Blvd.
Suite A
Portland, OR 97214
U.S.A.

facebook.com/onipress
twitter.com/onipress
onipress.tumblr.com
onipress.com

confessions123.com
artofmeganlevens.carbonmade.com/

First Edition: April 2015
ISBN 978-1-62010-208-4
eISBN 978-1-62010-209-1

Printed in China

Library of Congress Control Number: 2014949474

1 2 3 4 5 6 7 8 9 10

# CHAPTER ONE

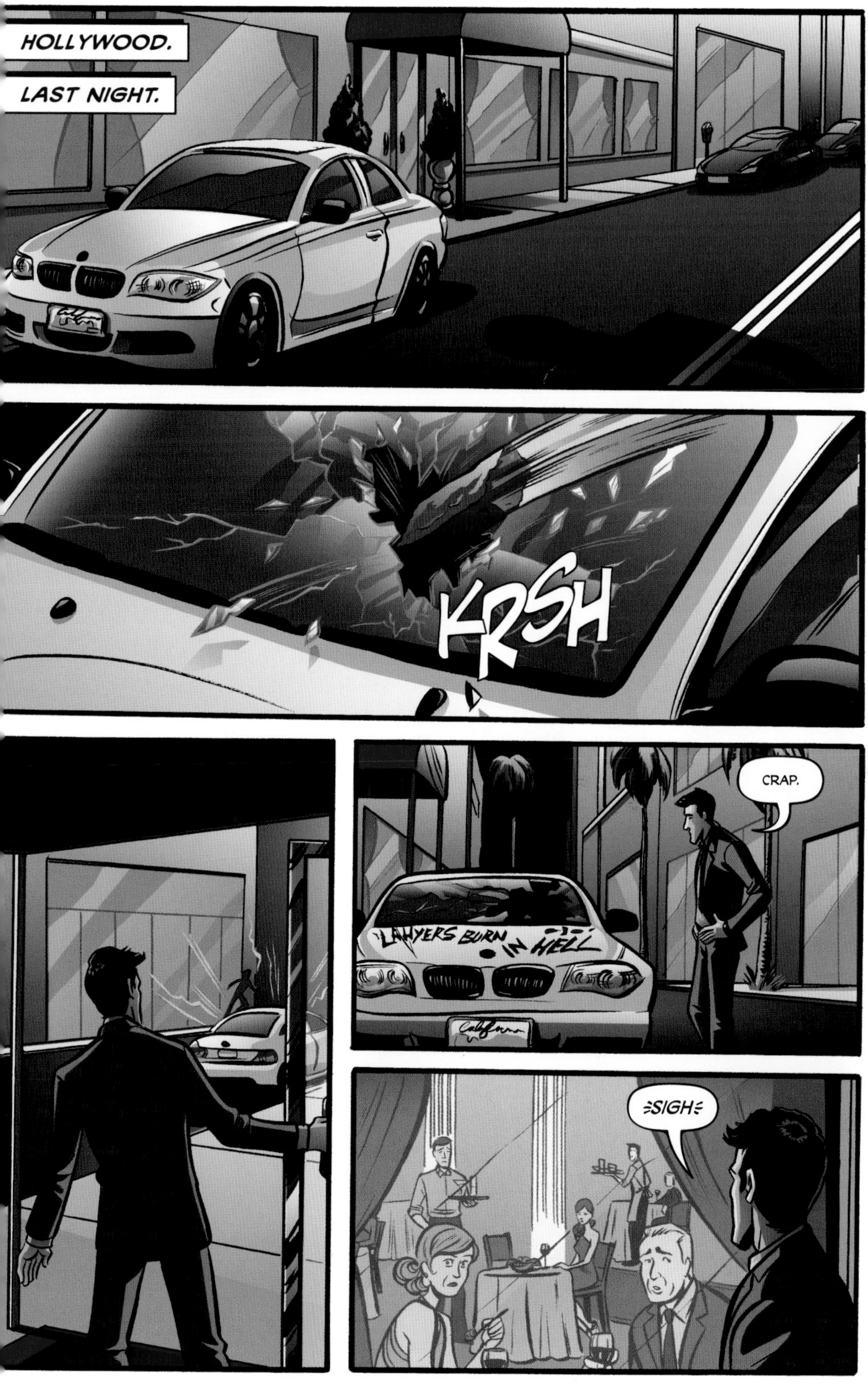

HOLLYWOOD.
LAST NIGHT.
KRSH
LAWYERS BURN IN HELL
CRAP.
SIGH

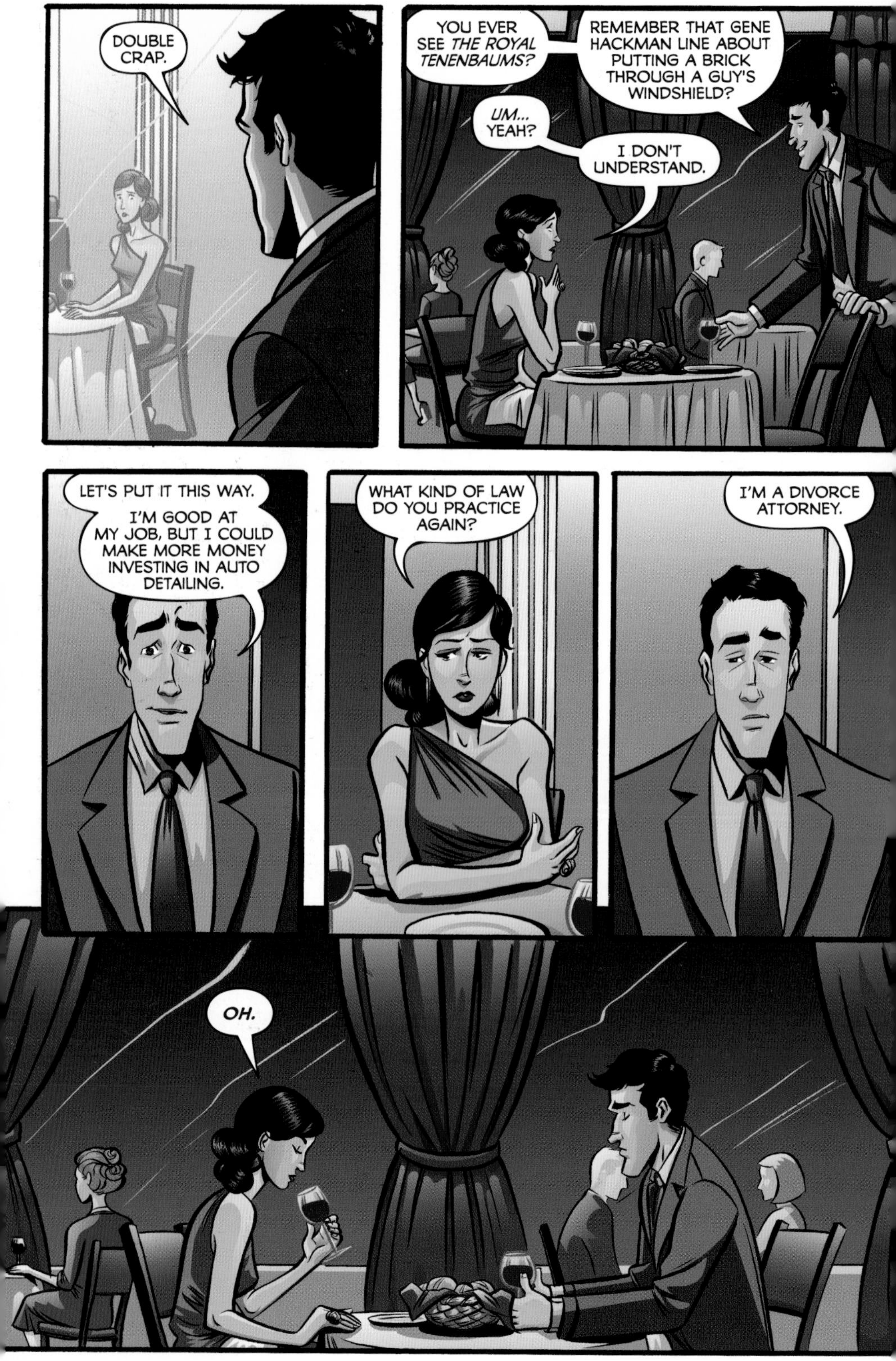
DOUBLE CRAP.
YOU EVER SEE *THE ROYAL TENENBAUMS?*
*UM...* YEAH?
REMEMBER THAT GENE HACKMAN LINE ABOUT PUTTING A BRICK THROUGH A GUY'S WINDSHIELD?
I DON'T UNDERSTAND.
LET'S PUT IT THIS WAY.
I'M GOOD AT MY JOB, BUT I COULD MAKE MORE MONEY INVESTING IN AUTO DETAILING.
WHAT KIND OF LAW DO YOU PRACTICE AGAIN?
I'M A DIVORCE ATTORNEY.
*OH.*

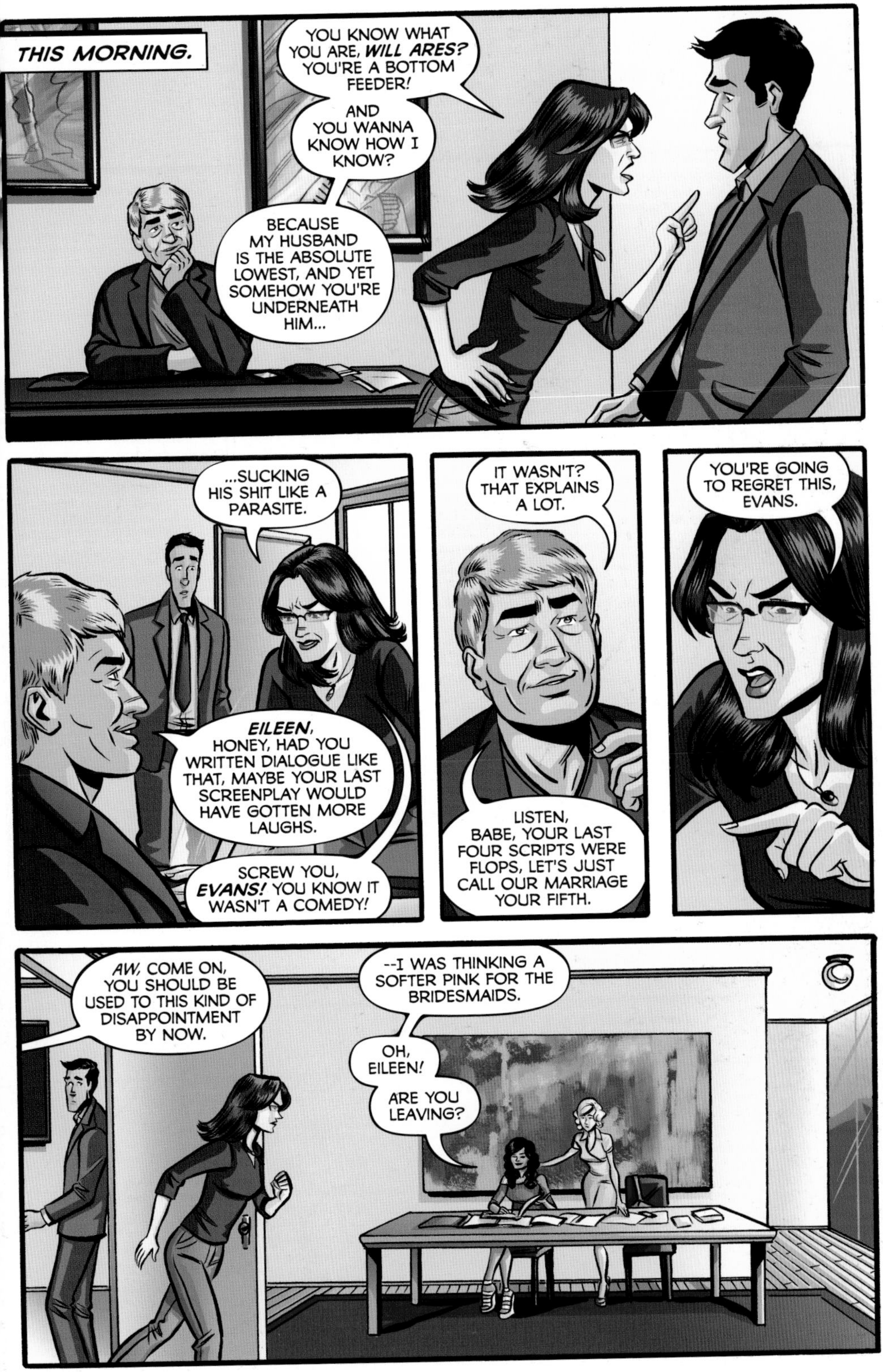
THIS MORNING.
YOU KNOW WHAT YOU ARE, WILL ARES? YOU'RE A BOTTOM FEEDER!
AND YOU WANNA KNOW HOW I KNOW?
BECAUSE MY HUSBAND IS THE ABSOLUTE LOWEST, AND YET SOMEHOW YOU'RE UNDERNEATH HIM...
...SUCKING HIS SHIT LIKE A PARASITE.
EILEEN, HONEY, HAD YOU WRITTEN DIALOGUE LIKE THAT, MAYBE YOUR LAST SCREENPLAY WOULD HAVE GOTTEN MORE LAUGHS.
SCREW YOU, EVANS! YOU KNOW IT WASN'T A COMEDY!
IT WASN'T? THAT EXPLAINS A LOT.
LISTEN, BABE, YOUR LAST FOUR SCRIPTS WERE FLOPS, LET'S JUST CALL OUR MARRIAGE YOUR FIFTH.
YOU'RE GOING TO REGRET THIS, EVANS.
AW, COME ON, YOU SHOULD BE USED TO THIS KIND OF DISAPPOINTMENT BY NOW.
--I WAS THINKING A SOFTER PINK FOR THE BRIDESMAIDS.
OH, EILEEN!
ARE YOU LEAVING?

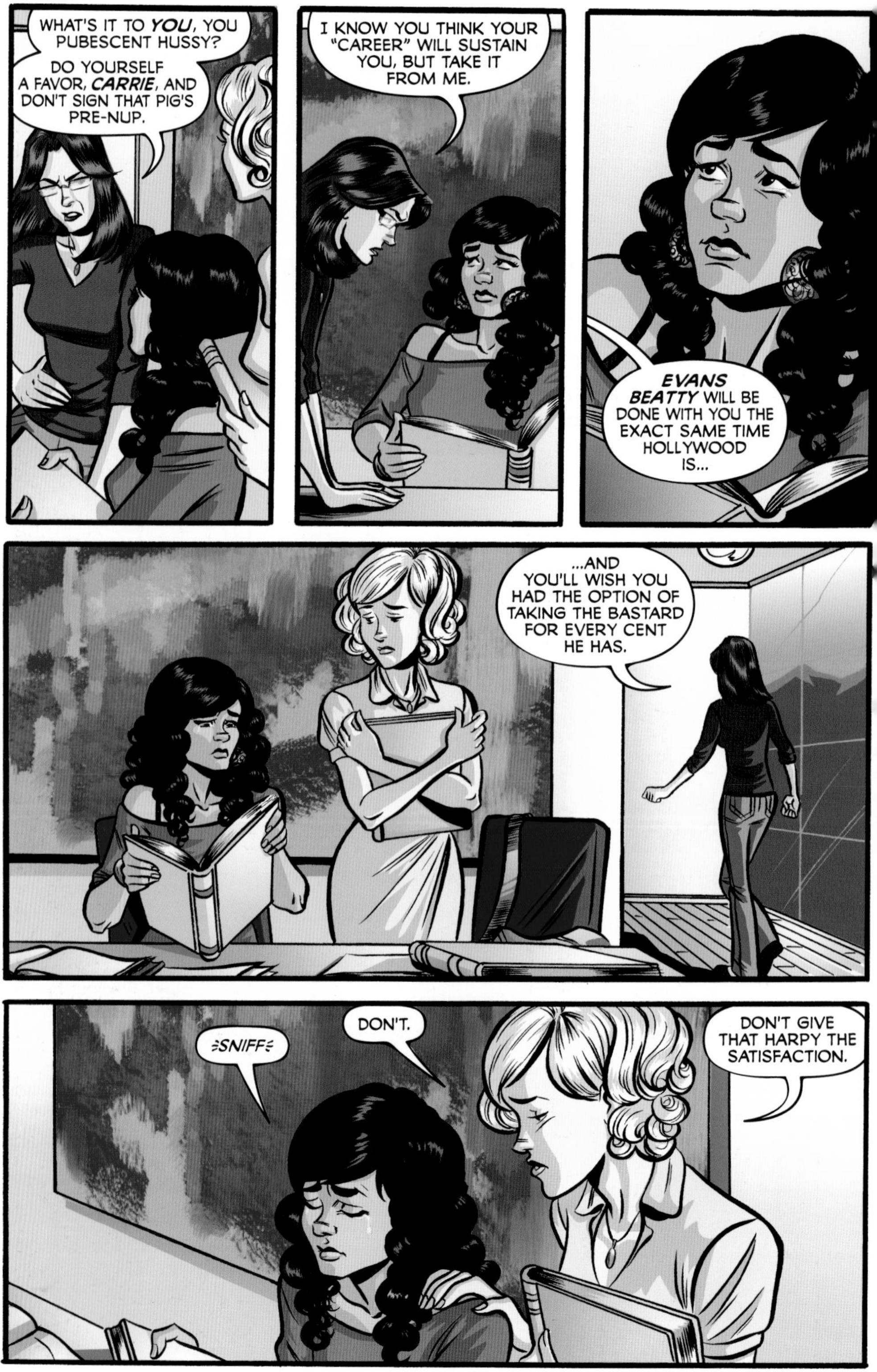

WHAT'S IT TO *YOU*, YOU PUBESCENT HUSSY?
DO YOURSELF A FAVOR, *CARRIE*, AND DON'T SIGN THAT PIG'S PRE-NUP.
I KNOW YOU THINK YOUR "CAREER" WILL SUSTAIN YOU, BUT TAKE IT FROM ME.
*EVANS BEATTY* WILL BE DONE WITH YOU THE EXACT SAME TIME HOLLYWOOD IS...
...AND YOU'LL WISH YOU HAD THE OPTION OF TAKING THE BASTARD FOR EVERY CENT HE HAS.
*SNIFF*
DON'T.
DON'T GIVE THAT HARPY THE SATISFACTION.

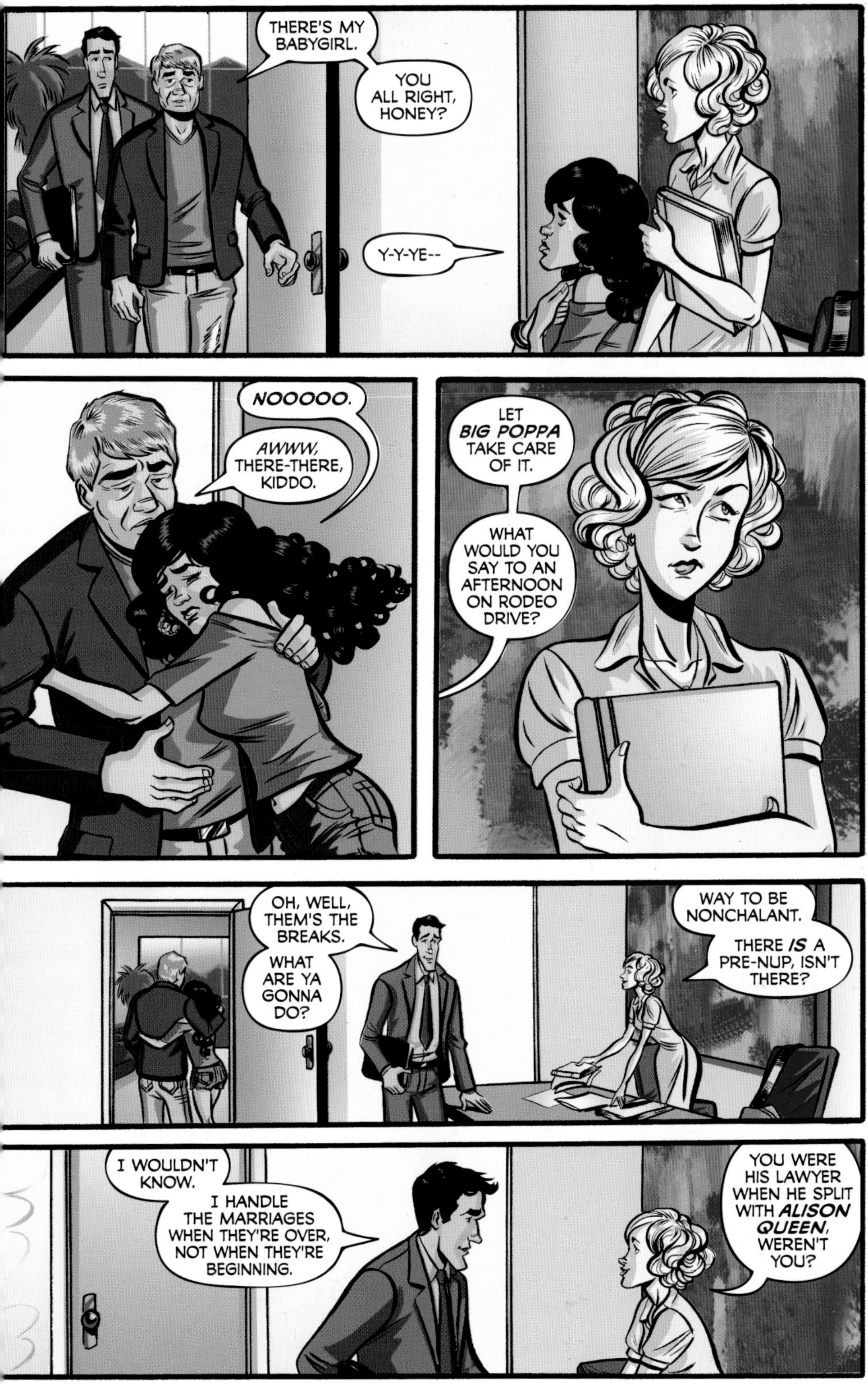
THERE'S MY BABYGIRL.
YOU ALL RIGHT, HONEY?
Y-Y-YE--
NOOOOO.
AWWW, THERE-THERE, KIDDO.
LET BIG POPPA TAKE CARE OF IT.
WHAT WOULD YOU SAY TO AN AFTERNOON ON RODEO DRIVE?
OH, WELL, THEM'S THE BREAKS.
WHAT ARE YA GONNA DO?
WAY TO BE NONCHALANT.
THERE IS A PRE-NUP, ISN'T THERE?
I WOULDN'T KNOW.
I HANDLE THE MARRIAGES WHEN THEY'RE OVER, NOT WHEN THEY'RE BEGINNING.
YOU WERE HIS LAWYER WHEN HE SPLIT WITH ALISON QUEEN, WEREN'T YOU?

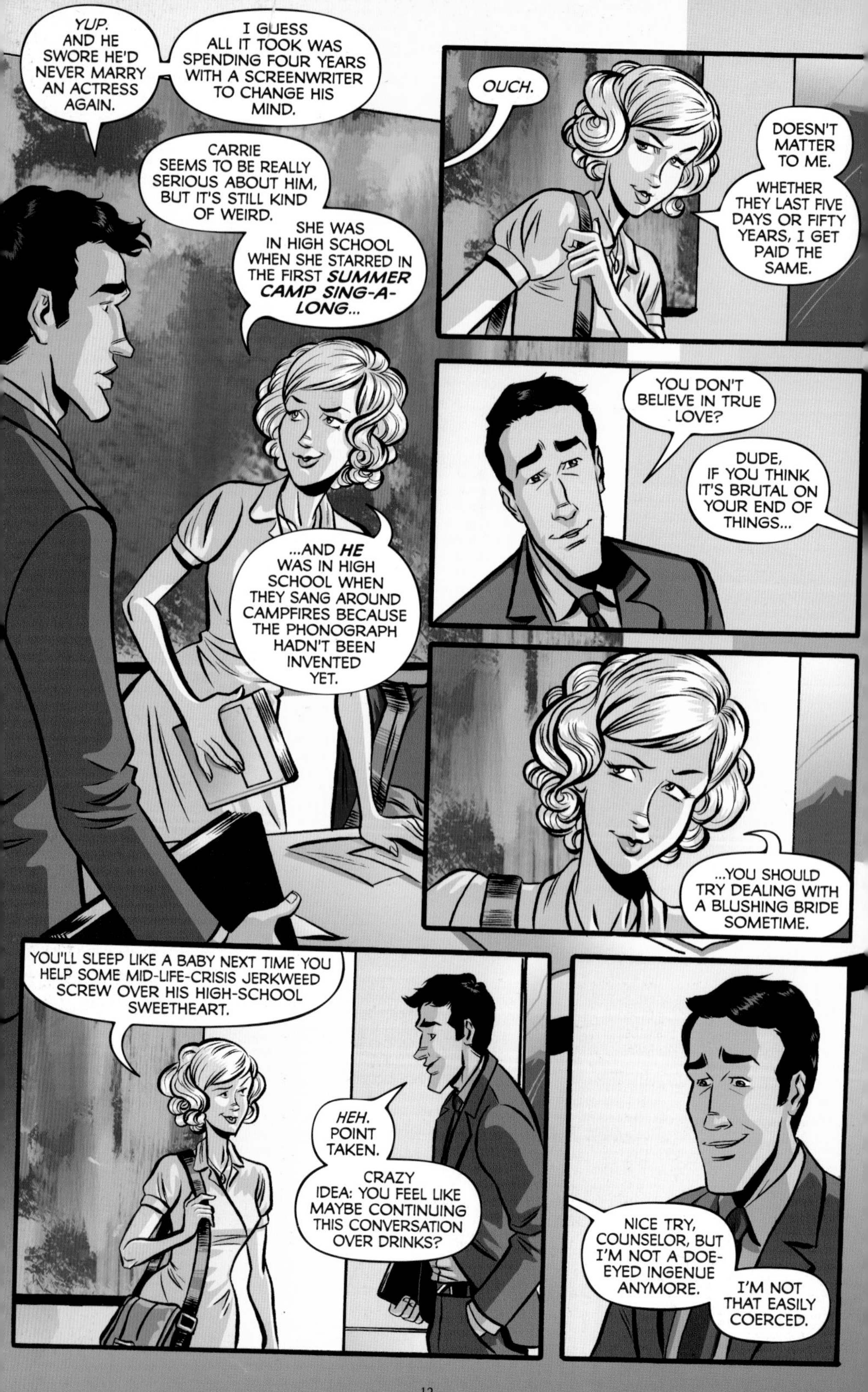
YUP. AND HE SWORE HE'D NEVER MARRY AN ACTRESS AGAIN.
I GUESS ALL IT TOOK WAS SPENDING FOUR YEARS WITH A SCREENWRITER TO CHANGE HIS MIND.
CARRIE SEEMS TO BE REALLY SERIOUS ABOUT HIM, BUT IT'S STILL KIND OF WEIRD.
SHE WAS IN HIGH SCHOOL WHEN SHE STARRED IN THE FIRST SUMMER CAMP SING-A-LONG...
...AND HE WAS IN HIGH SCHOOL WHEN THEY SANG AROUND CAMPFIRES BECAUSE THE PHONOGRAPH HADN'T BEEN INVENTED YET.
OUCH.
DOESN'T MATTER TO ME.
WHETHER THEY LAST FIVE DAYS OR FIFTY YEARS, I GET PAID THE SAME.
YOU DON'T BELIEVE IN TRUE LOVE?
DUDE, IF YOU THINK IT'S BRUTAL ON YOUR END OF THINGS...
...YOU SHOULD TRY DEALING WITH A BLUSHING BRIDE SOMETIME.
YOU'LL SLEEP LIKE A BABY NEXT TIME YOU HELP SOME MID-LIFE-CRISIS JERKWEED SCREW OVER HIS HIGH-SCHOOL SWEETHEART.
HEH. POINT TAKEN.
CRAZY IDEA: YOU FEEL LIKE MAYBE CONTINUING THIS CONVERSATION OVER DRINKS?
NICE TRY, COUNSELOR, BUT I'M NOT A DOE-EYED INGENUE ANYMORE.
I'M NOT THAT EASILY COERCED.

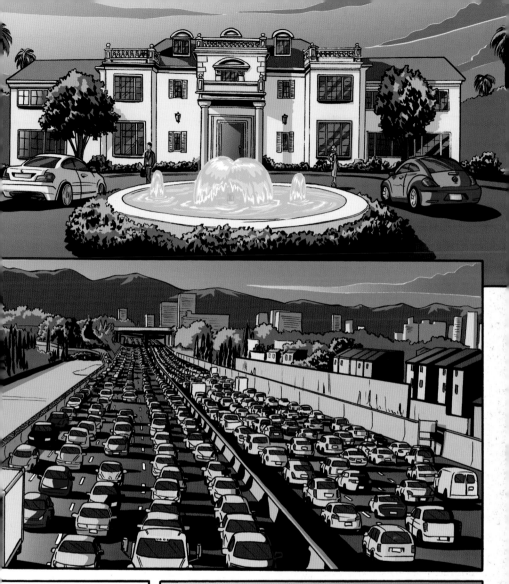

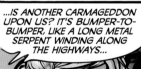

...IS ANOTHER CARMAGEDDON UPON US? IT'S BUMPER-TO-BUMPER, LIKE A LONG METAL SERPENT WINDING ALONG THE HIGHWAYS...
Goddess Of Love
Nuptials
WEDDINGS

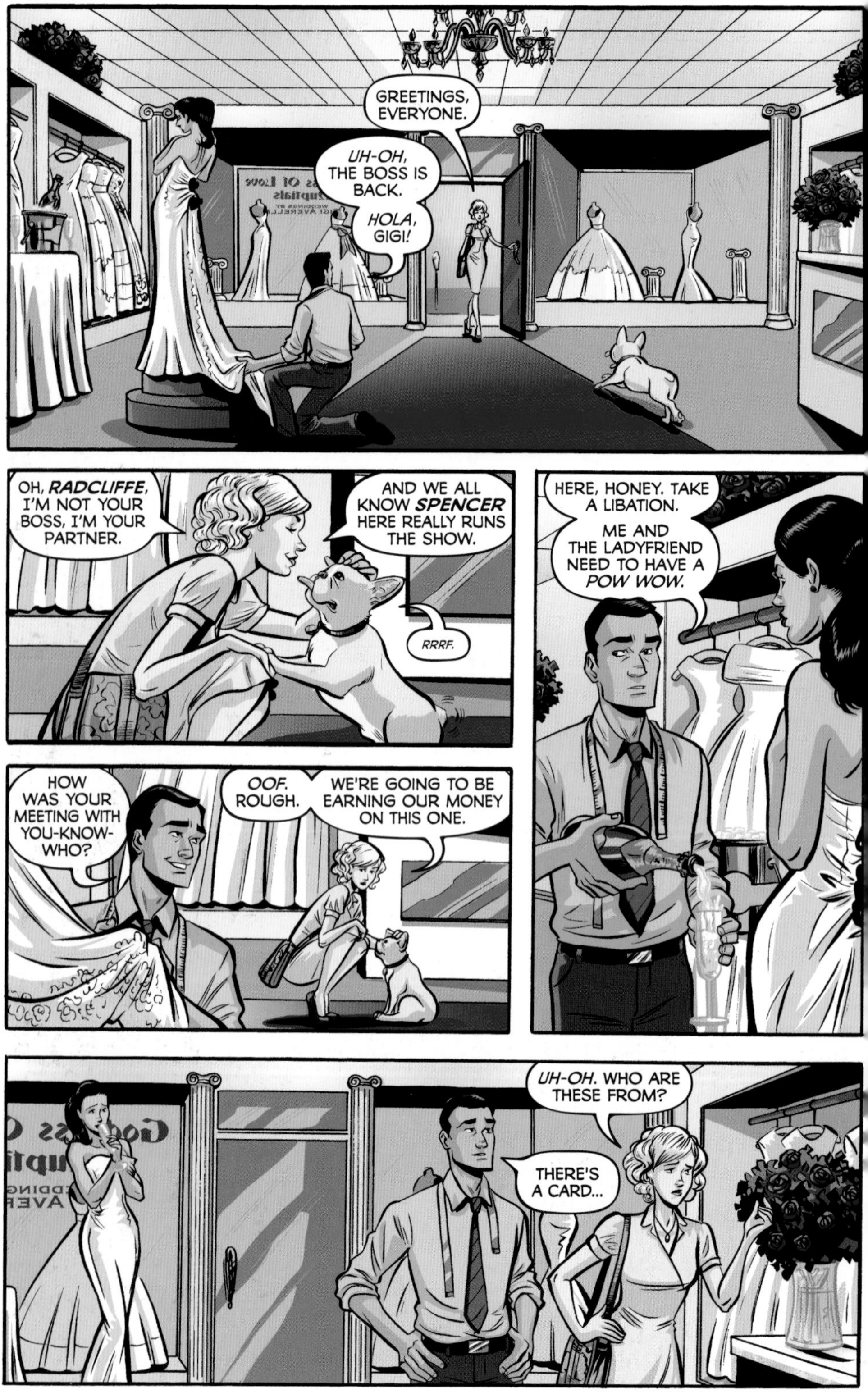
GREETINGS, EVERYONE.
UH-OH, THE BOSS IS BACK.
HOLA, GIGI!
OH, RADCLIFFE, I'M NOT YOUR BOSS, I'M YOUR PARTNER.
AND WE ALL KNOW SPENCER HERE REALLY RUNS THE SHOW.
RRRF.
HOW WAS YOUR MEETING WITH YOU-KNOW-WHO?
OOF. ROUGH.
WE'RE GOING TO BE EARNING OUR MONEY ON THIS ONE.
HERE, HONEY. TAKE A LIBATION.
ME AND THE LADYFRIEND NEED TO HAVE A POW WOW.
UH-OH. WHO ARE THESE FROM?
THERE'S A CARD...

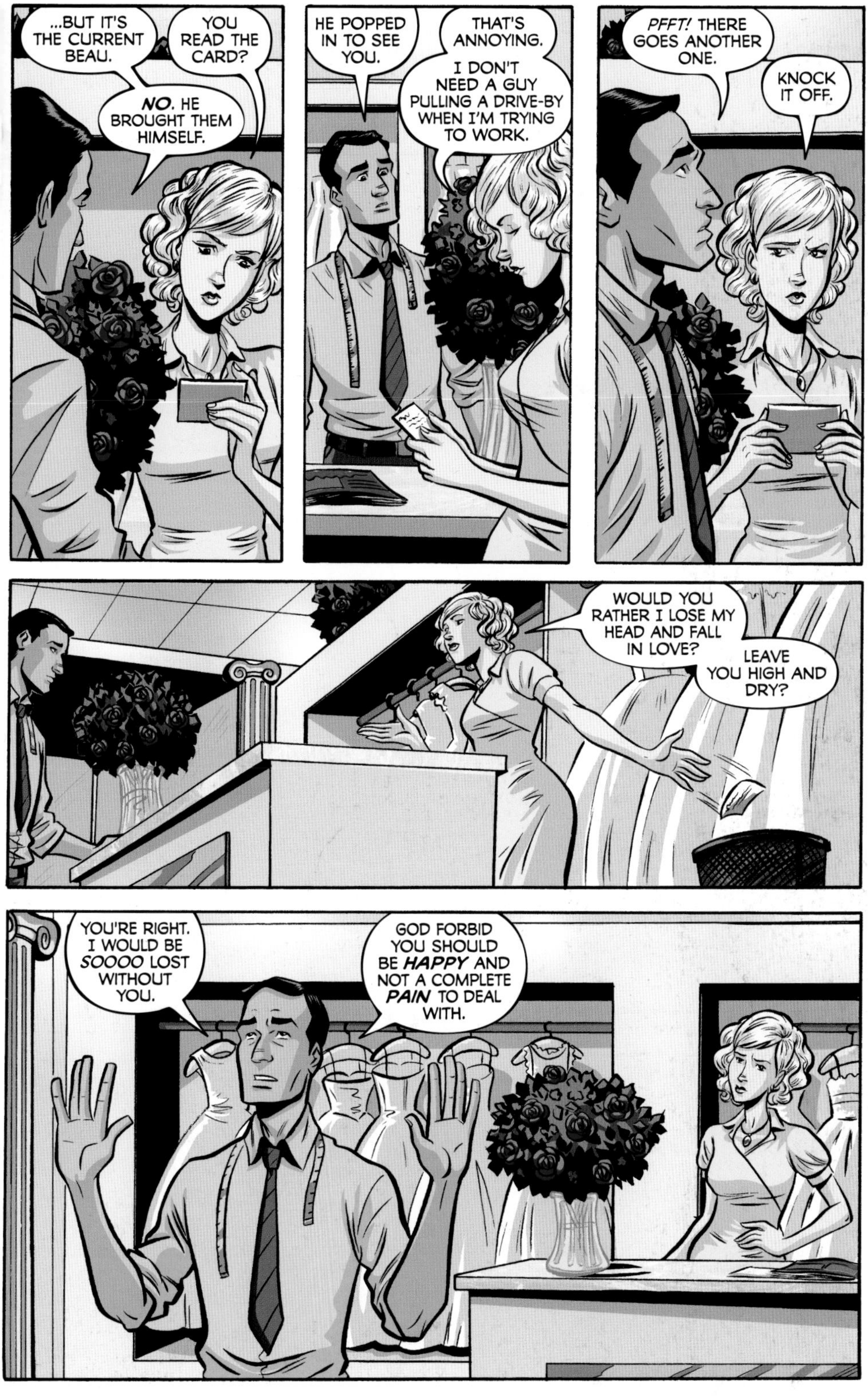

...BUT IT'S THE CURRENT BEAU.
YOU READ THE CARD?
NO. HE BROUGHT THEM HIMSELF.
HE POPPED IN TO SEE YOU.
THAT'S ANNOYING.
I DON'T NEED A GUY PULLING A DRIVE-BY WHEN I'M TRYING TO WORK.
PFFT! THERE GOES ANOTHER ONE.
KNOCK IT OFF.
WOULD YOU RATHER I LOSE MY HEAD AND FALL IN LOVE?
LEAVE YOU HIGH AND DRY?
YOU'RE RIGHT. I WOULD BE SOOOO LOST WITHOUT YOU.
GOD FORBID YOU SHOULD BE HAPPY AND NOT A COMPLETE PAIN TO DEAL WITH.

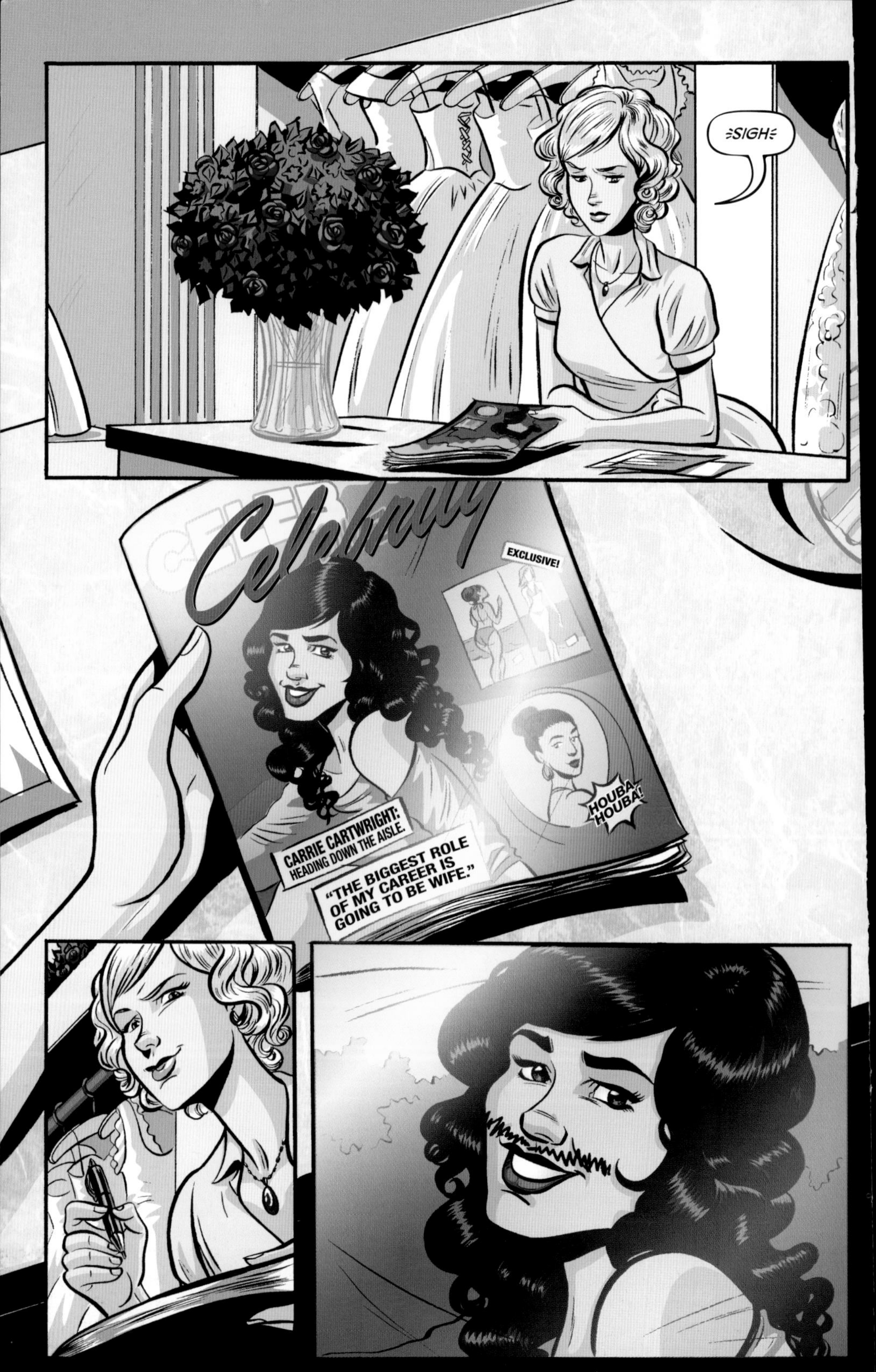
SIGH
Celebrity
EXCLUSIVE!
HOUBA HOUBA!
CARRIE CARTWRIGHT: HEADING DOWN THE AISLE.
"THE BIGGEST ROLE OF MY CAREER IS GOING TO BE WIFE."

# CHAPTER TWO

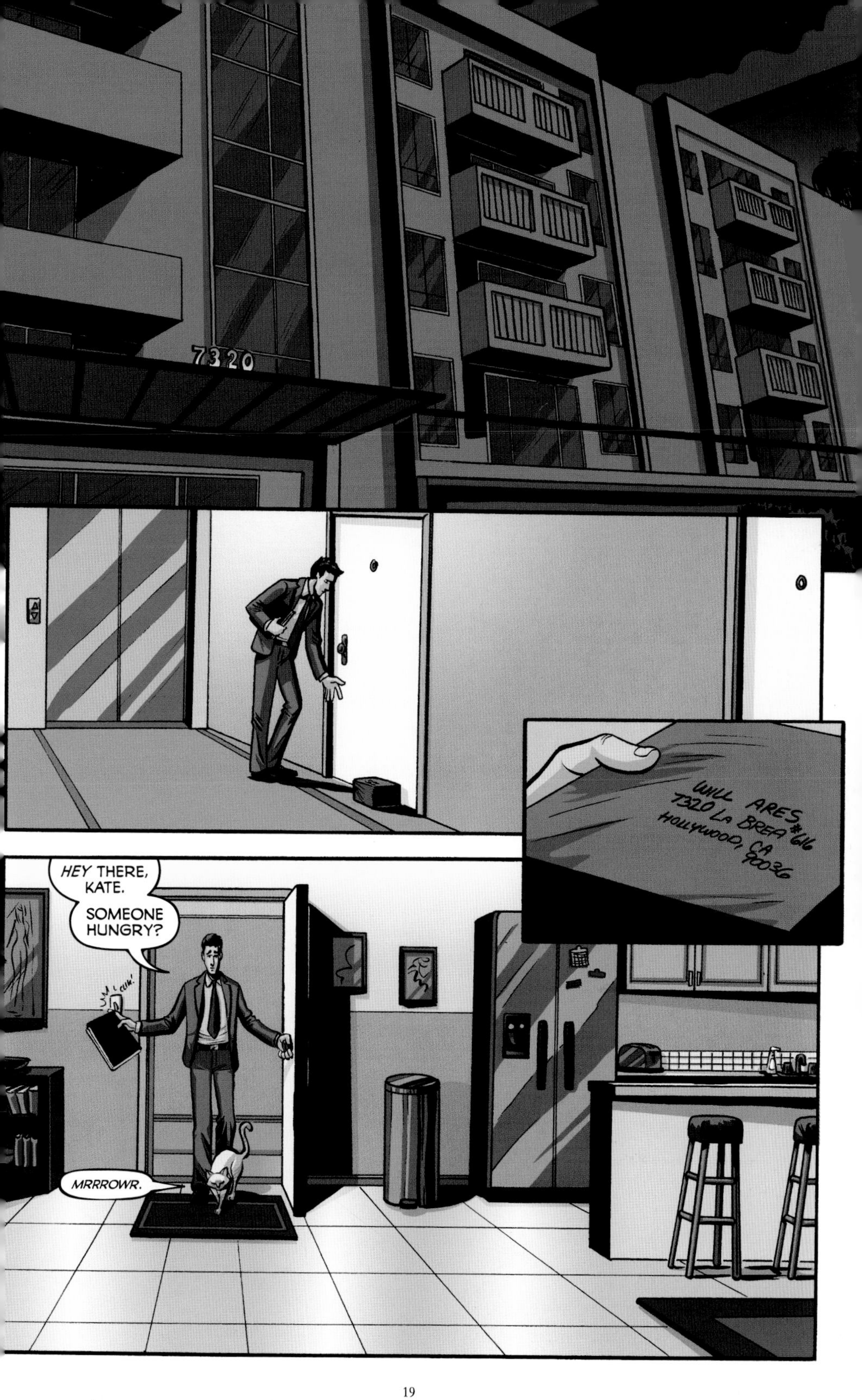
7320
WILL ARES
7320 La BREA #616
HOLLYWOOD, CA
90036
HEY THERE, KATE.
SOMEONE HUNGRY?
MRRROWR.

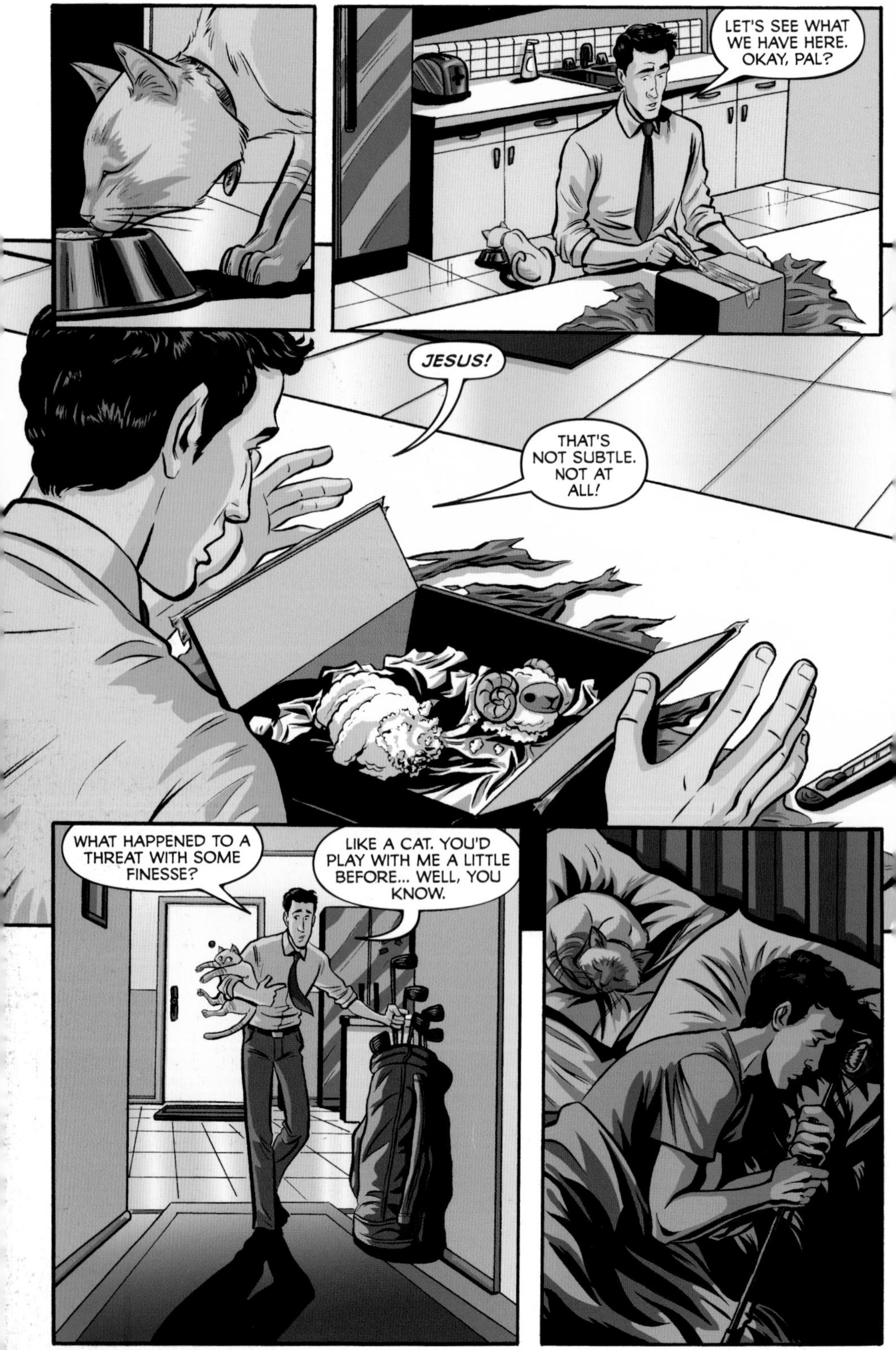
LET'S SEE WHAT WE HAVE HERE. OKAY, PAL?
JESUS!
THAT'S NOT SUBTLE. NOT AT ALL!
WHAT HAPPENED TO A THREAT WITH SOME FINESSE?
LIKE A CAT. YOU'D PLAY WITH ME A LITTLE BEFORE... WELL, YOU KNOW.

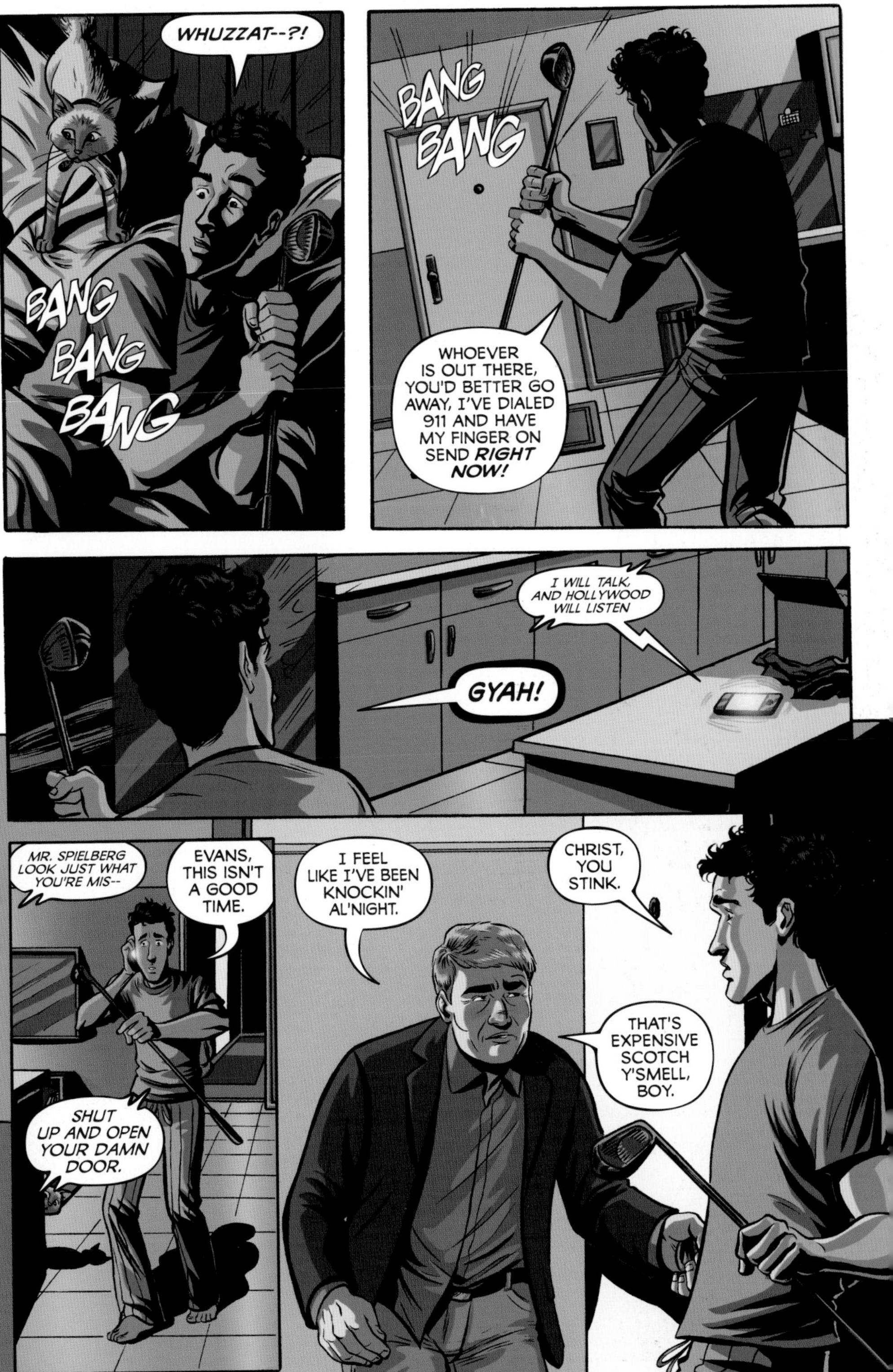
WHUZZAT--?!
BANG BANG BANG
BANG BANG
WHOEVER IS OUT THERE, YOU'D BETTER GO AWAY, I'VE DIALED 911 AND HAVE MY FINGER ON SEND RIGHT NOW!
I WILL TALK, AND HOLLYWOOD WILL LISTEN
GYAH!
MR. SPIELBERG LOOK JUST WHAT YOU'RE MIS--
EVANS, THIS ISN'T A GOOD TIME.
SHUT UP AND OPEN YOUR DAMN DOOR.
I FEEL LIKE I'VE BEEN KNOCKIN' AL'NIGHT.
CHRIST, YOU STINK.
THAT'S EXPENSIVE SCOTCH Y'SMELL, BOY.

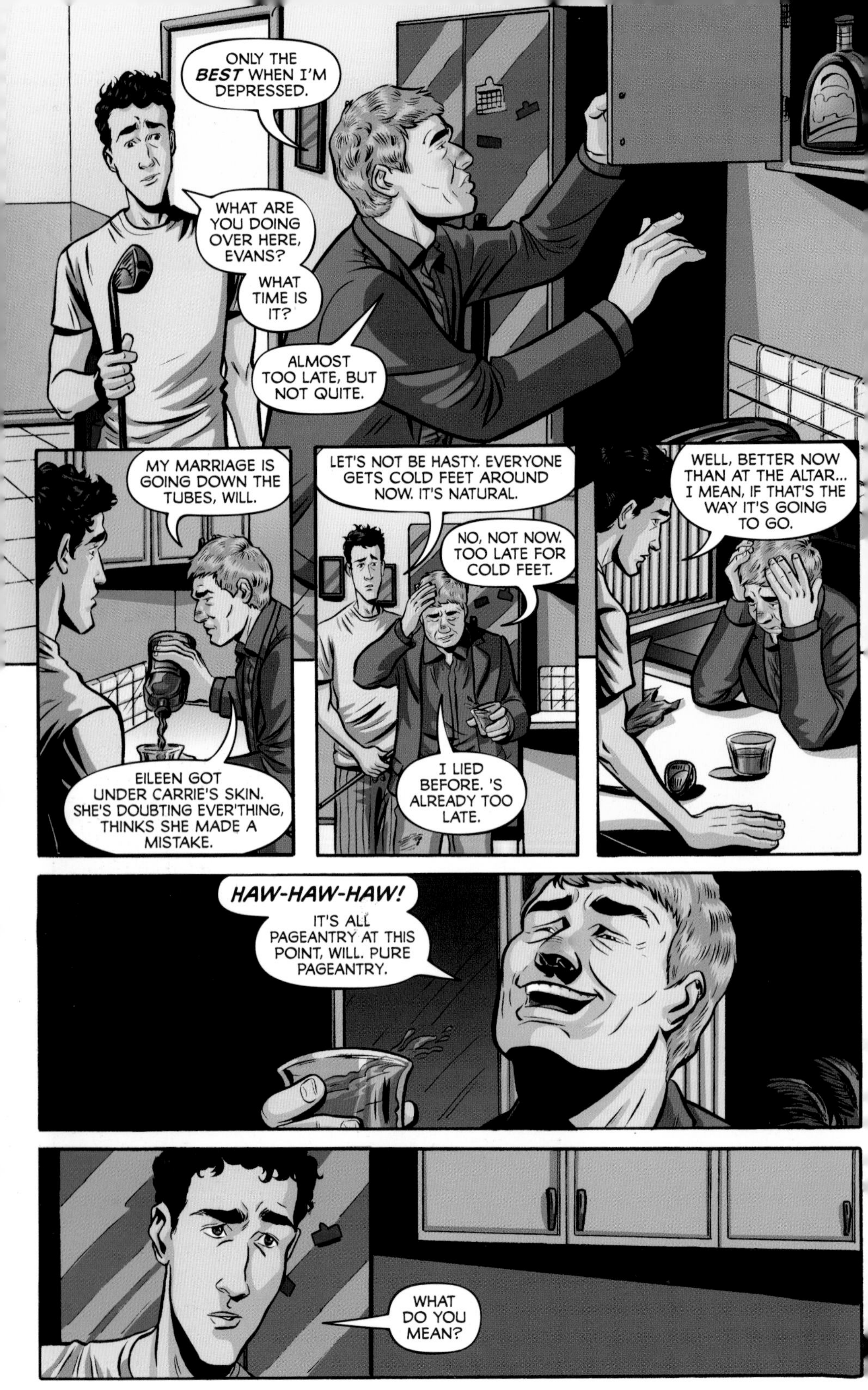
ONLY THE *BEST* WHEN I'M DEPRESSED.
WHAT ARE YOU DOING OVER HERE, EVANS?
WHAT TIME IS IT?
ALMOST TOO LATE, BUT NOT QUITE.
MY MARRIAGE IS GOING DOWN THE TUBES, WILL.
EILEEN GOT UNDER CARRIE'S SKIN. SHE'S DOUBTING EVER'THING, THINKS SHE MADE A MISTAKE.
LET'S NOT BE HASTY. EVERYONE GETS COLD FEET AROUND NOW. IT'S NATURAL.
NO, NOT NOW. TOO LATE FOR COLD FEET.
I LIED BEFORE. 'S ALREADY TOO LATE.
WELL, BETTER NOW THAN AT THE ALTAR... I MEAN, IF THAT'S THE WAY IT'S GOING TO GO.
HAW-HAW-HAW!
IT'S ALL PAGEANTRY AT THIS POINT, WILL. PURE PAGEANTRY.
WHAT DO YOU MEAN?

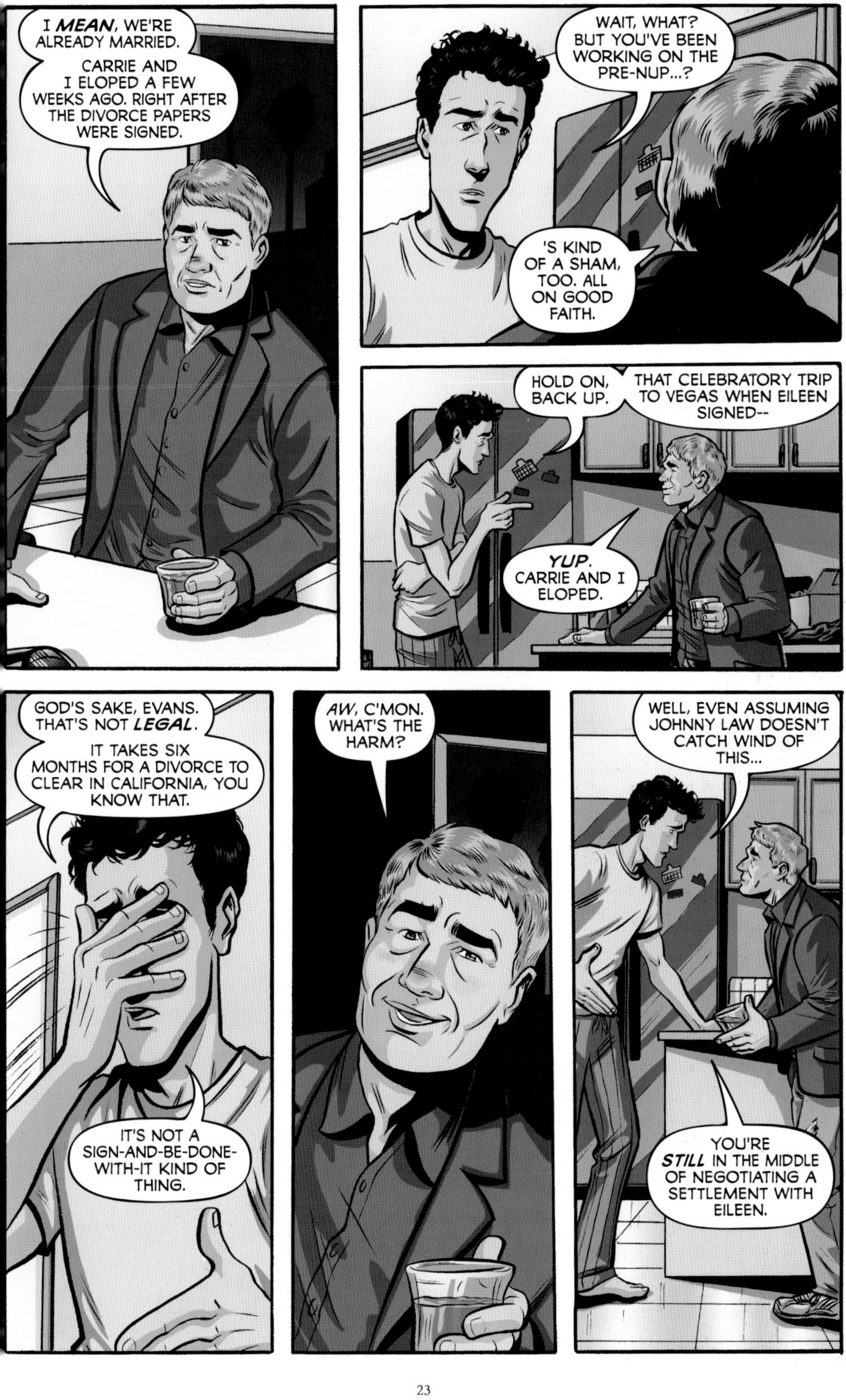
I MEAN, WE'RE ALREADY MARRIED.
CARRIE AND I ELOPED A FEW WEEKS AGO. RIGHT AFTER THE DIVORCE PAPERS WERE SIGNED.
WAIT, WHAT? BUT YOU'VE BEEN WORKING ON THE PRE-NUP...?
'S KIND OF A SHAM, TOO. ALL ON GOOD FAITH.
HOLD ON, BACK UP.
THAT CELEBRATORY TRIP TO VEGAS WHEN EILEEN SIGNED--
YUP. CARRIE AND I ELOPED.
GOD'S SAKE, EVANS. THAT'S NOT LEGAL.
IT TAKES SIX MONTHS FOR A DIVORCE TO CLEAR IN CALIFORNIA, YOU KNOW THAT.
IT'S NOT A SIGN-AND-BE-DONE-WITH-IT KIND OF THING.
AW, C'MON. WHAT'S THE HARM?
WELL, EVEN ASSUMING JOHNNY LAW DOESN'T CATCH WIND OF THIS...
YOU'RE STILL IN THE MIDDLE OF NEGOTIATING A SETTLEMENT WITH EILEEN.

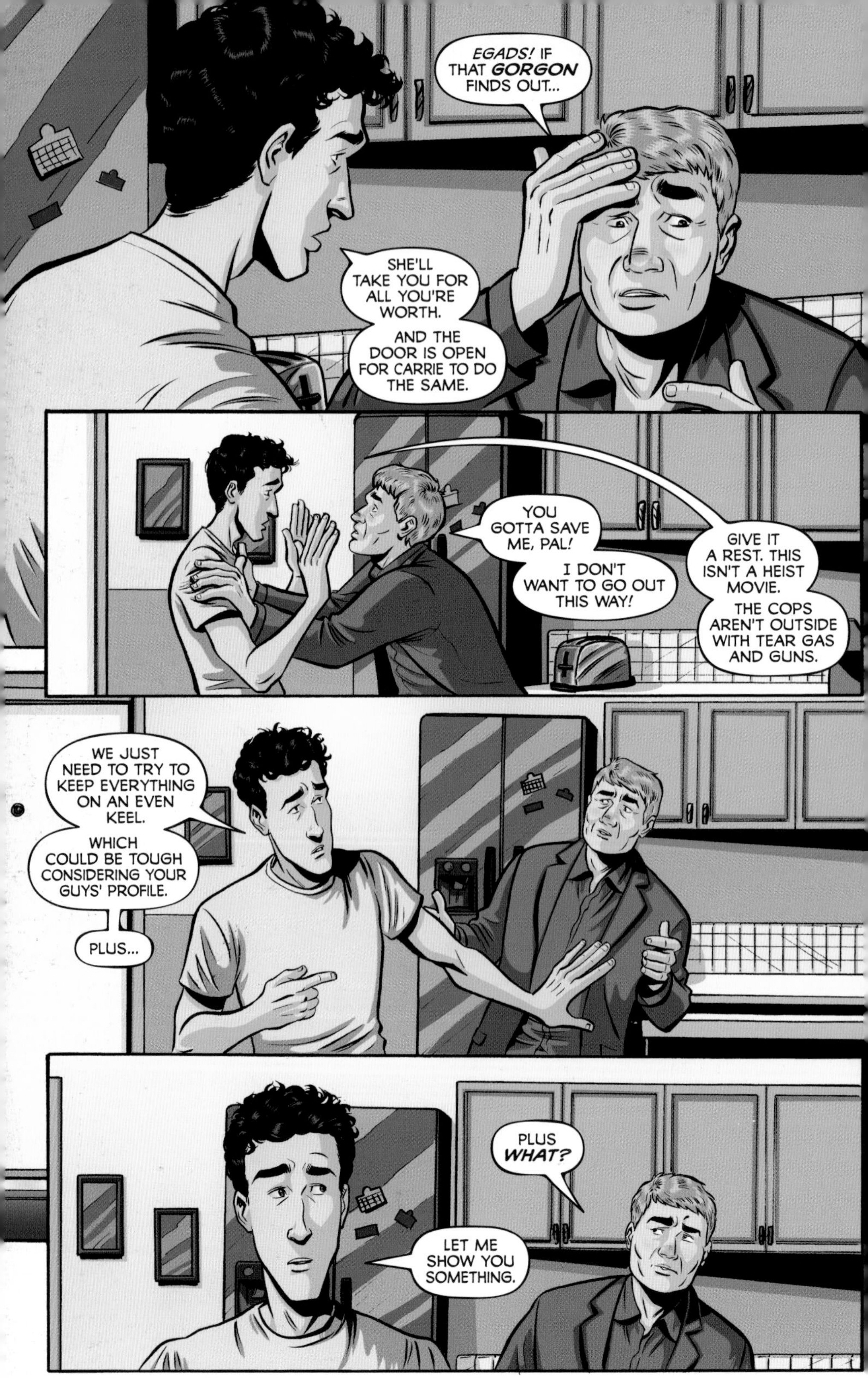
EGADS! IF THAT GORGON FINDS OUT...
SHE'LL TAKE YOU FOR ALL YOU'RE WORTH.
AND THE DOOR IS OPEN FOR CARRIE TO DO THE SAME.
YOU GOTTA SAVE ME, PAL!
I DON'T WANT TO GO OUT THIS WAY!
GIVE IT A REST. THIS ISN'T A HEIST MOVIE.
THE COPS AREN'T OUTSIDE WITH TEAR GAS AND GUNS.
WE JUST NEED TO TRY TO KEEP EVERYTHING ON AN EVEN KEEL.
WHICH COULD BE TOUGH CONSIDERING YOUR GUYS' PROFILE.
PLUS...
PLUS WHAT?
LET ME SHOW YOU SOMETHING.

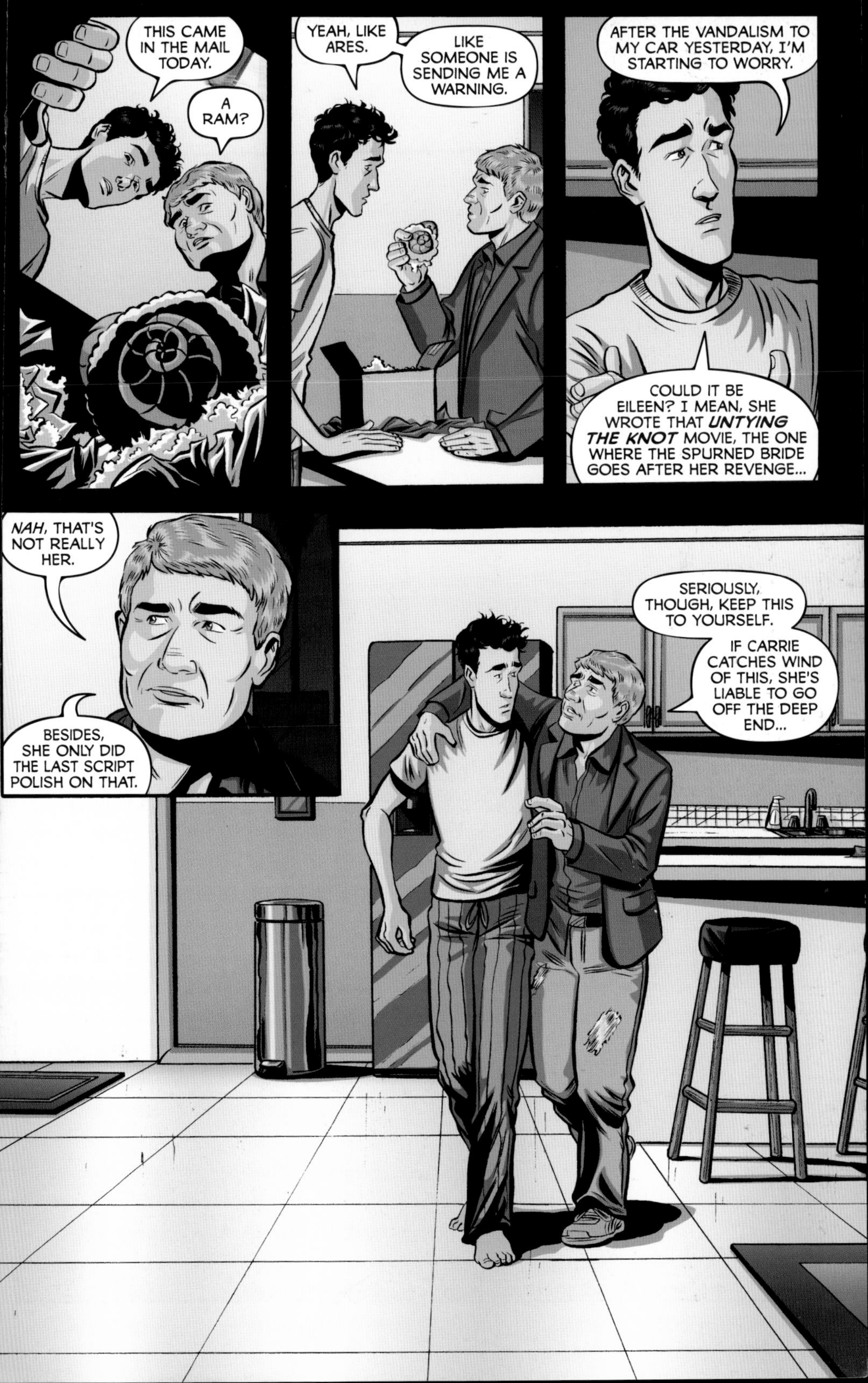
THIS CAME IN THE MAIL TODAY.
A RAM?
YEAH, LIKE ARES.
LIKE SOMEONE IS SENDING ME A WARNING.
AFTER THE VANDALISM TO MY CAR YESTERDAY, I'M STARTING TO WORRY.
COULD IT BE EILEEN? I MEAN, SHE WROTE THAT *UNTYING THE KNOT* MOVIE, THE ONE WHERE THE SPURNED BRIDE GOES AFTER HER REVENGE...
*NAH*, THAT'S NOT REALLY HER.
BESIDES, SHE ONLY DID THE LAST SCRIPT POLISH ON THAT.
SERIOUSLY, THOUGH, KEEP THIS TO YOURSELF.
IF CARRIE CATCHES WIND OF THIS, SHE'S LIABLE TO GO OFF THE DEEP END...

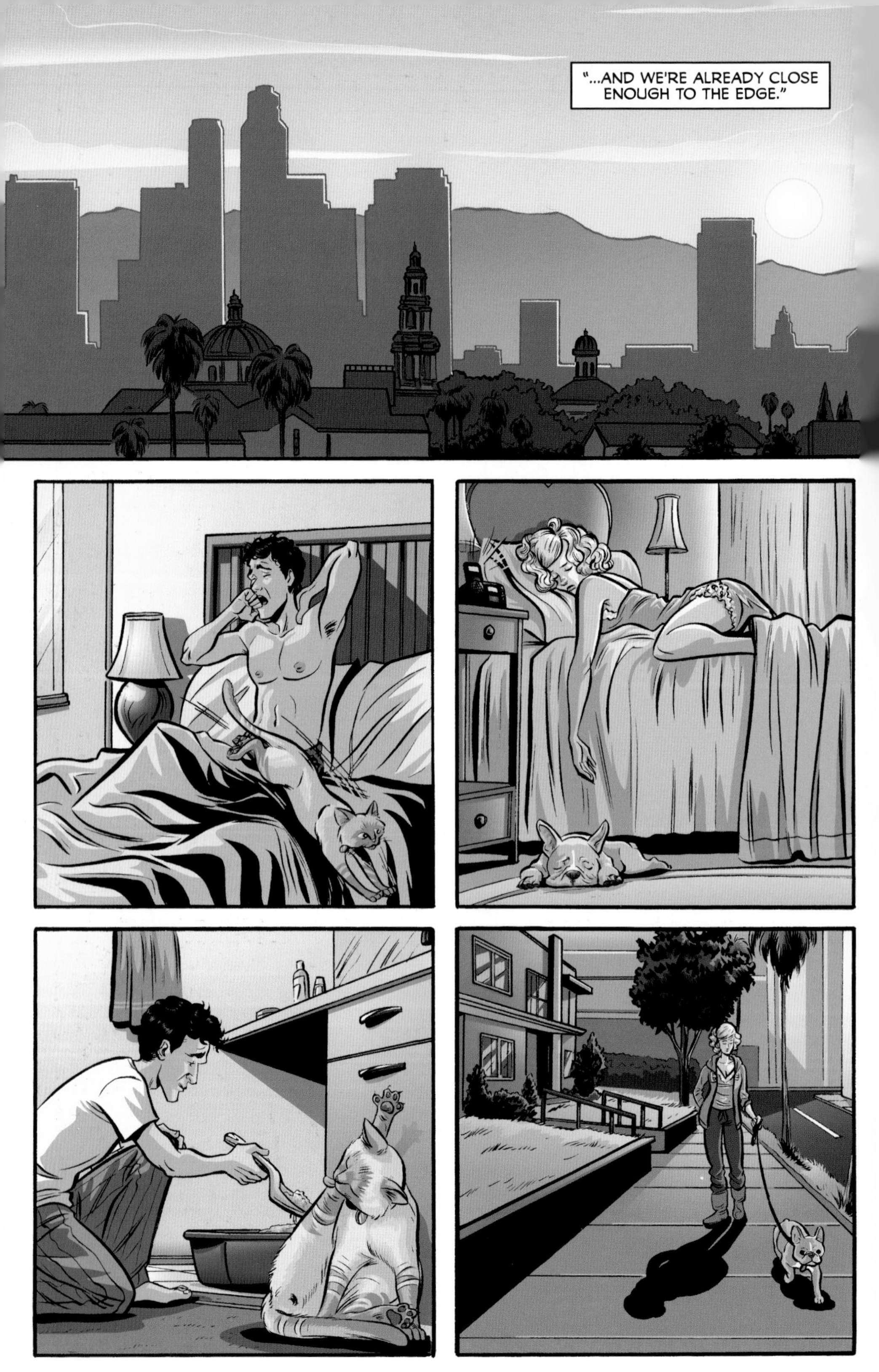
"...AND WE'RE ALREADY CLOSE ENOUGH TO THE EDGE."

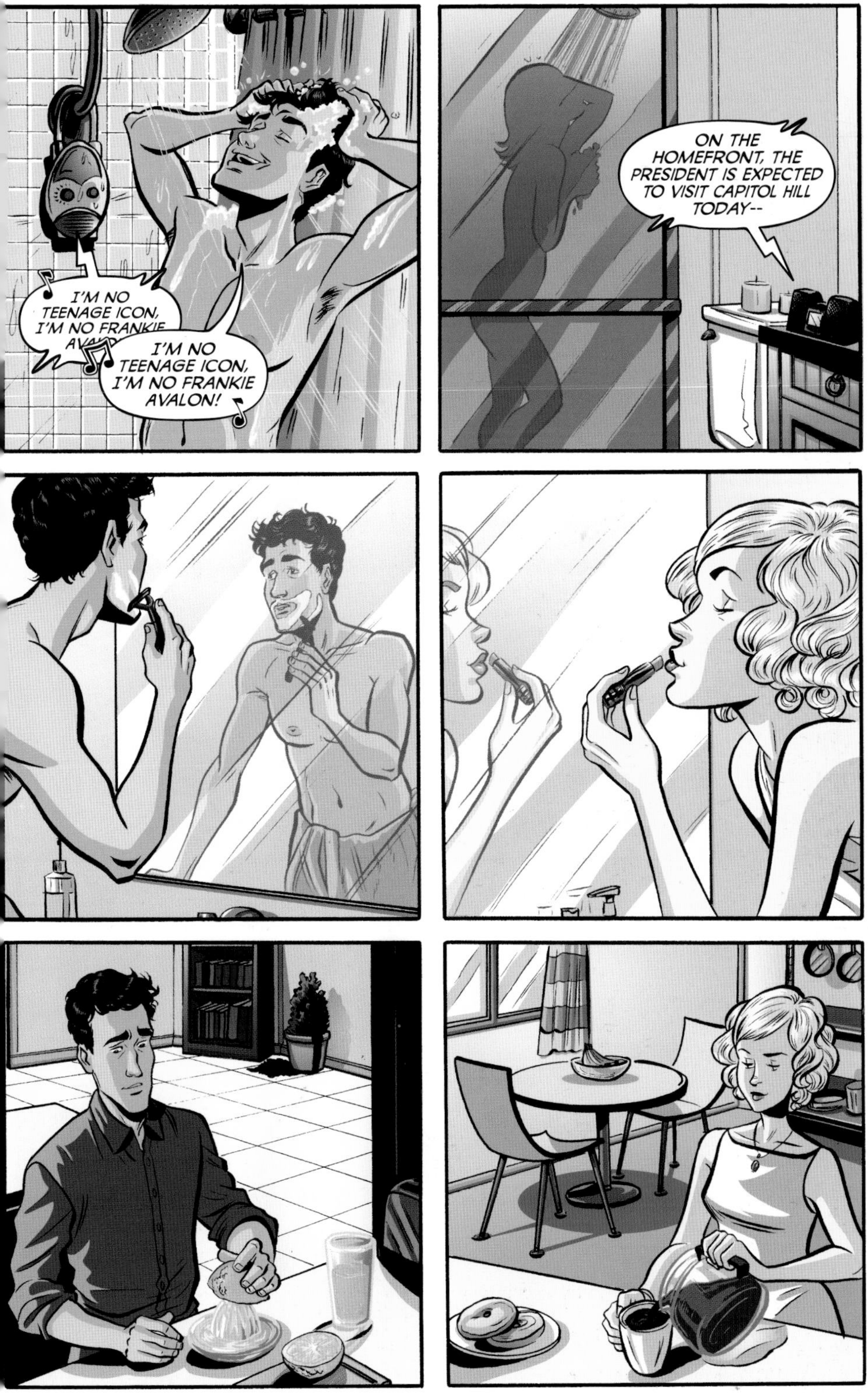

I'M NO TEENAGE ICON, I'M NO FRANKIE AVALON
I'M NO TEENAGE ICON, I'M NO FRANKIE AVALON!
ON THE HOMEFRONT, THE PRESIDENT IS EXPECTED TO VISIT CAPITOL HILL TODAY--

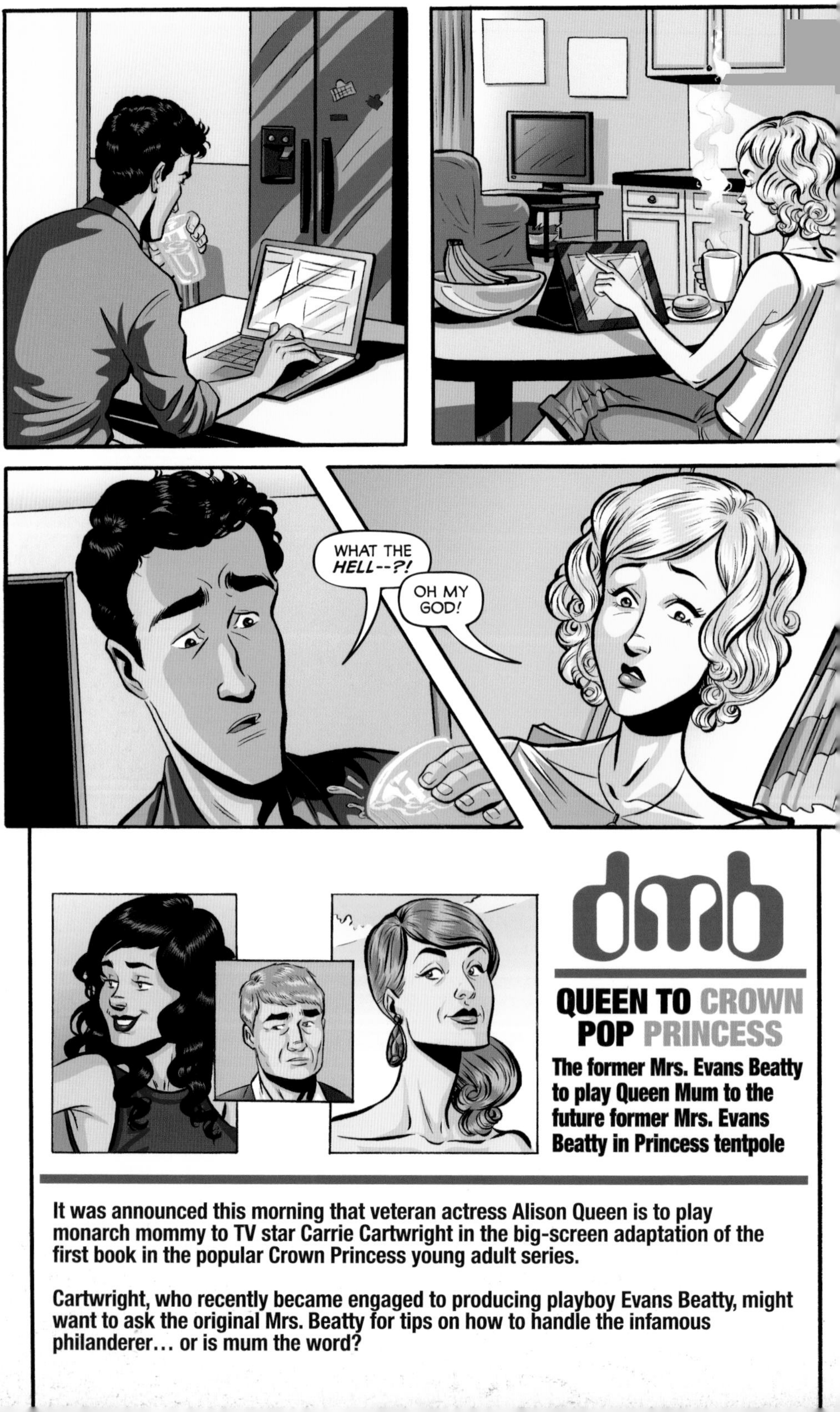
WHAT THE HELL--?!
OH MY GOD!
dmb
QUEEN TO CROWN POP PRINCESS
The former Mrs. Evans Beatty to play Queen Mum to the future former Mrs. Evans Beatty in Princess tentpole
It was announced this morning that veteran actress Alison Queen is to play monarch mommy to TV star Carrie Cartwright in the big-screen adaptation of the first book in the popular Crown Princess young adult series.
Cartwright, who recently became engaged to producing playboy Evans Beatty, might want to ask the original Mrs. Beatty for tips on how to handle the infamous philanderer… or is mum the word?

# CHAPTER THREE

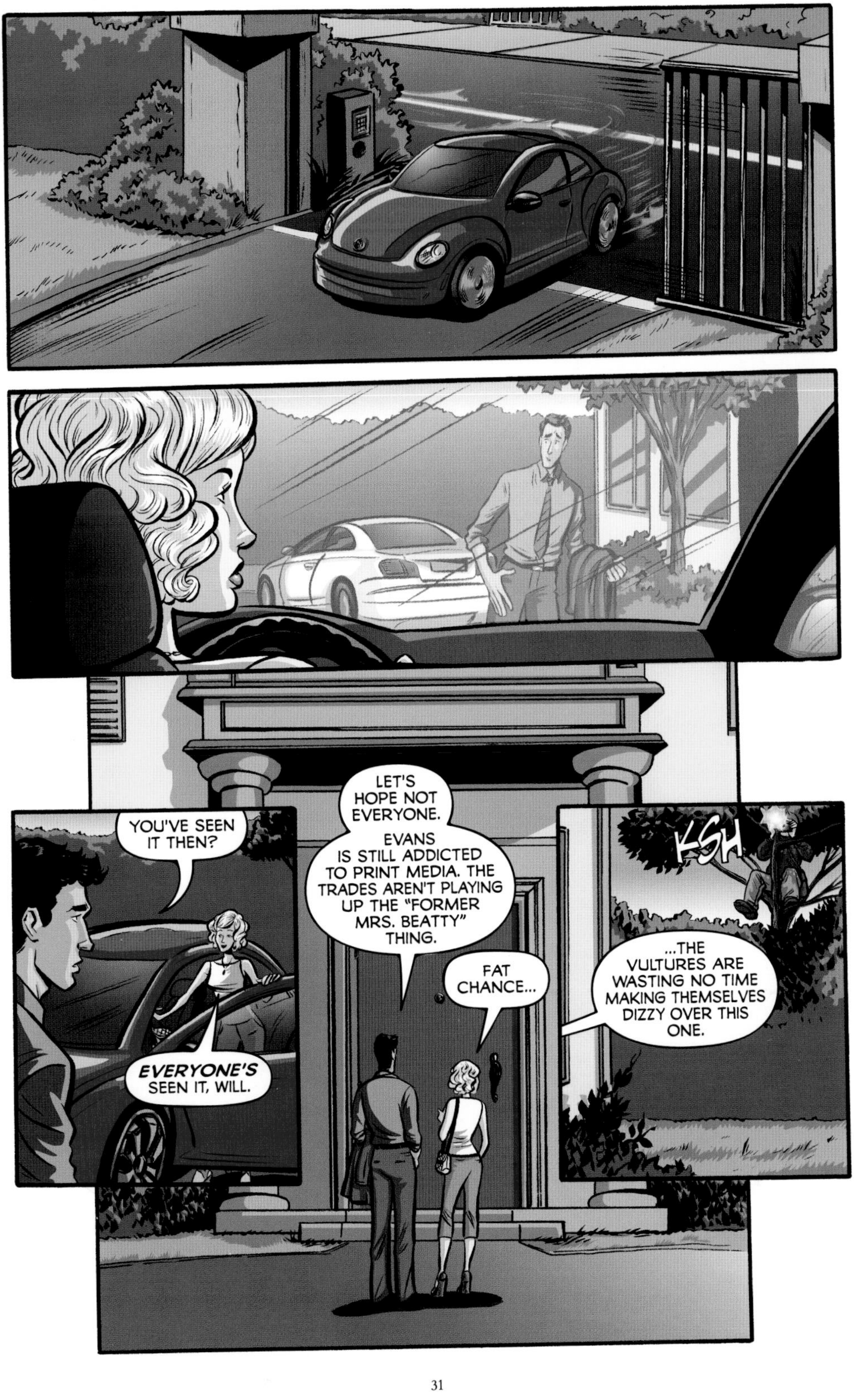
YOU'VE SEEN IT THEN?
EVERYONE'S SEEN IT, WILL.
LET'S HOPE NOT EVERYONE.
EVANS IS STILL ADDICTED TO PRINT MEDIA. THE TRADES AREN'T PLAYING UP THE "FORMER MRS. BEATTY" THING.
FAT CHANCE...
KSH
...THE VULTURES ARE WASTING NO TIME MAKING THEMSELVES DIZZY OVER THIS ONE.

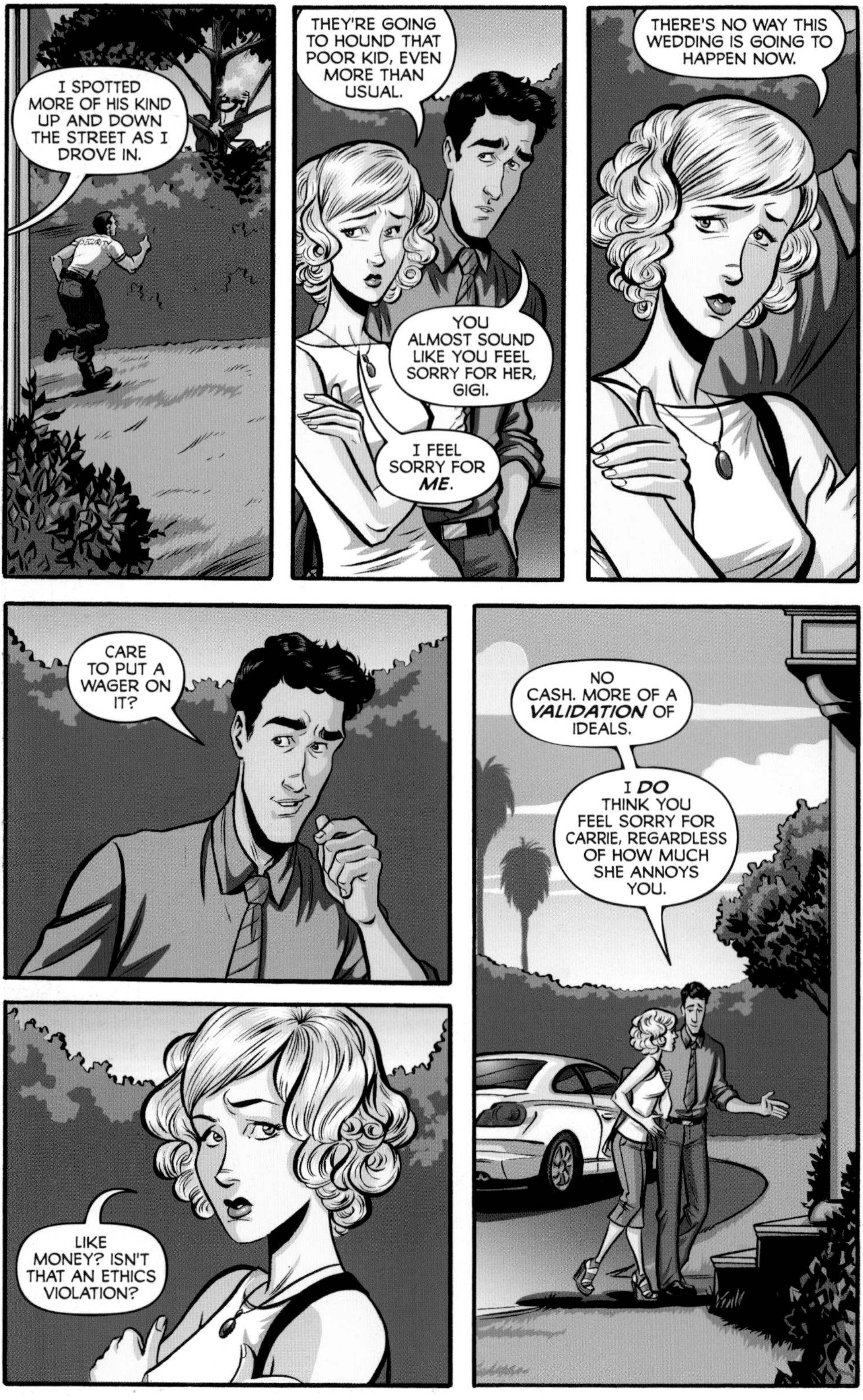
I SPOTTED MORE OF HIS KIND UP AND DOWN THE STREET AS I DROVE IN.
SECURITY
THEY'RE GOING TO HOUND THAT POOR KID, EVEN MORE THAN USUAL.
YOU ALMOST SOUND LIKE YOU FEEL SORRY FOR HER, GIGI.
I FEEL SORRY FOR ***ME***.
THERE'S NO WAY THIS WEDDING IS GOING TO HAPPEN NOW.
CARE TO PUT A WAGER ON IT?
LIKE MONEY? ISN'T THAT AN ETHICS VIOLATION?
NO CASH. MORE OF A ***VALIDATION*** OF IDEALS.
I ***DO*** THINK YOU FEEL SORRY FOR CARRIE, REGARDLESS OF HOW MUCH SHE ANNOYS YOU.

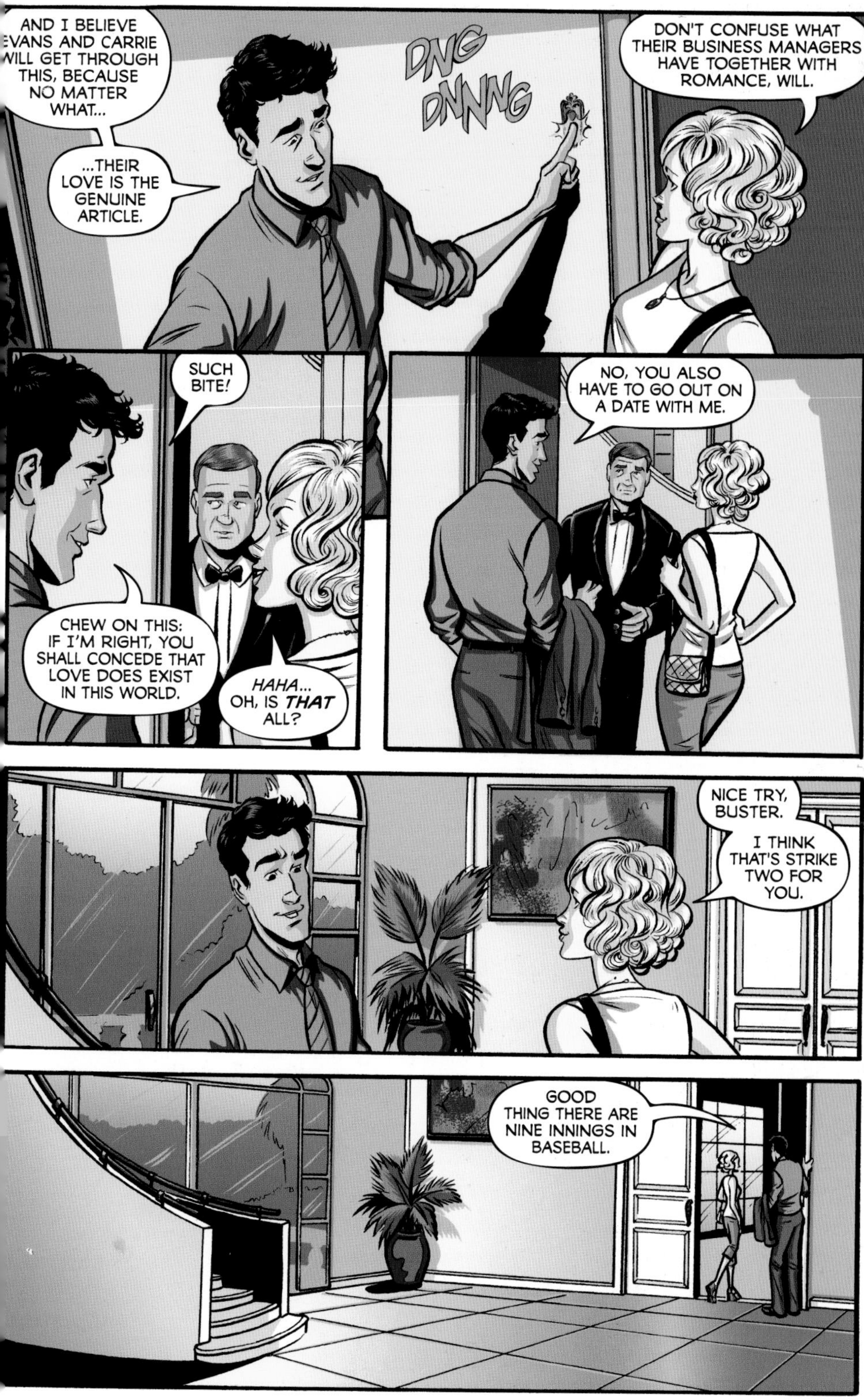
AND I BELIEVE EVANS AND CARRIE WILL GET THROUGH THIS, BECAUSE NO MATTER WHAT...
DNG DNNNG
...THEIR LOVE IS THE GENUINE ARTICLE.
DON'T CONFUSE WHAT THEIR BUSINESS MANAGERS HAVE TOGETHER WITH ROMANCE, WILL.
SUCH BITE!
CHEW ON THIS: IF I'M RIGHT, YOU SHALL CONCEDE THAT LOVE DOES EXIST IN THIS WORLD.
HAHA... OH, IS THAT ALL?
NO, YOU ALSO HAVE TO GO OUT ON A DATE WITH ME.
NICE TRY, BUSTER.
I THINK THAT'S STRIKE TWO FOR YOU.
GOOD THING THERE ARE NINE INNINGS IN BASEBALL.

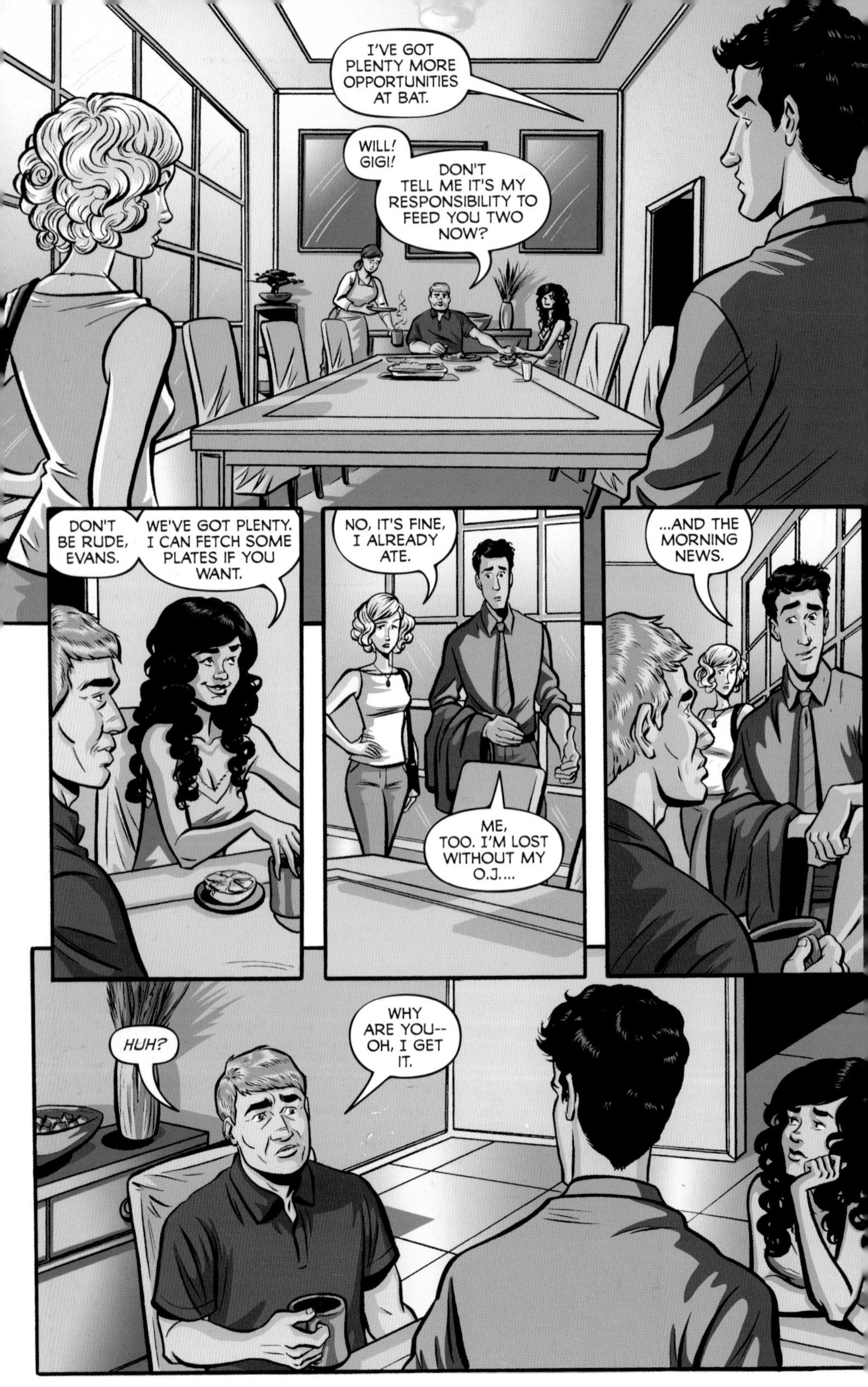
I'VE GOT PLENTY MORE OPPORTUNITIES AT BAT.
WILL! GIGI!
DON'T TELL ME IT'S MY RESPONSIBILITY TO FEED YOU TWO NOW?
DON'T BE RUDE, EVANS.
WE'VE GOT PLENTY. I CAN FETCH SOME PLATES IF YOU WANT.
NO, IT'S FINE, I ALREADY ATE.
ME, TOO. I'M LOST WITHOUT MY O.J....
...AND THE MORNING NEWS.
HUH?
WHY ARE YOU-- OH, I GET IT.

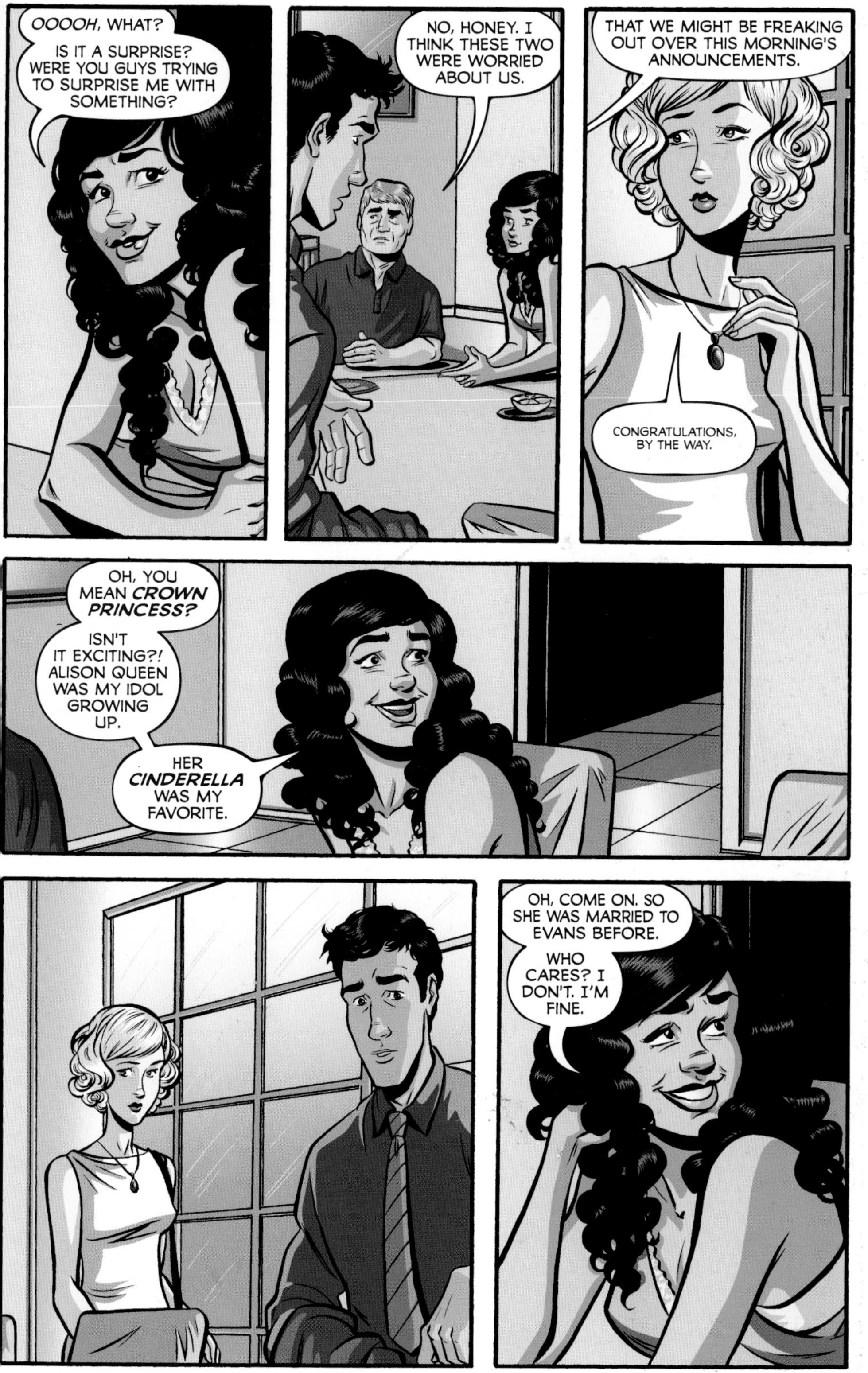

*OOOOH,* WHAT?
IS IT A SURPRISE? WERE YOU GUYS TRYING TO SURPRISE ME WITH SOMETHING?
NO, HONEY. I THINK THESE TWO WERE WORRIED ABOUT US.
THAT WE MIGHT BE FREAKING OUT OVER THIS MORNING'S ANNOUNCEMENTS.
CONGRATULATIONS, BY THE WAY.
OH, YOU MEAN ***CROWN PRINCESS?***
ISN'T IT EXCITING?! ALISON QUEEN WAS MY IDOL GROWING UP.
HER ***CINDERELLA*** WAS MY FAVORITE.
OH, COME ON. SO SHE WAS MARRIED TO EVANS BEFORE.
WHO CARES? I DON'T. I'M FINE.

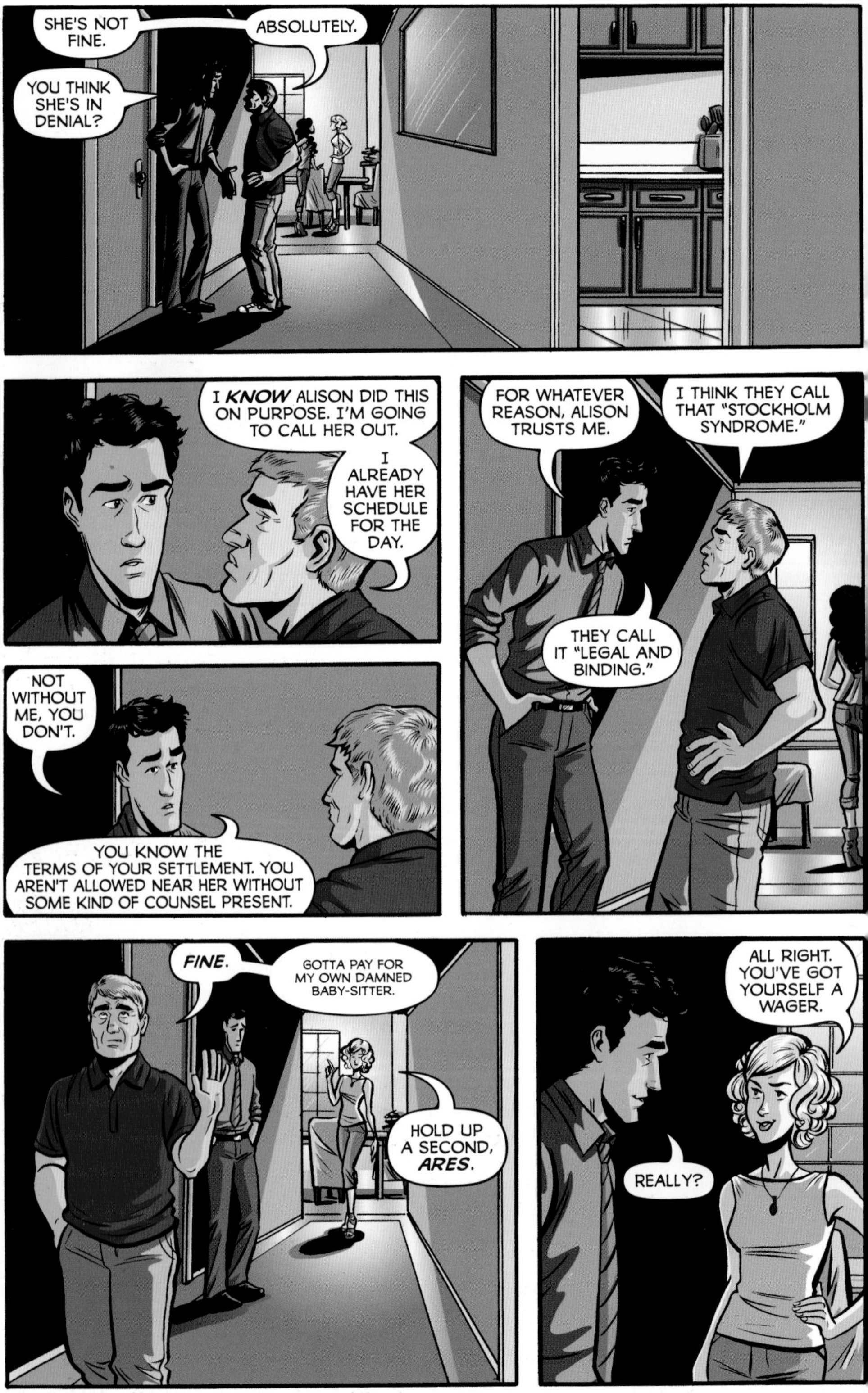
SHE'S NOT FINE.
ABSOLUTELY.
YOU THINK SHE'S IN DENIAL?
I *KNOW* ALISON DID THIS ON PURPOSE. I'M GOING TO CALL HER OUT.
I ALREADY HAVE HER SCHEDULE FOR THE DAY.
NOT WITHOUT ME, YOU DON'T.
YOU KNOW THE TERMS OF YOUR SETTLEMENT. YOU AREN'T ALLOWED NEAR HER WITHOUT SOME KIND OF COUNSEL PRESENT.
FOR WHATEVER REASON, ALISON TRUSTS ME.
I THINK THEY CALL THAT "STOCKHOLM SYNDROME."
THEY CALL IT "LEGAL AND BINDING."
*FINE*.
GOTTA PAY FOR MY OWN DAMNED BABY-SITTER.
HOLD UP A SECOND, *ARES*.
ALL RIGHT. YOU'VE GOT YOURSELF A WAGER.
REALLY?

"AS GOOD AS THIS GIG IS FOR ME..."

HOLLYWOOD

"...I'M GOING TO END UP RIGHT REGARDLESS..."

"...SO I MIGHT AS WELL GET SOMETHING OUT OF IT."

START THINKING NOW ABOUT WHERE YOU WANT ME TO TAKE YOU.

YEAH, RIGHT. IT'LL BE WORTH THE LOST INCOME JUST TO SEE YOUR BELIEF IN FAIRY TALES TURNED TO STONE.

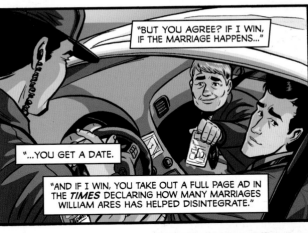

"BUT YOU AGREE? IF I WIN, IF THE MARRIAGE HAPPENS..."

"...YOU GET A DATE.

"AND IF I WIN, YOU TAKE OUT A FULL PAGE AD IN THE *TIMES* DECLARING HOW MANY MARRIAGES WILLIAM ARES HAS HELPED DISINTEGRATE."

I WANT YOU TO DECLARE TO THE WORLD THAT LOVE IS A LIE.

HELL, YOU COULD EVEN PUBLISH THEIR NAMES.

THAT COULD GET DICEY. LET'S NOT DESTROY MY PRACTICE ON A LARK.

*FINE*, Y'SISSY.

HOW ABOUT THIS...

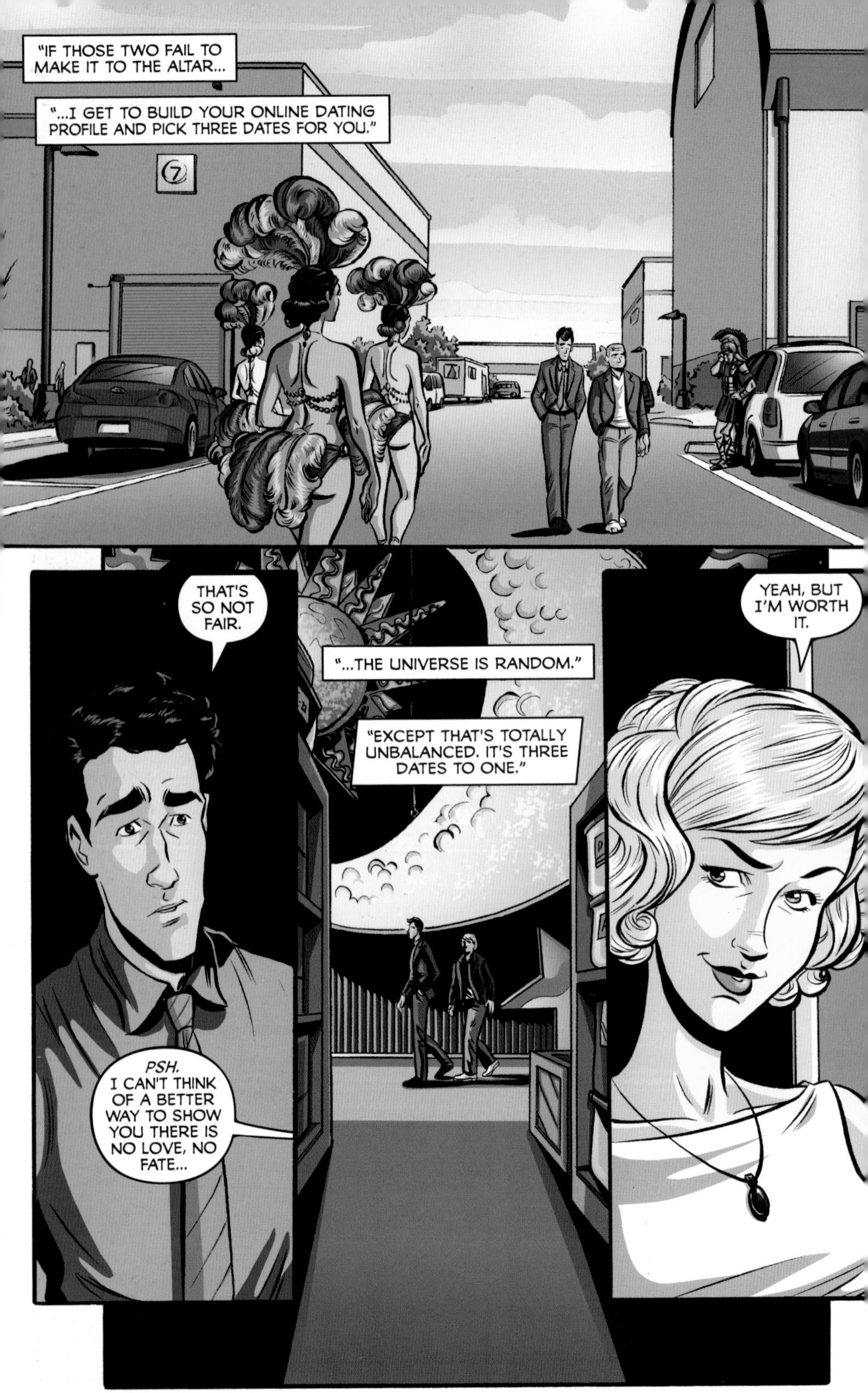
"IF THOSE TWO FAIL TO MAKE IT TO THE ALTAR...
"...I GET TO BUILD YOUR ONLINE DATING PROFILE AND PICK THREE DATES FOR YOU."
7
THAT'S SO NOT FAIR.
YEAH, BUT I'M WORTH IT.
"...THE UNIVERSE IS RANDOM."
"EXCEPT THAT'S TOTALLY UNBALANCED. IT'S THREE DATES TO ONE."
PSH. I CAN'T THINK OF A BETTER WAY TO SHOW YOU THERE IS NO LOVE, NO FATE...

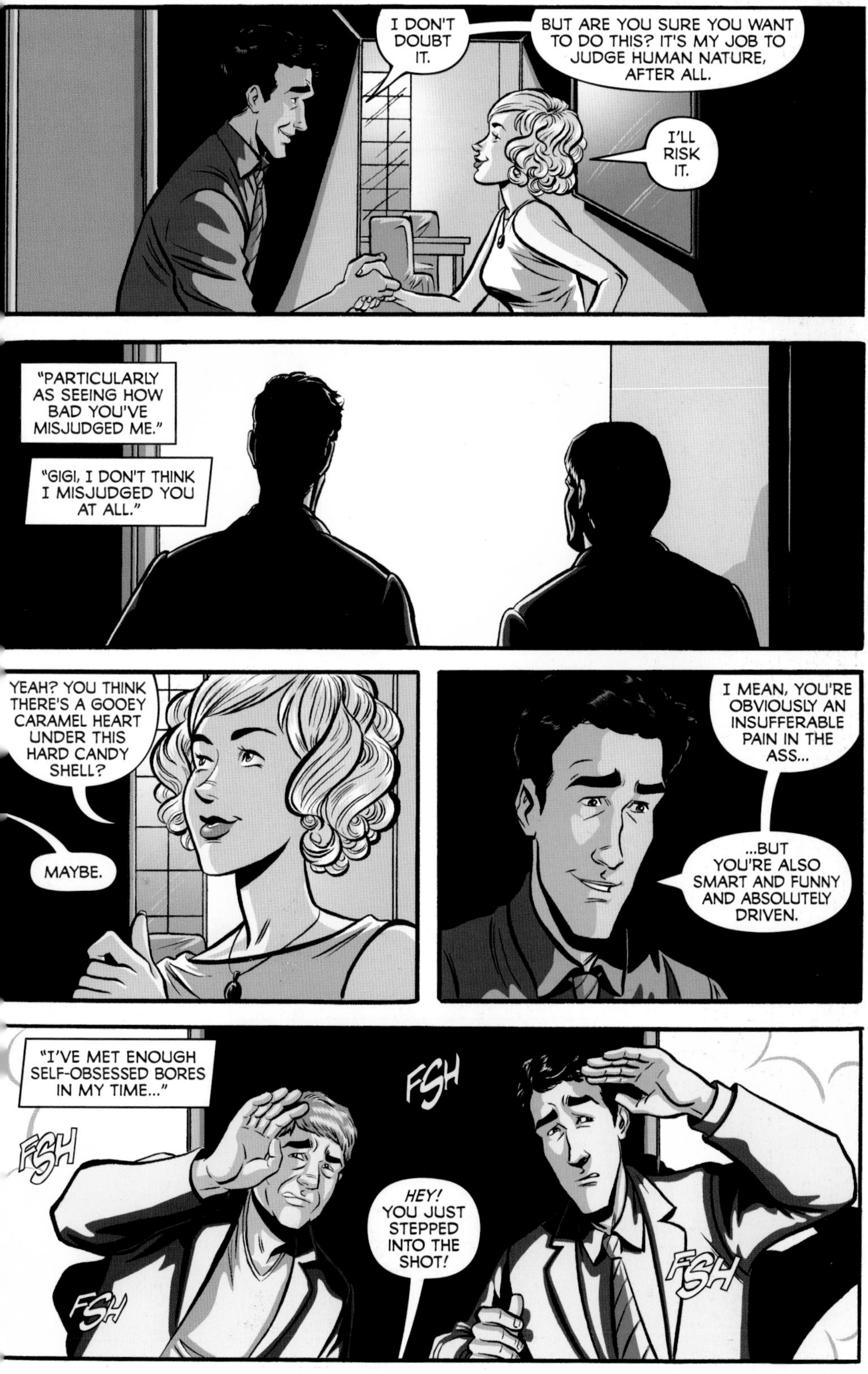

I DON'T DOUBT IT.
BUT ARE YOU SURE YOU WANT TO DO THIS? IT'S MY JOB TO JUDGE HUMAN NATURE, AFTER ALL.
I'LL RISK IT.
"PARTICULARLY AS SEEING HOW BAD YOU'VE MISJUDGED ME."
"GIGI, I DON'T THINK I MISJUDGED YOU AT ALL."
YEAH? YOU THINK THERE'S A GOOEY CARAMEL HEART UNDER THIS HARD CANDY SHELL?
MAYBE.
I MEAN, YOU'RE OBVIOUSLY AN INSUFFERABLE PAIN IN THE ASS...
...BUT YOU'RE ALSO SMART AND FUNNY AND ABSOLUTELY DRIVEN.
"I'VE MET ENOUGH SELF-OBSESSED BORES IN MY TIME..."
FSH
FSH
HEY! YOU JUST STEPPED INTO THE SHOT!
FSH
FSH

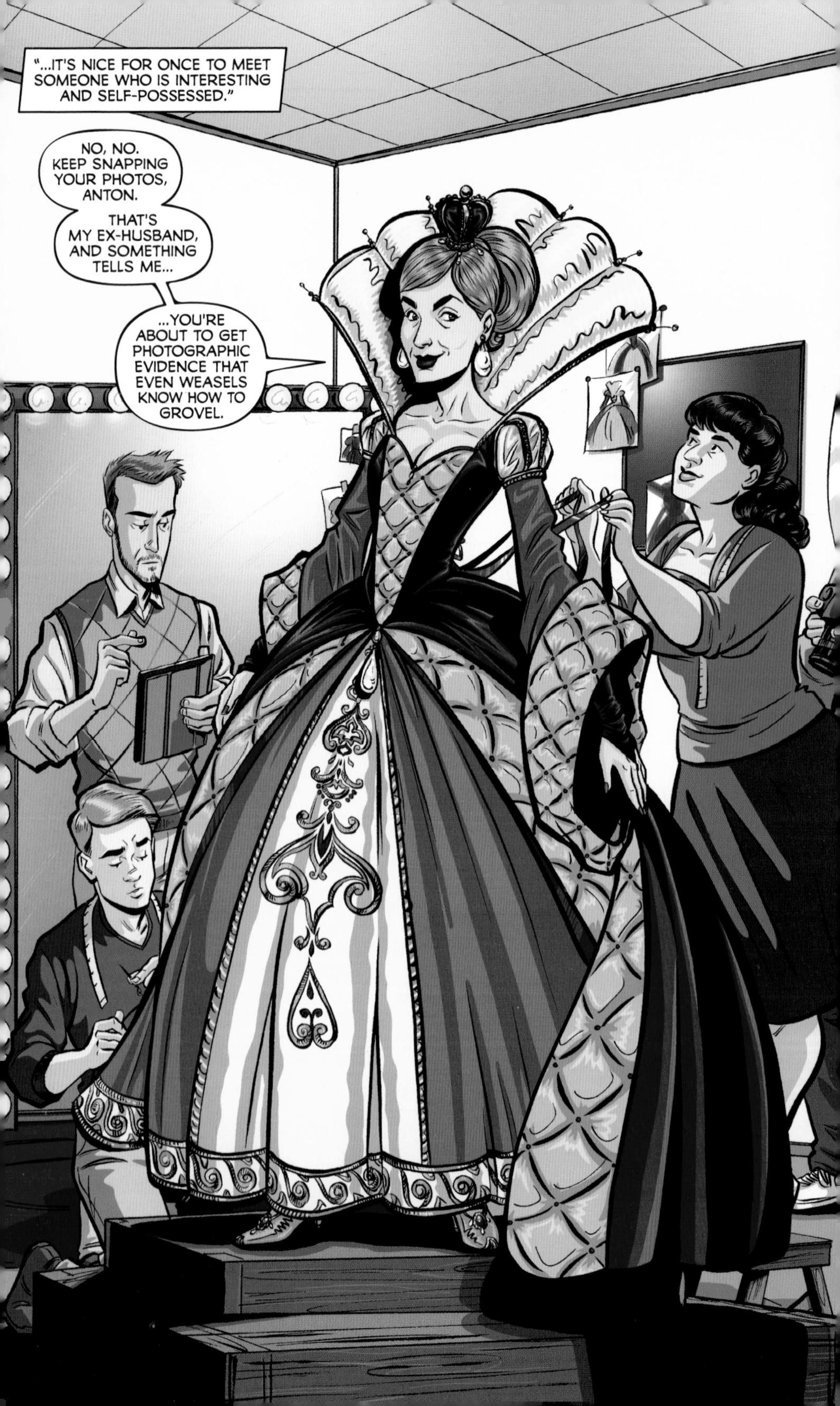
"...IT'S NICE FOR ONCE TO MEET SOMEONE WHO IS INTERESTING AND SELF-POSSESSED."
NO, NO. KEEP SNAPPING YOUR PHOTOS, ANTON.
THAT'S MY EX-HUSBAND, AND SOMETHING TELLS ME...
...YOU'RE ABOUT TO GET PHOTOGRAPHIC EVIDENCE THAT EVEN WEASELS KNOW HOW TO GROVEL.

# CHAPTER FOUR

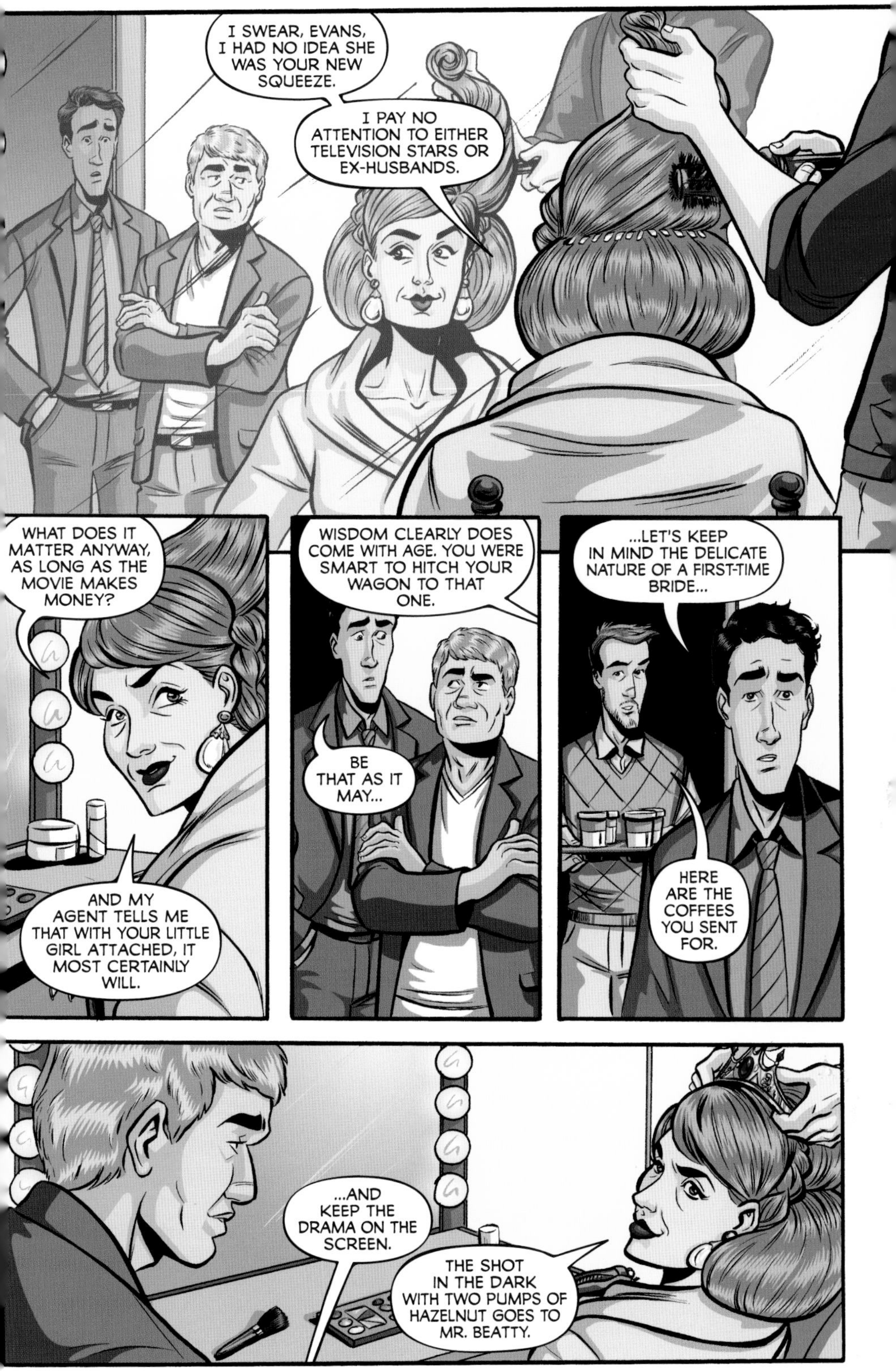
I SWEAR, EVANS, I HAD NO IDEA SHE WAS YOUR NEW SQUEEZE.
I PAY NO ATTENTION TO EITHER TELEVISION STARS OR EX-HUSBANDS.
WHAT DOES IT MATTER ANYWAY, AS LONG AS THE MOVIE MAKES MONEY?
AND MY AGENT TELLS ME THAT WITH YOUR LITTLE GIRL ATTACHED, IT MOST CERTAINLY WILL.
WISDOM CLEARLY DOES COME WITH AGE. YOU WERE SMART TO HITCH YOUR WAGON TO THAT ONE.
BE THAT AS IT MAY...
...LET'S KEEP IN MIND THE DELICATE NATURE OF A FIRST-TIME BRIDE...
HERE ARE THE COFFEES YOU SENT FOR.
...AND KEEP THE DRAMA ON THE SCREEN.
THE SHOT IN THE DARK WITH TWO PUMPS OF HAZELNUT GOES TO MR. BEATTY.

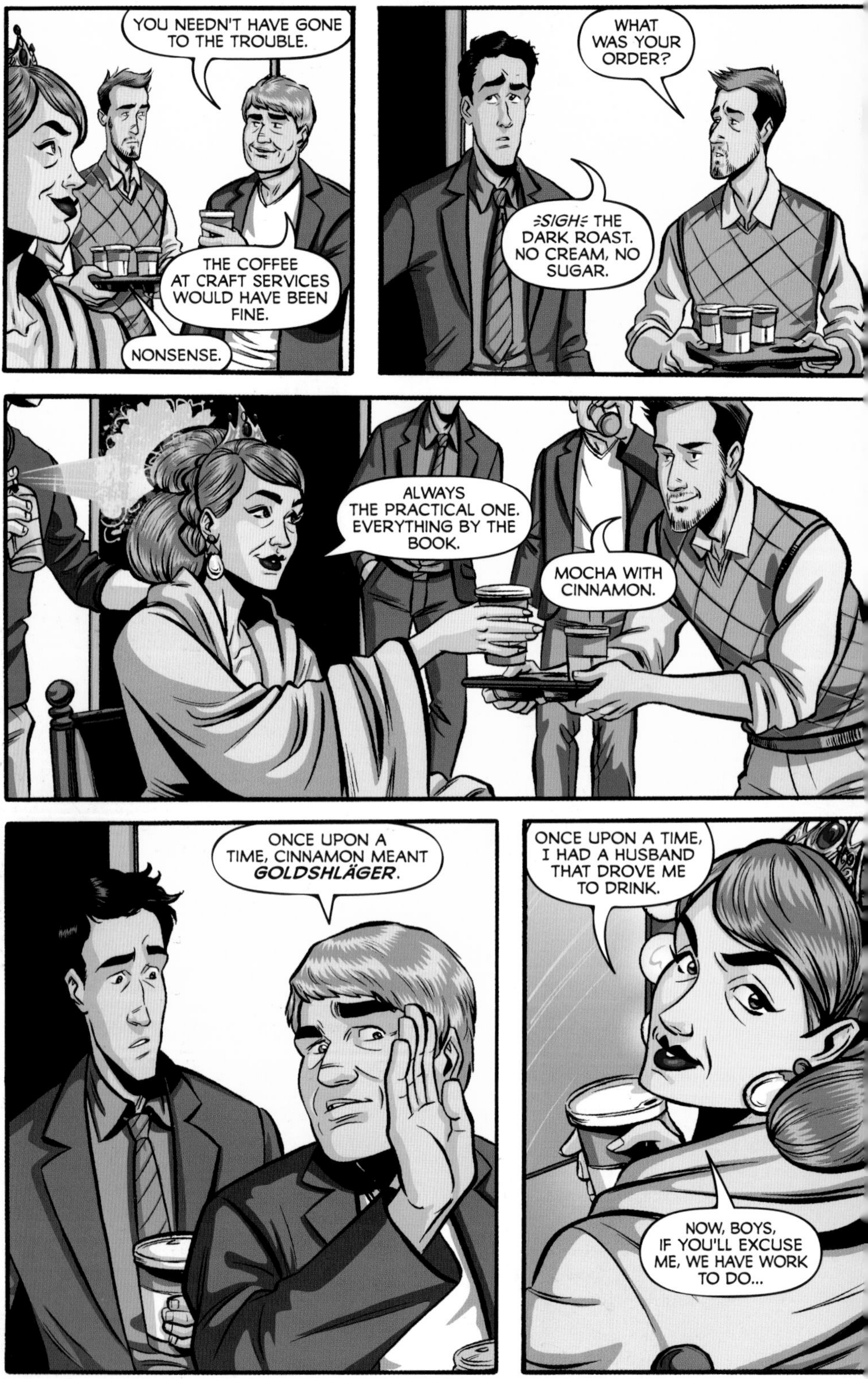
YOU NEEDN'T HAVE GONE TO THE TROUBLE.
THE COFFEE AT CRAFT SERVICES WOULD HAVE BEEN FINE.
NONSENSE.
WHAT WAS YOUR ORDER?
*SIGH* THE DARK ROAST. NO CREAM, NO SUGAR.
ALWAYS THE PRACTICAL ONE. EVERYTHING BY THE BOOK.
MOCHA WITH CINNAMON.
ONCE UPON A TIME, CINNAMON MEANT GOLDSHLÄGER.
ONCE UPON A TIME, I HAD A HUSBAND THAT DROVE ME TO DRINK.
NOW, BOYS, IF YOU'LL EXCUSE ME, WE HAVE WORK TO DO...

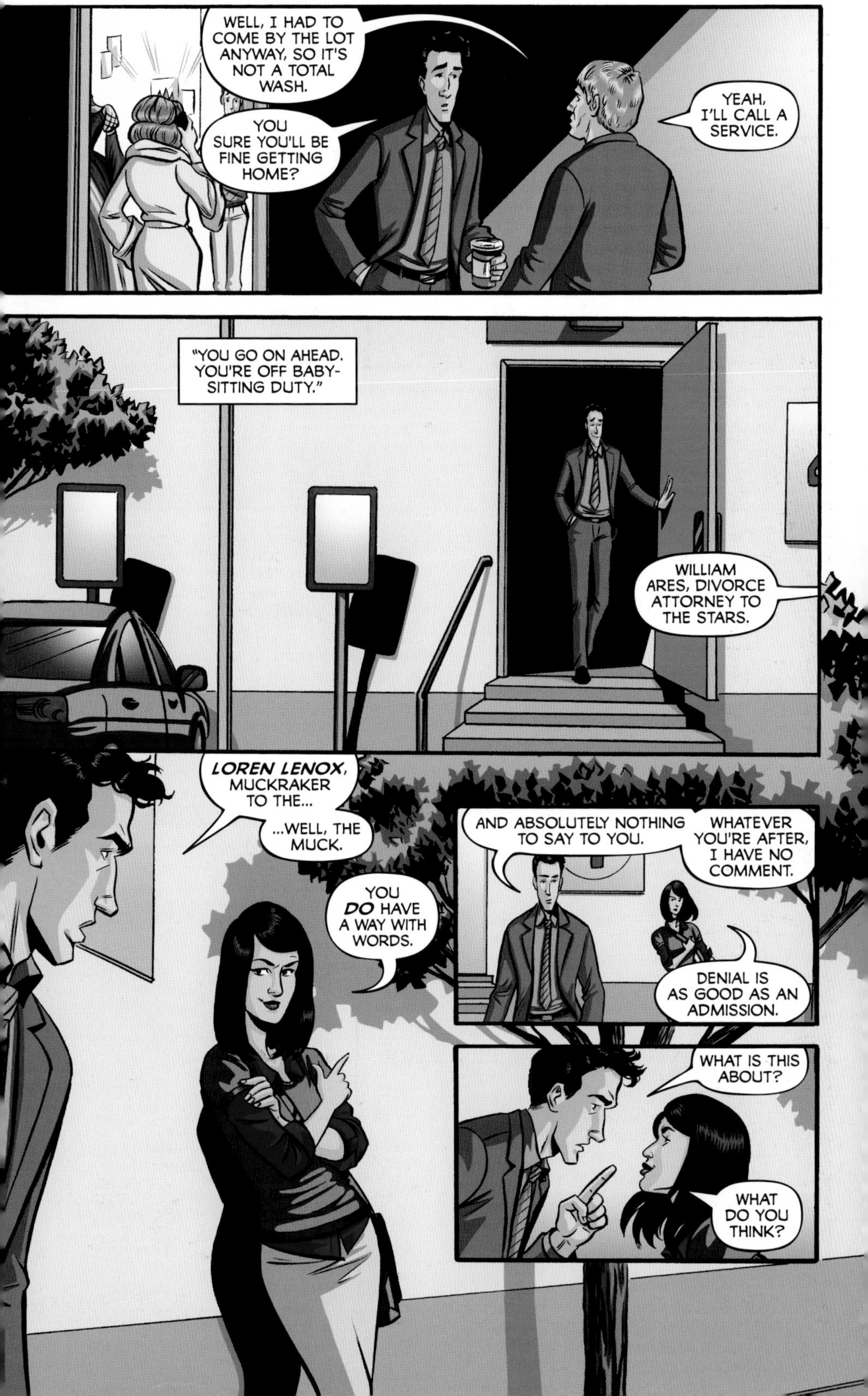
WELL, I HAD TO COME BY THE LOT ANYWAY, SO IT'S NOT A TOTAL WASH.
YOU SURE YOU'LL BE FINE GETTING HOME?
YEAH, I'LL CALL A SERVICE.
"YOU GO ON AHEAD. YOU'RE OFF BABY-SITTING DUTY."
WILLIAM ARES, DIVORCE ATTORNEY TO THE STARS.
LOREN LENOX, MUCKRAKER TO THE...
...WELL, THE MUCK.
YOU DO HAVE A WAY WITH WORDS.
WHATEVER YOU'RE AFTER, I HAVE NO COMMENT.
AND ABSOLUTELY NOTHING TO SAY TO YOU.
DENIAL IS AS GOOD AS AN ADMISSION.
WHAT IS THIS ABOUT?
WHAT DO YOU THINK?

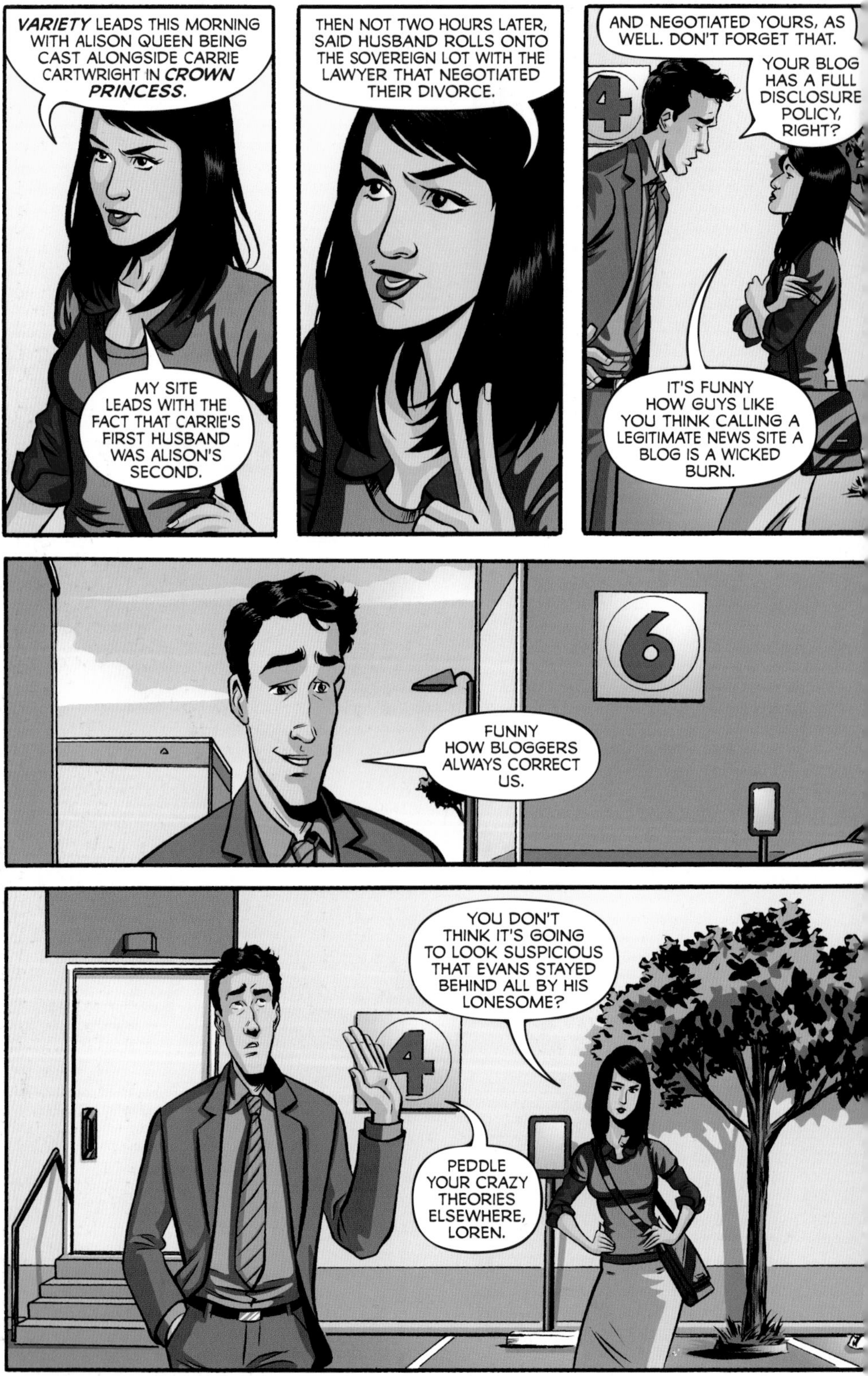
*VARIETY* LEADS THIS MORNING WITH ALISON QUEEN BEING CAST ALONGSIDE CARRIE CARTWRIGHT IN *CROWN PRINCESS*.
MY SITE LEADS WITH THE FACT THAT CARRIE'S FIRST HUSBAND WAS ALISON'S SECOND.
THEN NOT TWO HOURS LATER, SAID HUSBAND ROLLS ONTO THE SOVEREIGN LOT WITH THE LAWYER THAT NEGOTIATED THEIR DIVORCE.
AND NEGOTIATED YOURS, AS WELL. DON'T FORGET THAT.
YOUR BLOG HAS A FULL DISCLOSURE POLICY, RIGHT?
4
IT'S FUNNY HOW GUYS LIKE YOU THINK CALLING A LEGITIMATE NEWS SITE A BLOG IS A WICKED BURN.
6
FUNNY HOW BLOGGERS ALWAYS CORRECT US.
YOU DON'T THINK IT'S GOING TO LOOK SUSPICIOUS THAT EVANS STAYED BEHIND ALL BY HIS LONESOME?
4
PEDDLE YOUR CRAZY THEORIES ELSEWHERE, LOREN.

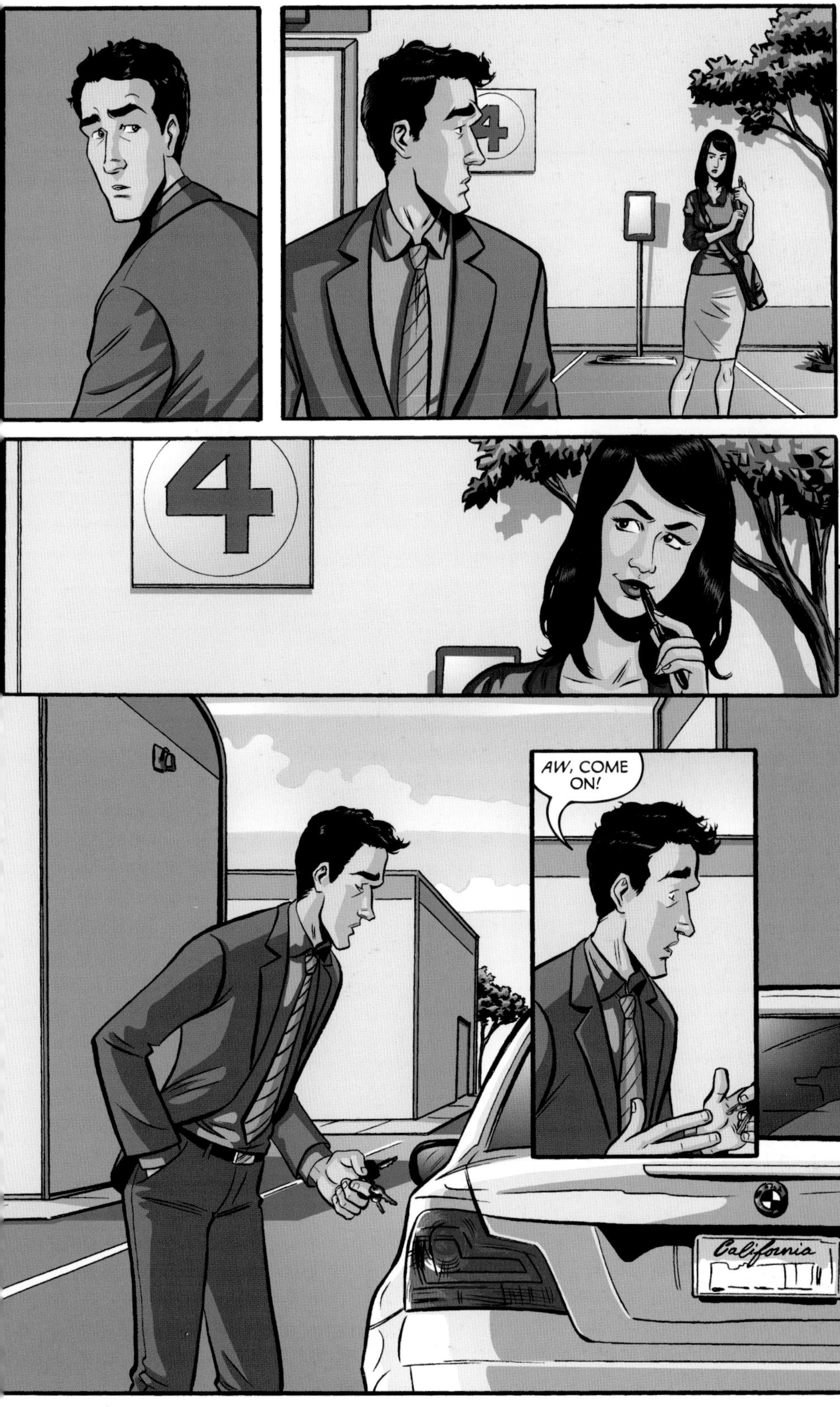
AW, COME ON!
California

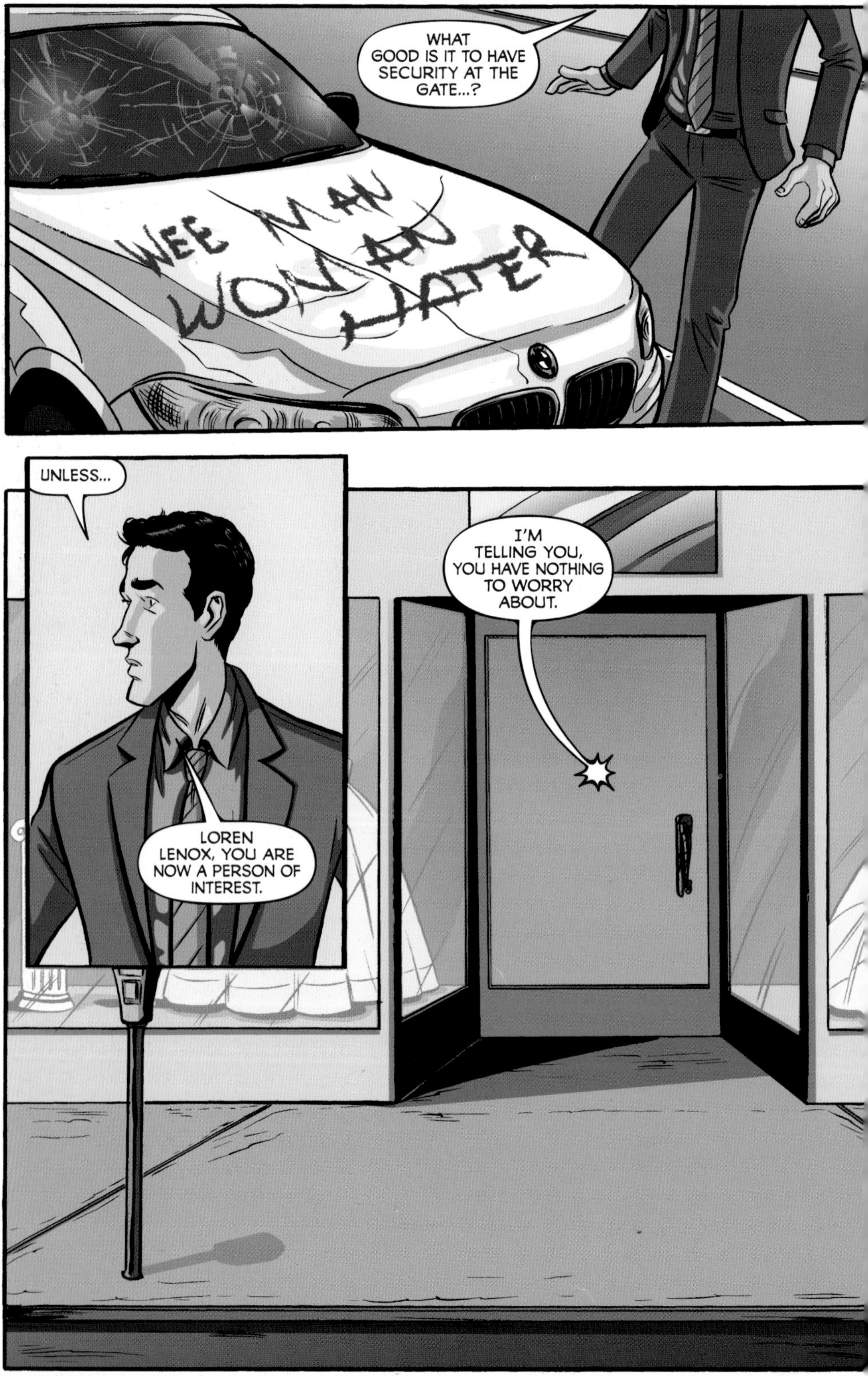
WHAT GOOD IS IT TO HAVE SECURITY AT THE GATE...?
WEE MAN WON AN HATER
UNLESS...
LOREN LENOX, YOU ARE NOW A PERSON OF INTEREST.
I'M TELLING YOU, YOU HAVE NOTHING TO WORRY ABOUT.

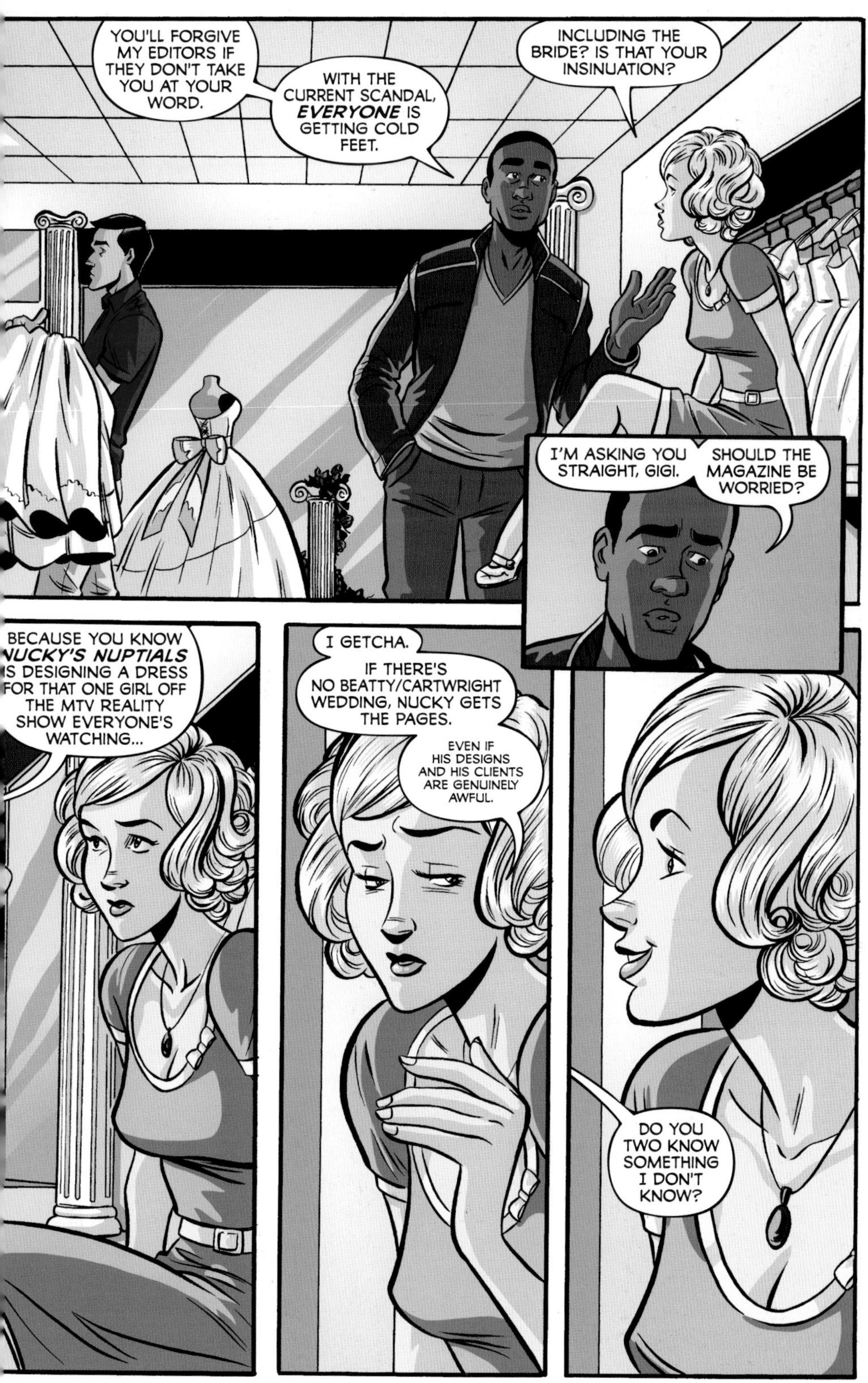

YOU'LL FORGIVE MY EDITORS IF THEY DON'T TAKE YOU AT YOUR WORD.
WITH THE CURRENT SCANDAL, *EVERYONE* IS GETTING COLD FEET.
INCLUDING THE BRIDE? IS THAT YOUR INSINUATION?
I'M ASKING YOU STRAIGHT, GIGI.
SHOULD THE MAGAZINE BE WORRIED?
BECAUSE YOU KNOW *NUCKY'S NUPTIALS* IS DESIGNING A DRESS FOR THAT ONE GIRL OFF THE MTV REALITY SHOW EVERYONE'S WATCHING...
I GETCHA.
IF THERE'S NO BEATTY/CARTWRIGHT WEDDING, NUCKY GETS THE PAGES.
EVEN IF HIS DESIGNS AND HIS CLIENTS ARE GENUINELY AWFUL.
DO YOU TWO KNOW SOMETHING I DON'T KNOW?

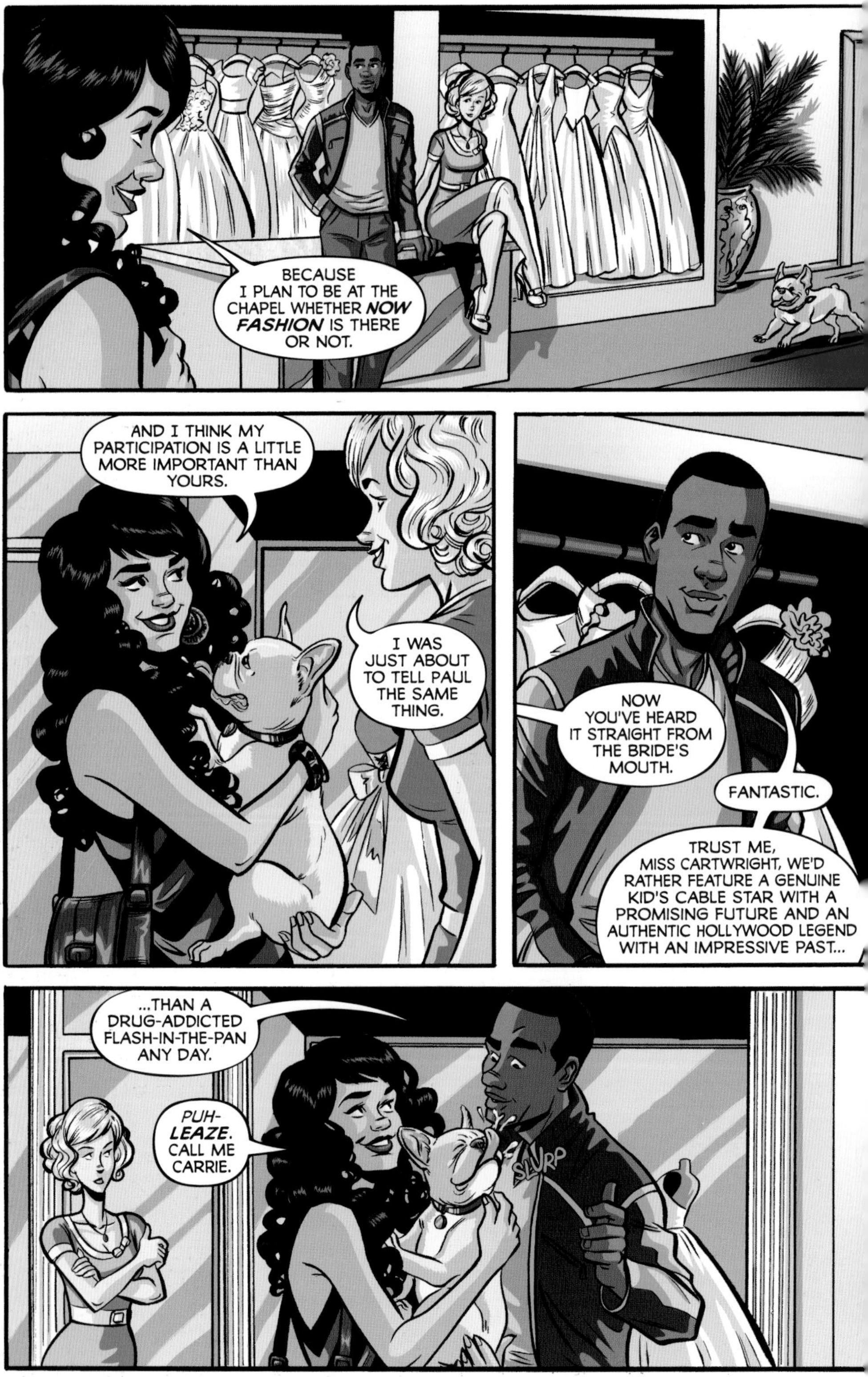
BECAUSE I PLAN TO BE AT THE CHAPEL WHETHER *NOW FASHION* IS THERE OR NOT.
AND I THINK MY PARTICIPATION IS A LITTLE MORE IMPORTANT THAN YOURS.
I WAS JUST ABOUT TO TELL PAUL THE SAME THING.
NOW YOU'VE HEARD IT STRAIGHT FROM THE BRIDE'S MOUTH.
FANTASTIC.
TRUST ME, MISS CARTWRIGHT, WE'D RATHER FEATURE A GENUINE KID'S CABLE STAR WITH A PROMISING FUTURE AND AN AUTHENTIC HOLLYWOOD LEGEND WITH AN IMPRESSIVE PAST...
...THAN A DRUG-ADDICTED FLASH-IN-THE-PAN ANY DAY.
*PUH-* ***LEAZE***. CALL ME CARRIE.
SLURP

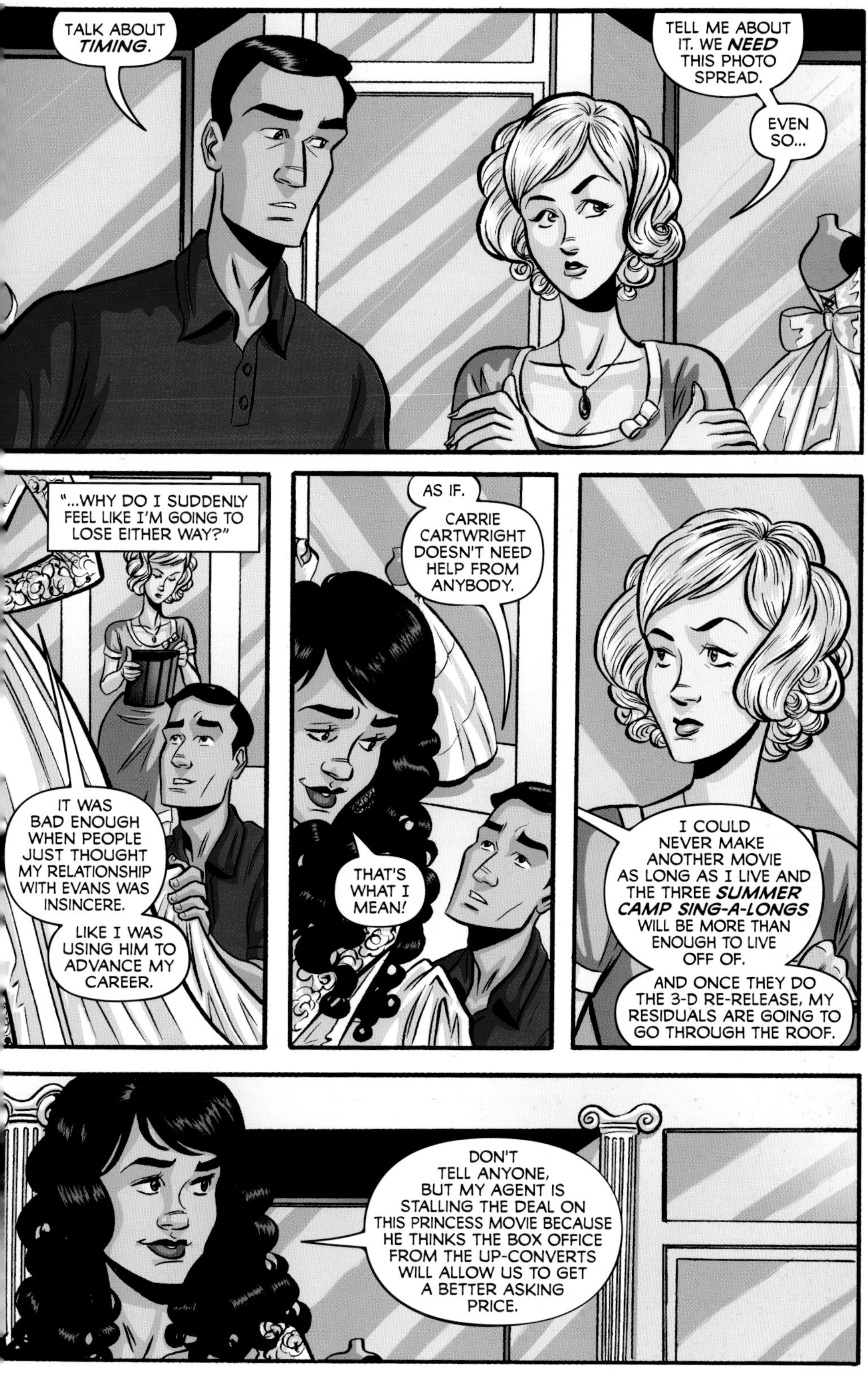
TALK ABOUT *TIMING*.
TELL ME ABOUT IT. WE ***NEED*** THIS PHOTO SPREAD.
EVEN SO...
"...WHY DO I SUDDENLY FEEL LIKE I'M GOING TO LOSE EITHER WAY?"
IT WAS BAD ENOUGH WHEN PEOPLE JUST THOUGHT MY RELATIONSHIP WITH EVANS WAS INSINCERE.
LIKE I WAS USING HIM TO ADVANCE MY CAREER.
AS IF.
CARRIE CARTWRIGHT DOESN'T NEED HELP FROM ANYBODY.
THAT'S WHAT I MEAN!
I COULD NEVER MAKE ANOTHER MOVIE AS LONG AS I LIVE AND THE THREE ***SUMMER CAMP SING-A-LONGS*** WILL BE MORE THAN ENOUGH TO LIVE OFF OF.
AND ONCE THEY DO THE 3-D RE-RELEASE, MY RESIDUALS ARE GOING TO GO THROUGH THE ROOF.
DON'T TELL ANYONE, BUT MY AGENT IS STALLING THE DEAL ON THIS PRINCESS MOVIE BECAUSE HE THINKS THE BOX OFFICE FROM THE UP-CONVERTS WILL ALLOW US TO GET A BETTER ASKING PRICE.

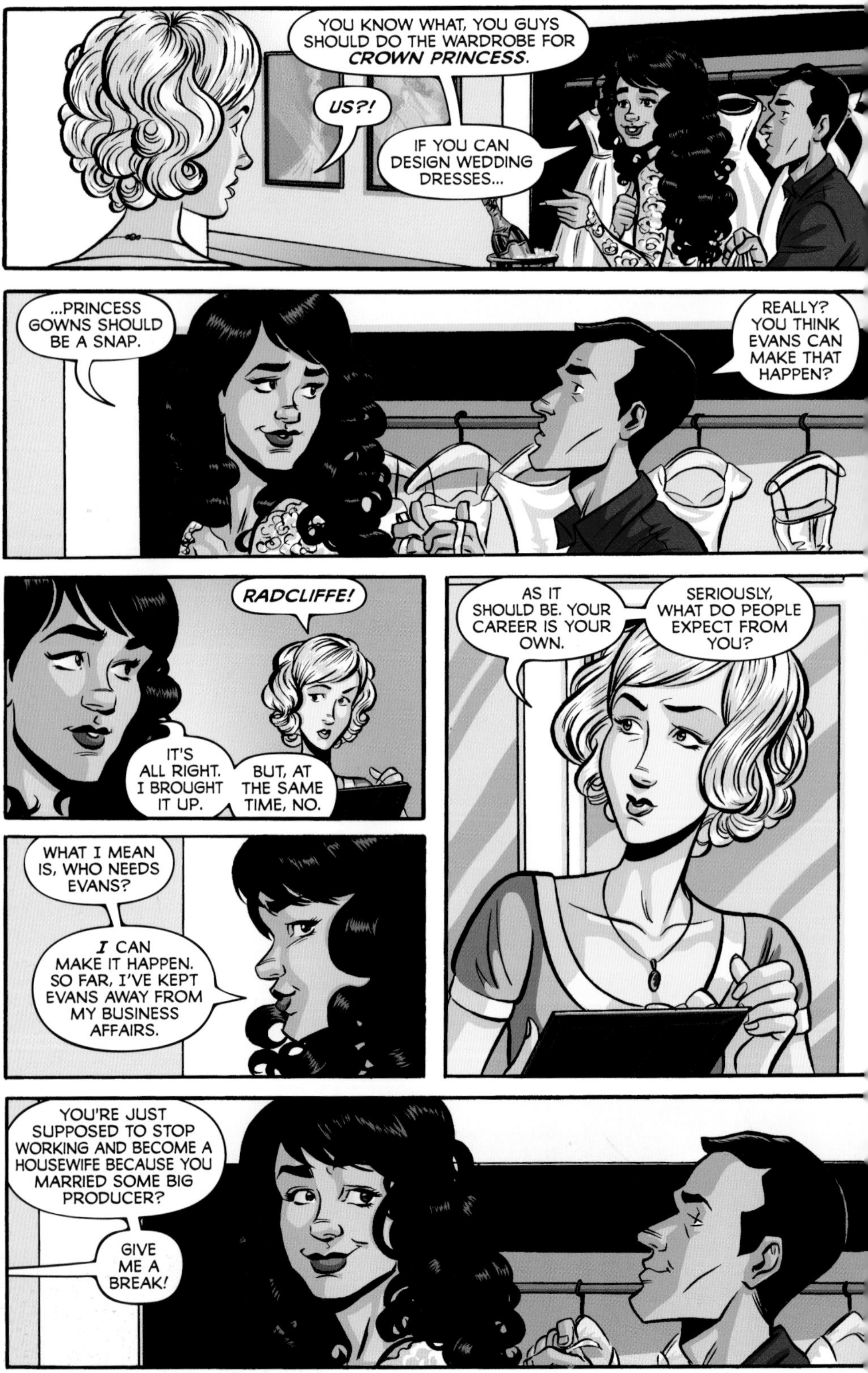
YOU KNOW WHAT, YOU GUYS SHOULD DO THE WARDROBE FOR *CROWN PRINCESS*.
*US?!*
IF YOU CAN DESIGN WEDDING DRESSES...
...PRINCESS GOWNS SHOULD BE A SNAP.
REALLY? YOU THINK EVANS CAN MAKE THAT HAPPEN?
*RADCLIFFE!*
IT'S ALL RIGHT. I BROUGHT IT UP.
BUT, AT THE SAME TIME, NO.
WHAT I MEAN IS, WHO NEEDS EVANS?
*I* CAN MAKE IT HAPPEN. SO FAR, I'VE KEPT EVANS AWAY FROM MY BUSINESS AFFAIRS.
AS IT SHOULD BE. YOUR CAREER IS YOUR OWN.
SERIOUSLY, WHAT DO PEOPLE EXPECT FROM YOU?
YOU'RE JUST SUPPOSED TO STOP WORKING AND BECOME A HOUSEWIFE BECAUSE YOU MARRIED SOME BIG PRODUCER?
GIVE ME A BREAK!

# CHAPTER FIVE

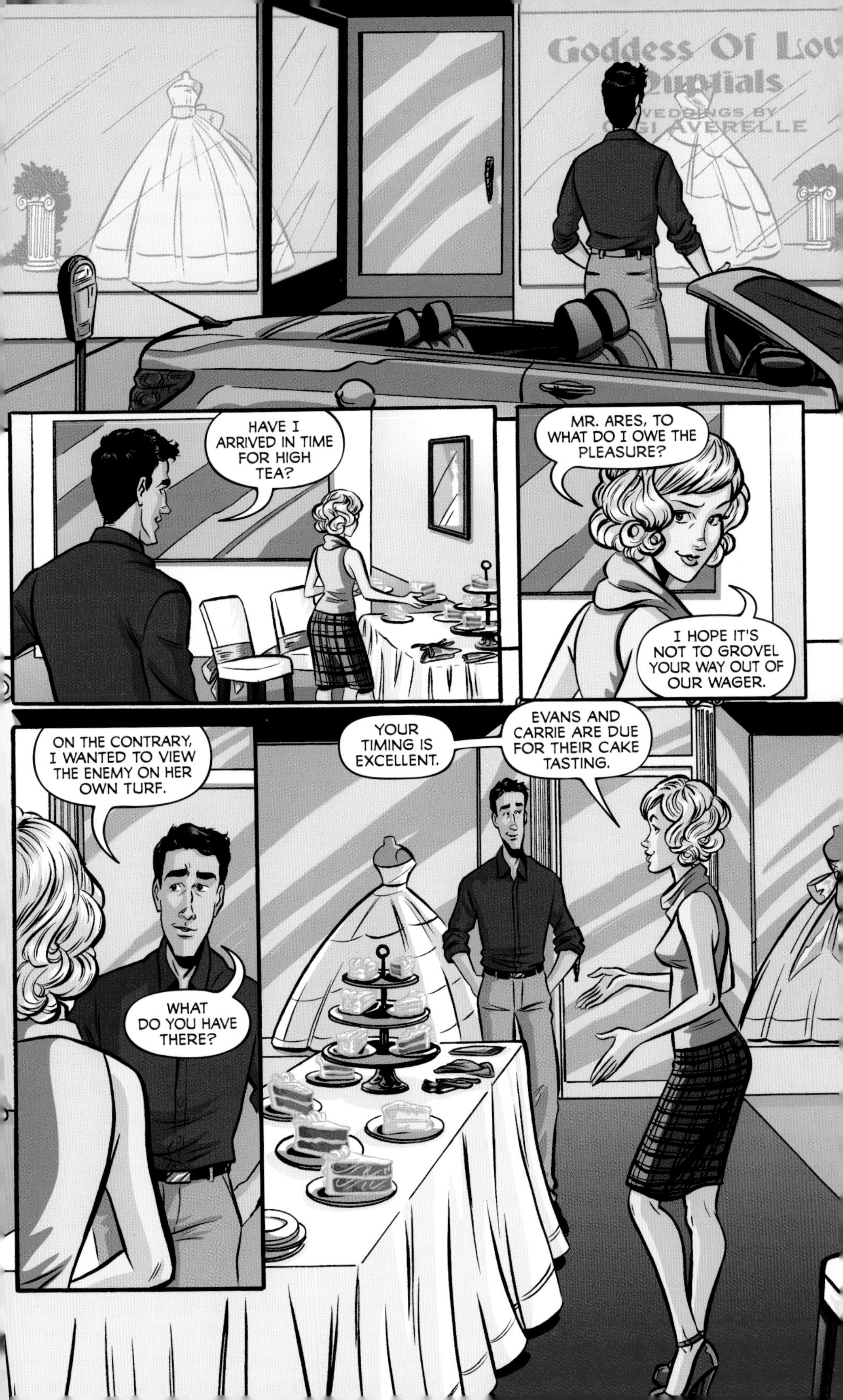
Goddess Of Lov
Nuptials
WEDDINGS BY
HAVE I ARRIVED IN TIME FOR HIGH TEA?
MR. ARES, TO WHAT DO I OWE THE PLEASURE?
I HOPE IT'S NOT TO GROVEL YOUR WAY OUT OF OUR WAGER.
ON THE CONTRARY, I WANTED TO VIEW THE ENEMY ON HER OWN TURF.
YOUR TIMING IS EXCELLENT.
EVANS AND CARRIE ARE DUE FOR THEIR CAKE TASTING.
WHAT DO YOU HAVE THERE?

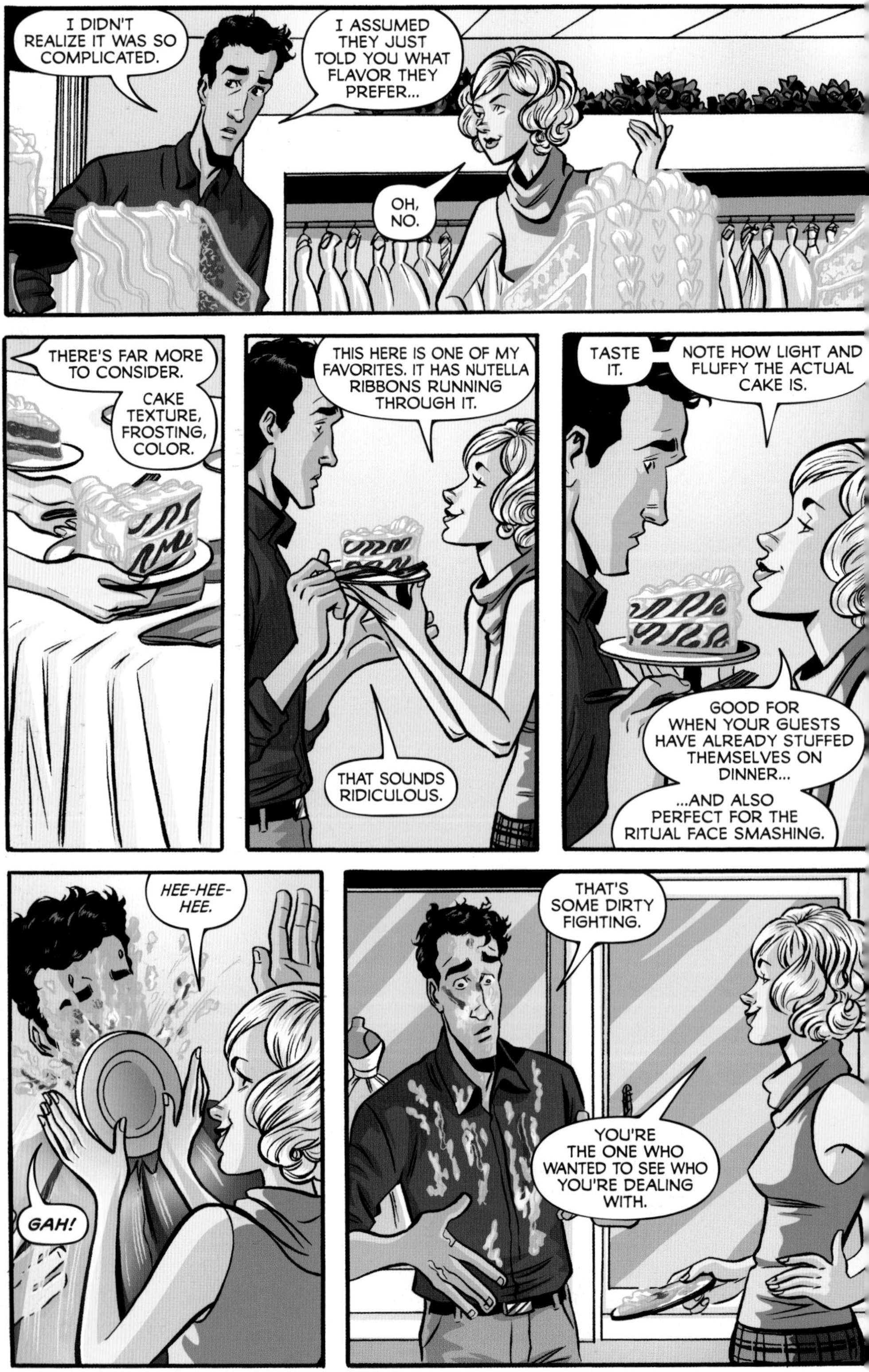
I DIDN'T REALIZE IT WAS SO COMPLICATED.
I ASSUMED THEY JUST TOLD YOU WHAT FLAVOR THEY PREFER...
OH, NO.
THERE'S FAR MORE TO CONSIDER.
CAKE TEXTURE, FROSTING, COLOR.
THIS HERE IS ONE OF MY FAVORITES. IT HAS NUTELLA RIBBONS RUNNING THROUGH IT.
THAT SOUNDS RIDICULOUS.
TASTE IT.
NOTE HOW LIGHT AND FLUFFY THE ACTUAL CAKE IS.
GOOD FOR WHEN YOUR GUESTS HAVE ALREADY STUFFED THEMSELVES ON DINNER...
...AND ALSO PERFECT FOR THE RITUAL FACE SMASHING.
HEE-HEE-HEE.
GAH!
THAT'S SOME DIRTY FIGHTING.
YOU'RE THE ONE WHO WANTED TO SEE WHO YOU'RE DEALING WITH.

DULY NOTED.

HA-HA-HA!

I'M GLAD YOU TWO ARE HAVING FUN.

SORRY. WE GOT STARTED WITHOUT YOU.

WHERE'S CARRIE?

THAT'S WHAT I'D LIKE TO KNOW.

SHE'S DISAPPEARED.

IS EVERYTHING ALL RIGHT? WHAT HAPPENED?

I SUPPOSE YOU'RE GOING TO SEE THESE EVENTUALLY...

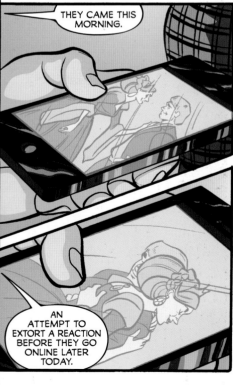

THEY CAME THIS MORNING.

AN ATTEMPT TO EXTORT A REACTION BEFORE THEY GO ONLINE LATER TODAY.

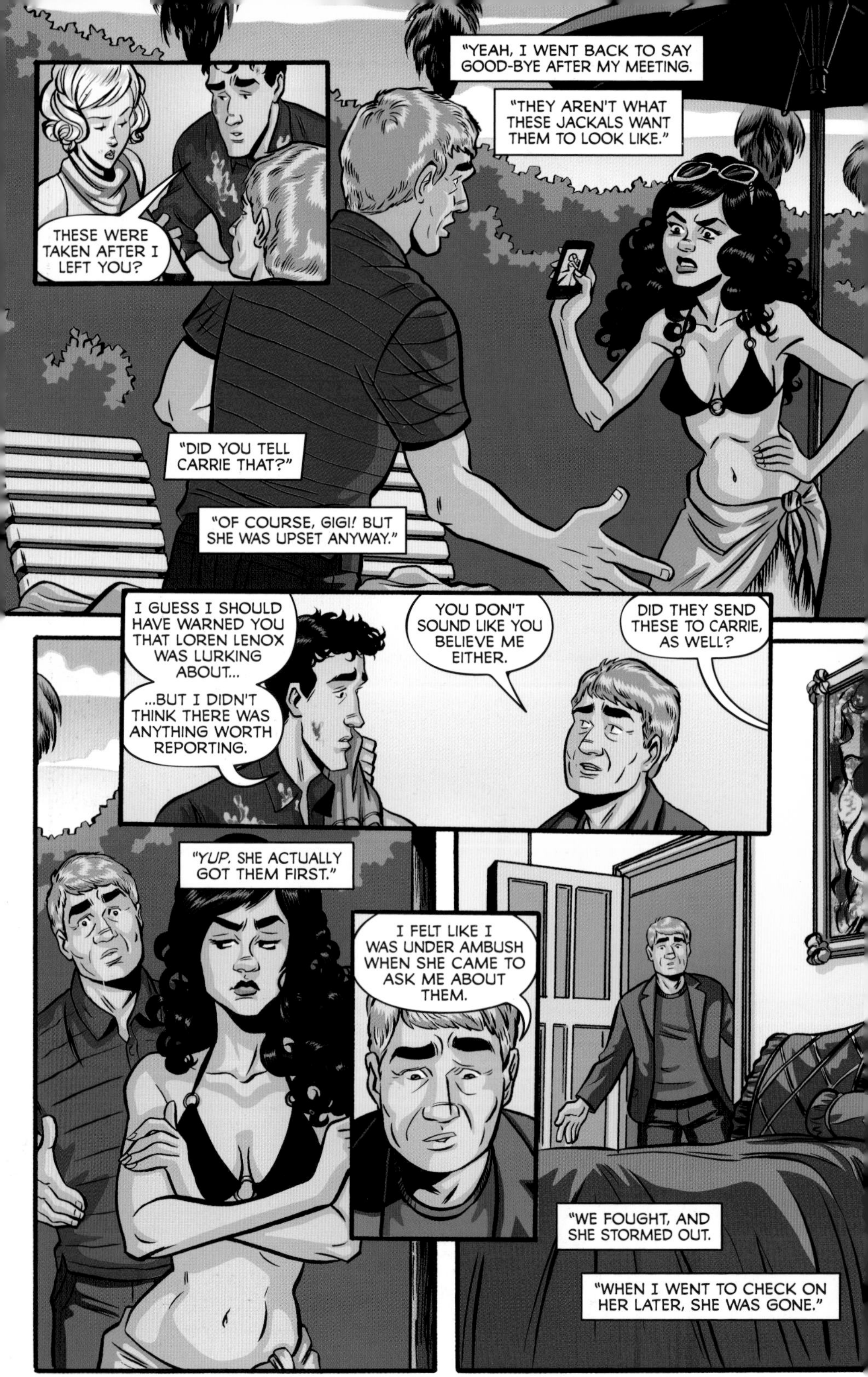
"YEAH, I WENT BACK TO SAY GOOD-BYE AFTER MY MEETING.
THESE WERE TAKEN AFTER I LEFT YOU?
"THEY AREN'T WHAT THESE JACKALS WANT THEM TO LOOK LIKE."
"DID YOU TELL CARRIE THAT?"
"OF COURSE, GIGI! BUT SHE WAS UPSET ANYWAY."
I GUESS I SHOULD HAVE WARNED YOU THAT LOREN LENOX WAS LURKING ABOUT...
...BUT I DIDN'T THINK THERE WAS ANYTHING WORTH REPORTING.
YOU DON'T SOUND LIKE YOU BELIEVE ME EITHER.
DID THEY SEND THESE TO CARRIE, AS WELL?
"YUP. SHE ACTUALLY GOT THEM FIRST."
I FELT LIKE I WAS UNDER AMBUSH WHEN SHE CAME TO ASK ME ABOUT THEM.
"WE FOUGHT, AND SHE STORMED OUT.
"WHEN I WENT TO CHECK ON HER LATER, SHE WAS GONE."

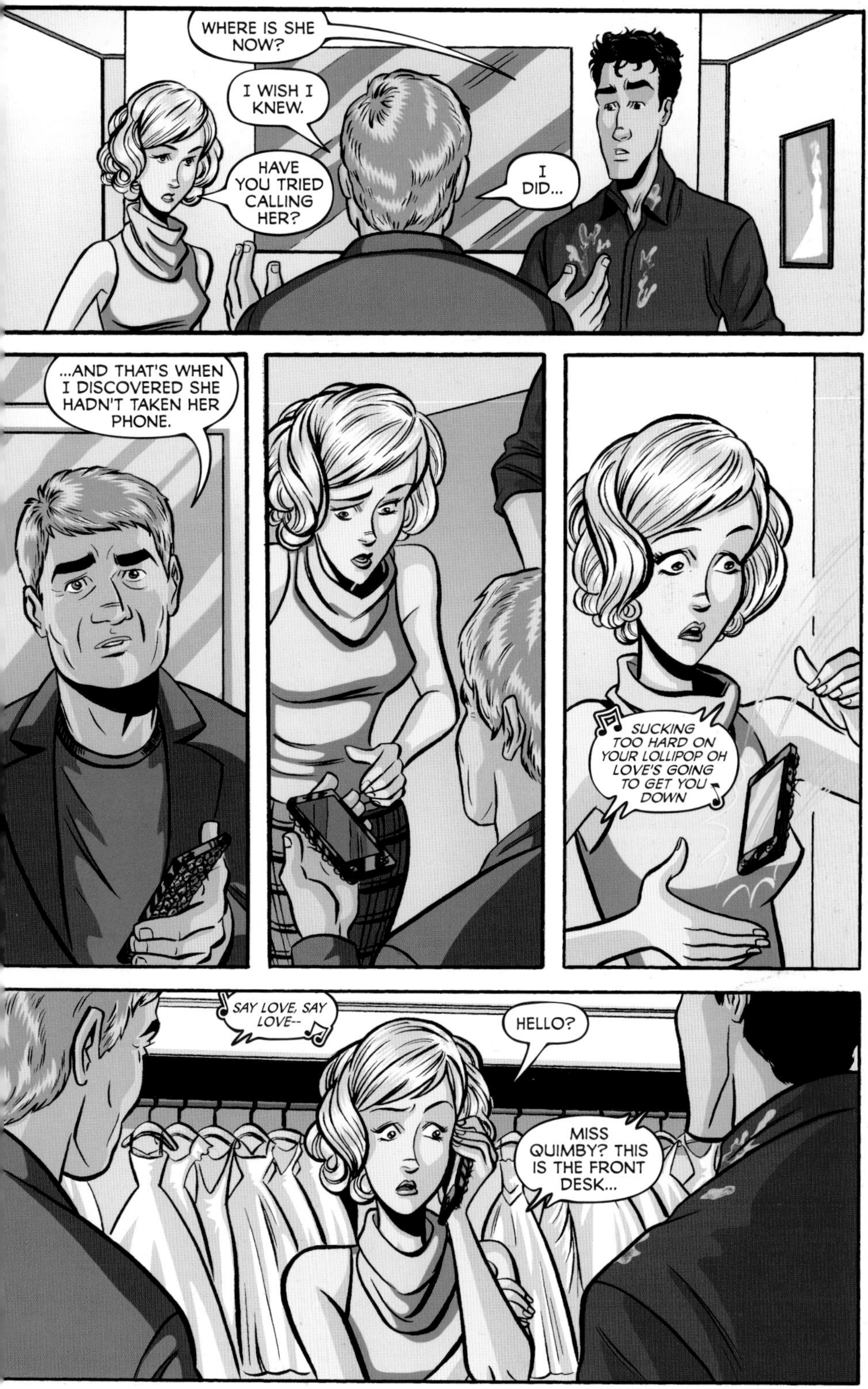
WHERE IS SHE NOW?
I WISH I KNEW.
HAVE YOU TRIED CALLING HER?
I DID...
...AND THAT'S WHEN I DISCOVERED SHE HADN'T TAKEN HER PHONE.
SUCKING TOO HARD ON YOUR LOLLIPOP OH LOVE'S GOING TO GET YOU DOWN
SAY LOVE, SAY LOVE--
HELLO?
MISS QUIMBY? THIS IS THE FRONT DESK...

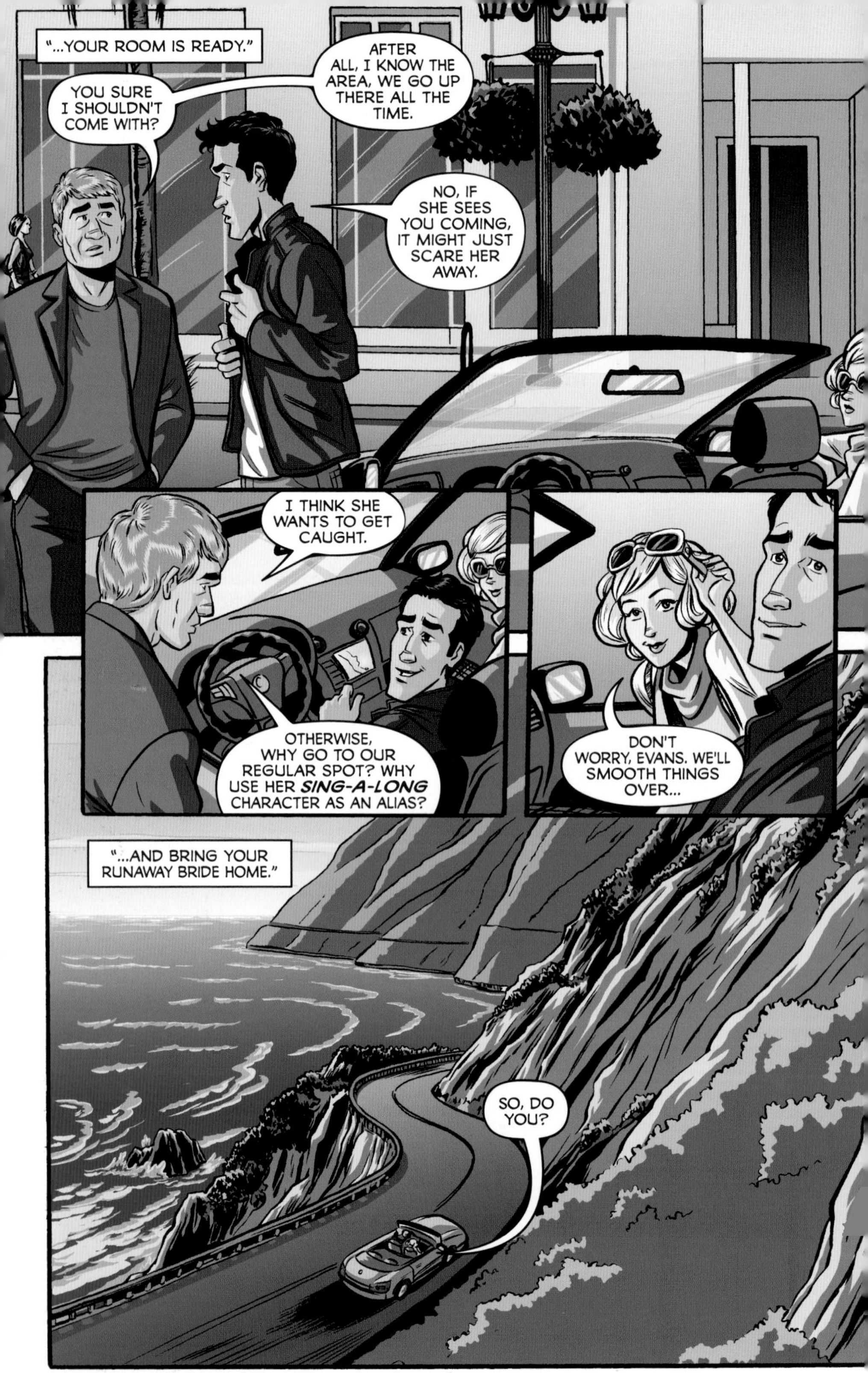
"...YOUR ROOM IS READY."
YOU SURE I SHOULDN'T COME WITH?
AFTER ALL, I KNOW THE AREA, WE GO UP THERE ALL THE TIME.
NO, IF SHE SEES YOU COMING, IT MIGHT JUST SCARE HER AWAY.
I THINK SHE WANTS TO GET CAUGHT.
OTHERWISE, WHY GO TO OUR REGULAR SPOT? WHY USE HER *SING-A-LONG* CHARACTER AS AN ALIAS?
DON'T WORRY, EVANS. WE'LL SMOOTH THINGS OVER...
"...AND BRING YOUR RUNAWAY BRIDE HOME."
SO, DO YOU?

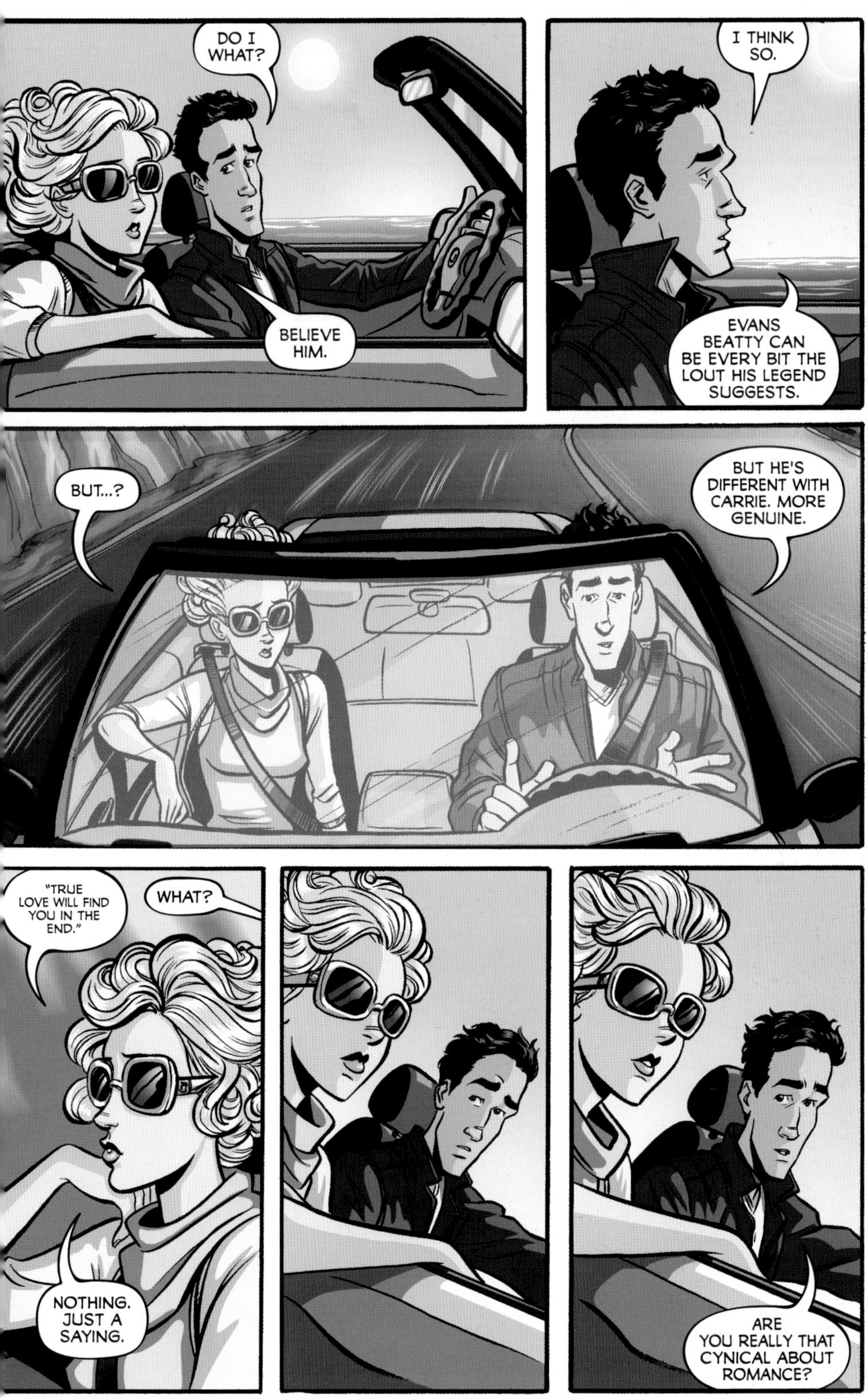
DO I WHAT?
BELIEVE HIM.
I THINK SO.
EVANS BEATTY CAN BE EVERY BIT THE LOUT HIS LEGEND SUGGESTS.
BUT...?
BUT HE'S DIFFERENT WITH CARRIE. MORE GENUINE.
"TRUE LOVE WILL FIND YOU IN THE END."
WHAT?
NOTHING. JUST A SAYING.
ARE YOU REALLY THAT CYNICAL ABOUT ROMANCE?

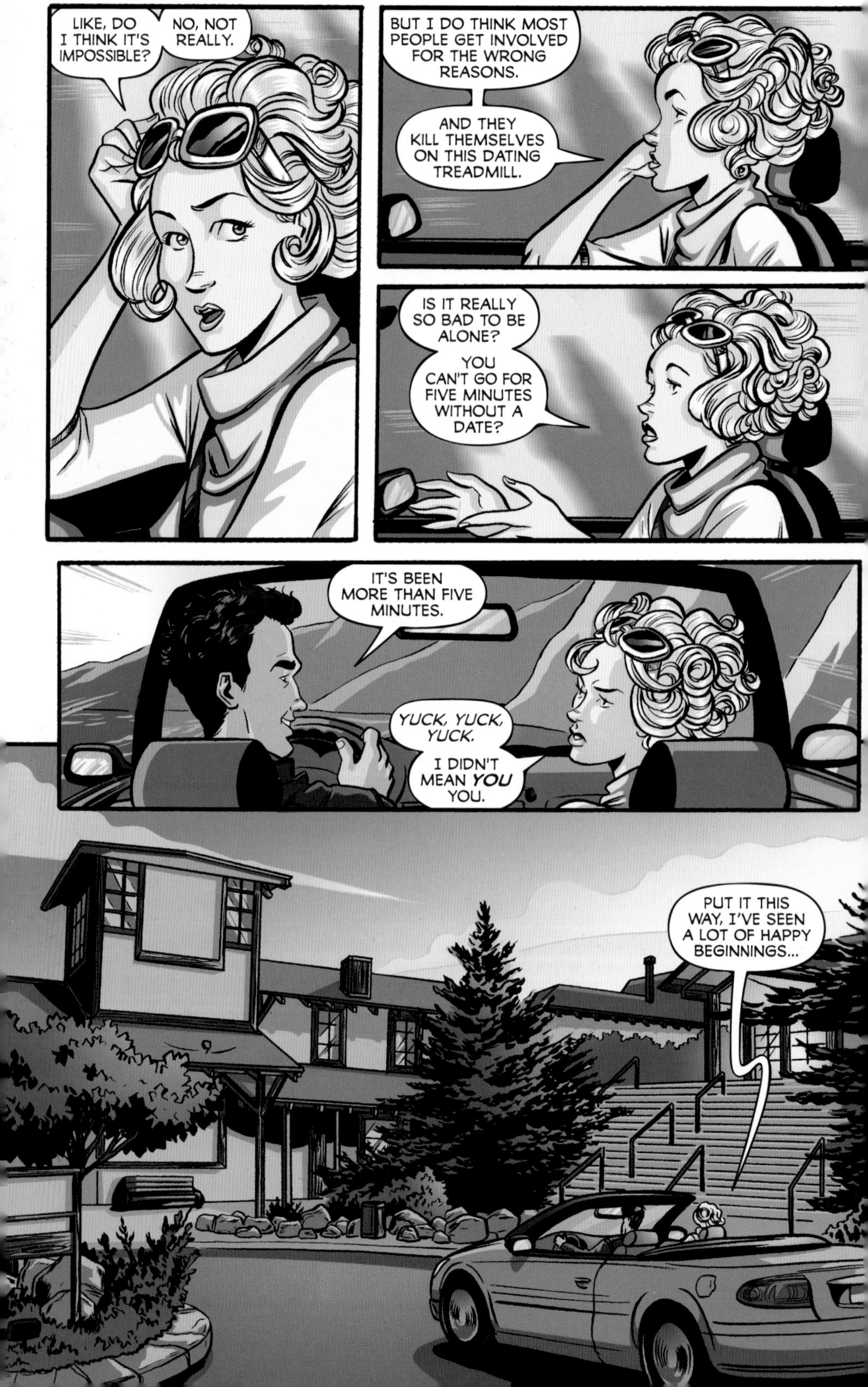

LIKE, DO I THINK IT'S IMPOSSIBLE?
NO, NOT REALLY.
BUT I DO THINK MOST PEOPLE GET INVOLVED FOR THE WRONG REASONS.
AND THEY KILL THEMSELVES ON THIS DATING TREADMILL.
IS IT REALLY SO BAD TO BE ALONE?
YOU CAN'T GO FOR FIVE MINUTES WITHOUT A DATE?
IT'S BEEN MORE THAN FIVE MINUTES.
*YUCK, YUCK, YUCK.*
I DIDN'T MEAN ***YOU*** YOU.
PUT IT THIS WAY, I'VE SEEN A LOT OF HAPPY BEGINNINGS...

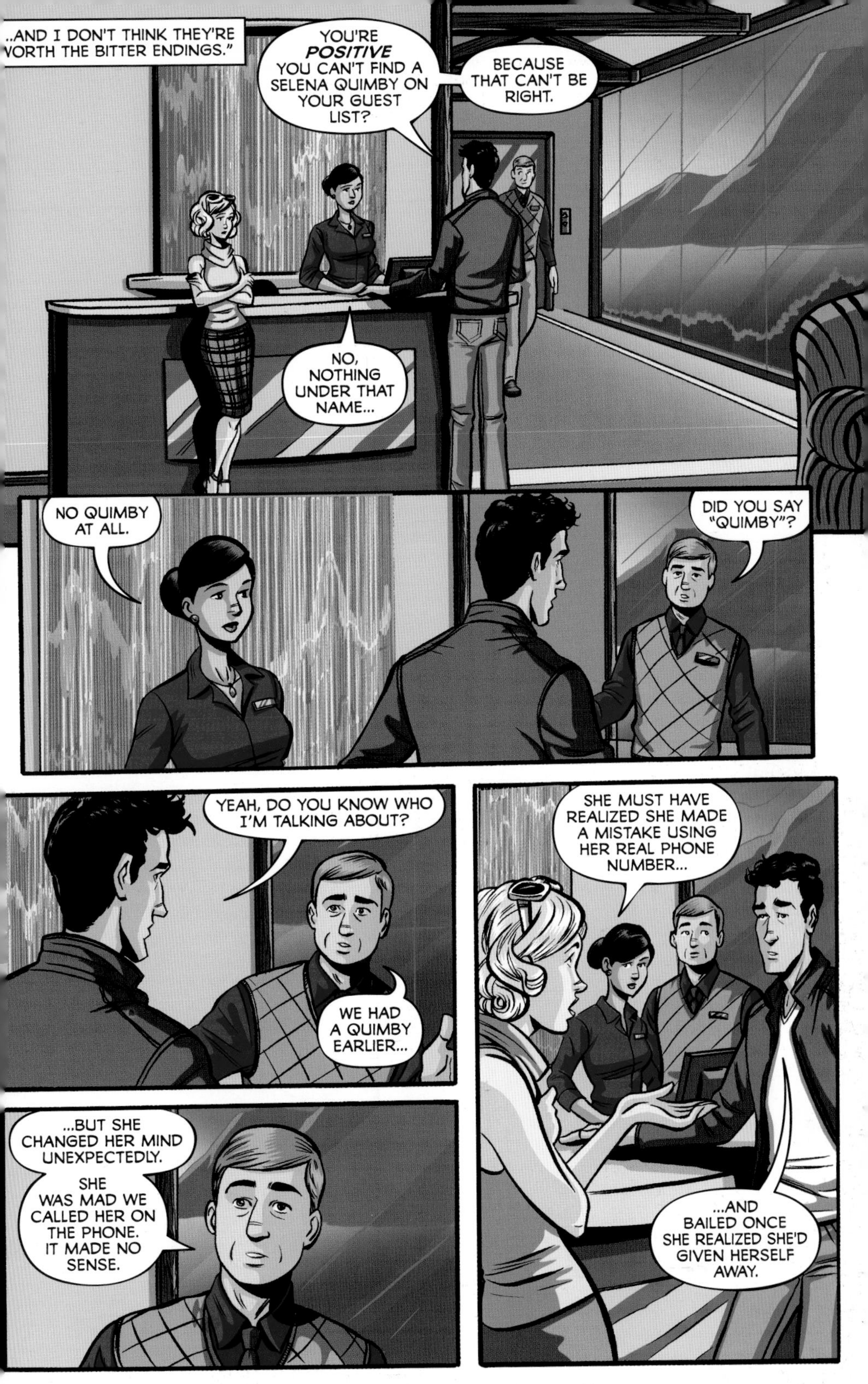
..AND I DON'T THINK THEY'RE
VORTH THE BITTER ENDINGS."
YOU'RE *POSITIVE* YOU CAN'T FIND A SELENA QUIMBY ON YOUR GUEST LIST?
BECAUSE THAT CAN'T BE RIGHT.
NO, NOTHING UNDER THAT NAME...
NO QUIMBY AT ALL.
DID YOU SAY "QUIMBY"?
YEAH, DO YOU KNOW WHO I'M TALKING ABOUT?
WE HAD A QUIMBY EARLIER...
...BUT SHE CHANGED HER MIND UNEXPECTEDLY.
SHE WAS MAD WE CALLED HER ON THE PHONE. IT MADE NO SENSE.
SHE MUST HAVE REALIZED SHE MADE A MISTAKE USING HER REAL PHONE NUMBER...
...AND BAILED ONCE SHE REALIZED SHE'D GIVEN HERSELF AWAY.

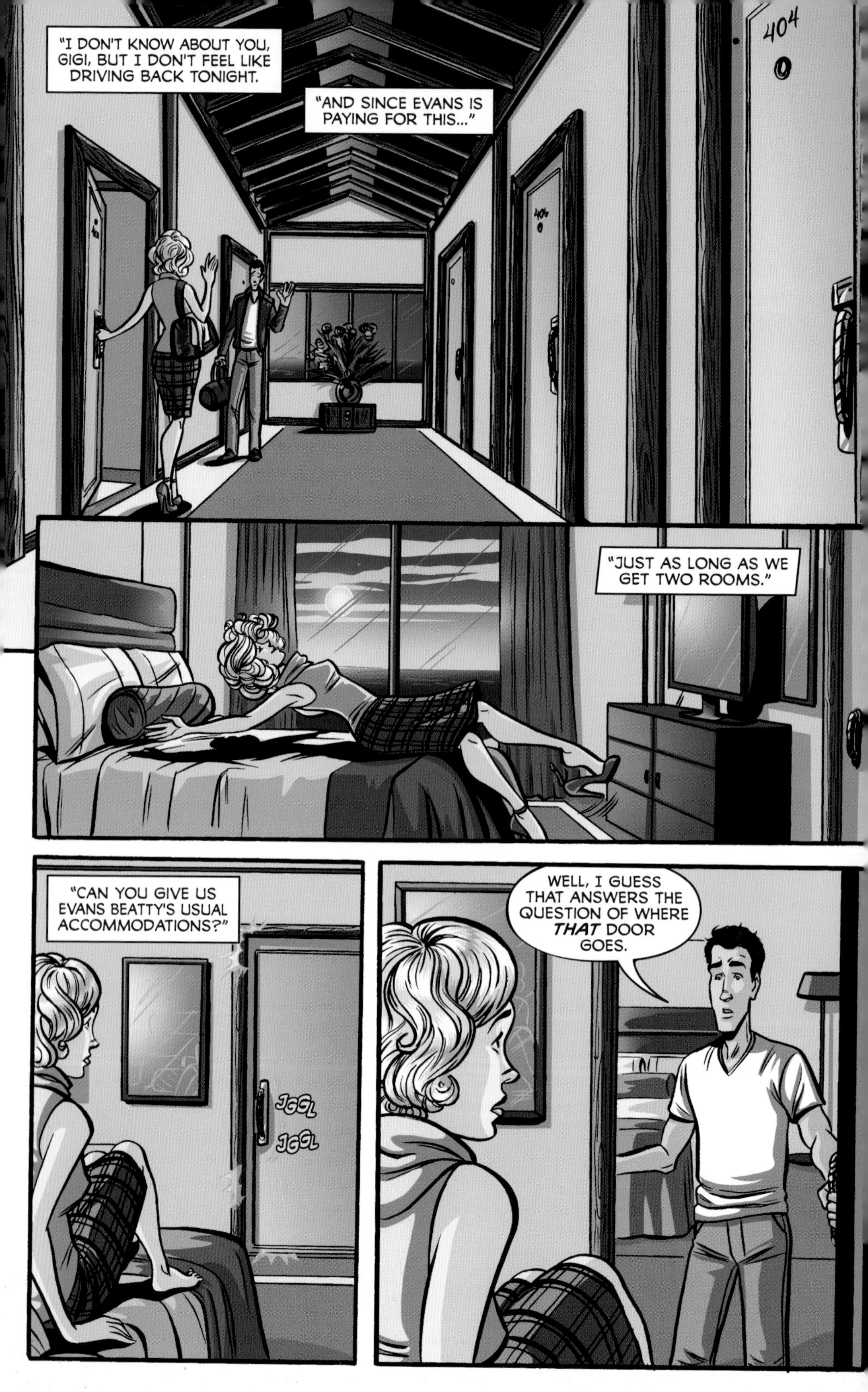
"I DON'T KNOW ABOUT YOU, GIGI, BUT I DON'T FEEL LIKE DRIVING BACK TONIGHT.
"AND SINCE EVANS IS PAYING FOR THIS..."
404
406
"JUST AS LONG AS WE GET TWO ROOMS."
"CAN YOU GIVE US EVANS BEATTY'S USUAL ACCOMMODATIONS?"
JGGL
JGGL
WELL, I GUESS THAT ANSWERS THE QUESTION OF WHERE *THAT* DOOR GOES.

# CHAPTER SIX

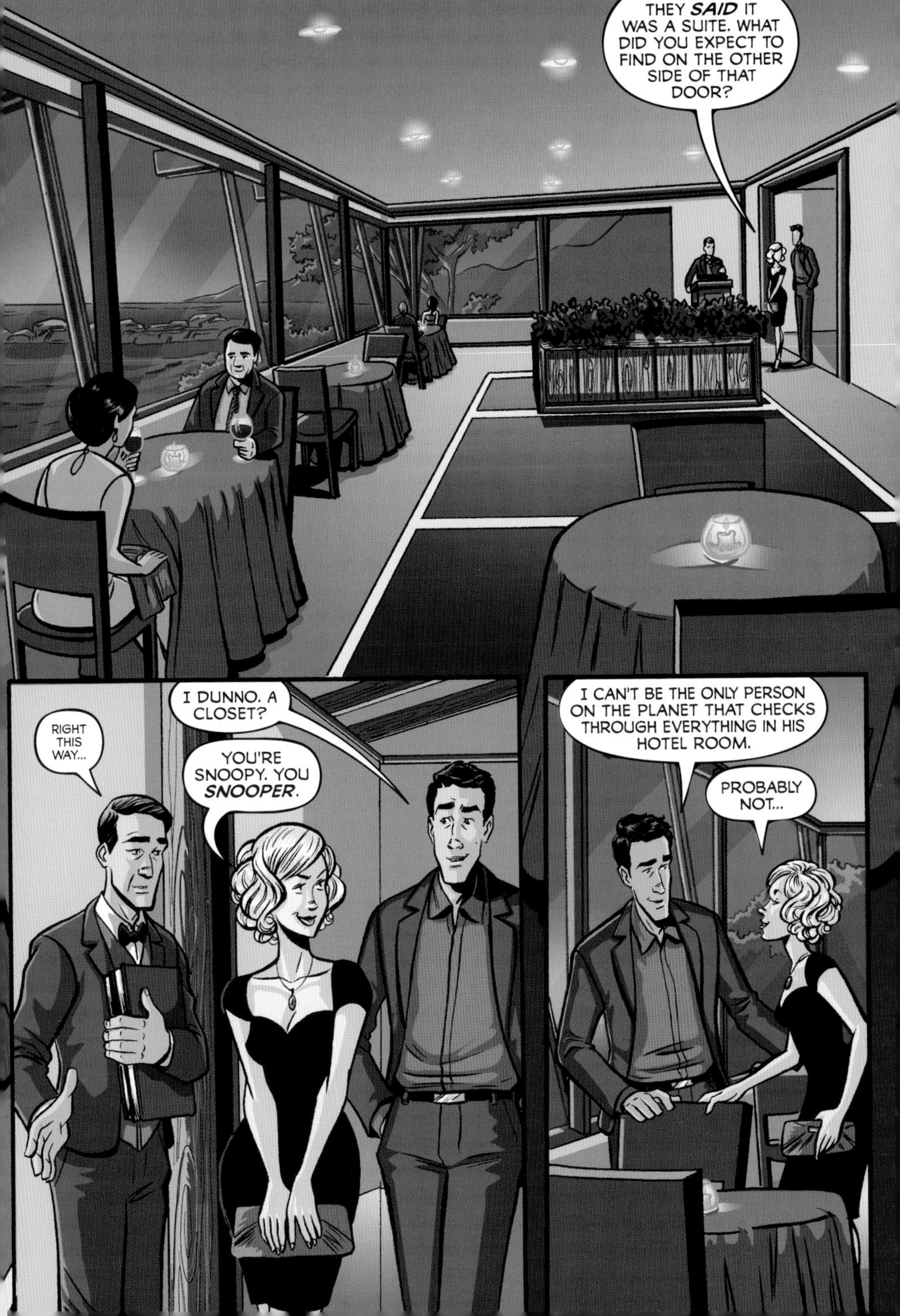
DUDE, THEY SAID IT WAS A SUITE. WHAT DID YOU EXPECT TO FIND ON THE OTHER SIDE OF THAT DOOR?
RIGHT THIS WAY...
I DUNNO. A CLOSET?
YOU'RE SNOOPY. YOU SNOOPER.
I CAN'T BE THE ONLY PERSON ON THE PLANET THAT CHECKS THROUGH EVERYTHING IN HIS HOTEL ROOM.
PROBABLY NOT...

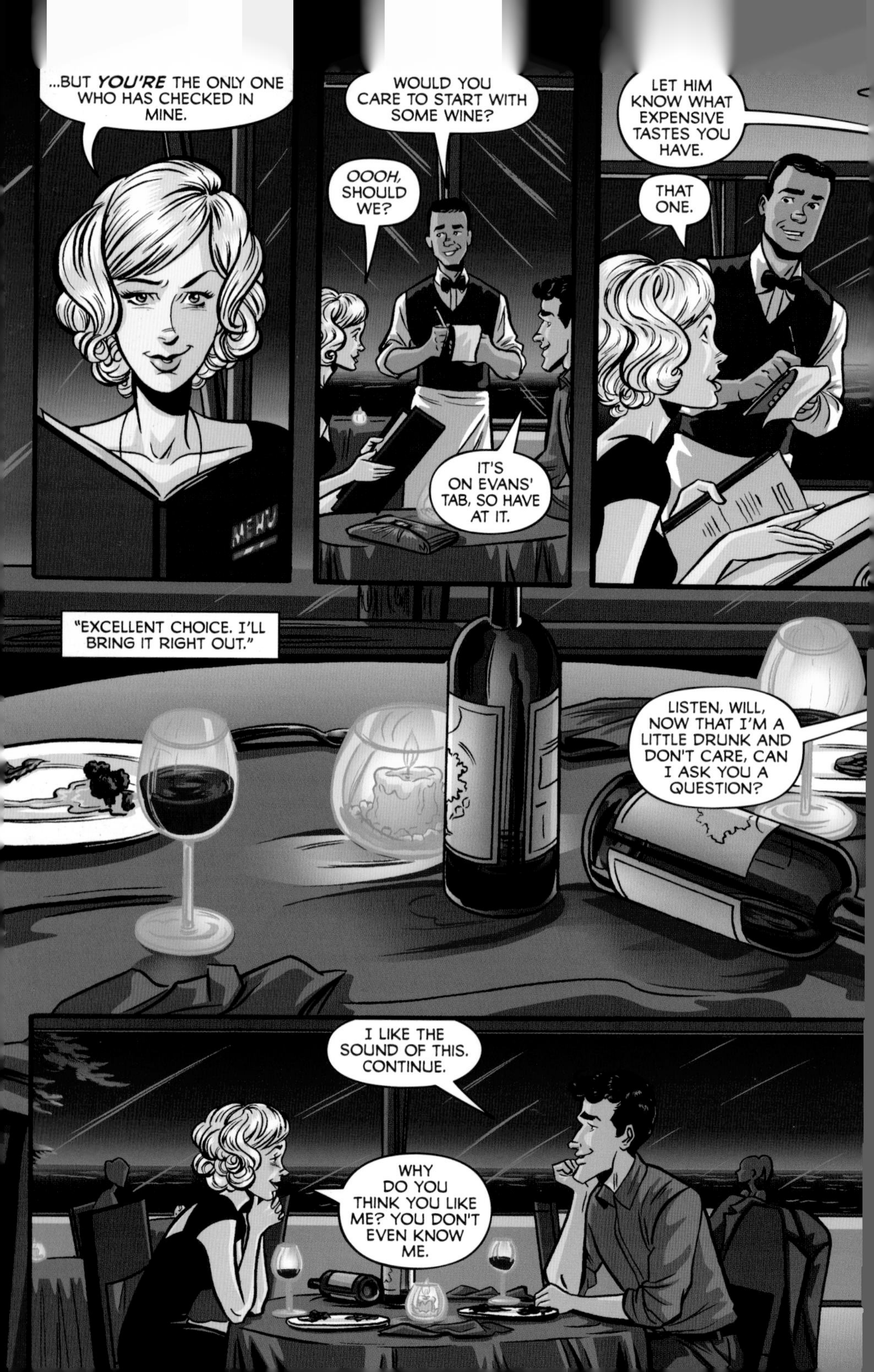
...BUT *YOU'RE* THE ONLY ONE WHO HAS CHECKED IN MINE.
MENU
WOULD YOU CARE TO START WITH SOME WINE?
OOOH, SHOULD WE?
IT'S ON EVANS' TAB, SO HAVE AT IT.
LET HIM KNOW WHAT EXPENSIVE TASTES YOU HAVE.
THAT ONE.
"EXCELLENT CHOICE. I'LL BRING IT RIGHT OUT."
LISTEN, WILL, NOW THAT I'M A LITTLE DRUNK AND DON'T CARE, CAN I ASK YOU A QUESTION?
I LIKE THE SOUND OF THIS. CONTINUE.
WHY DO YOU THINK YOU LIKE ME? YOU DON'T EVEN KNOW ME.

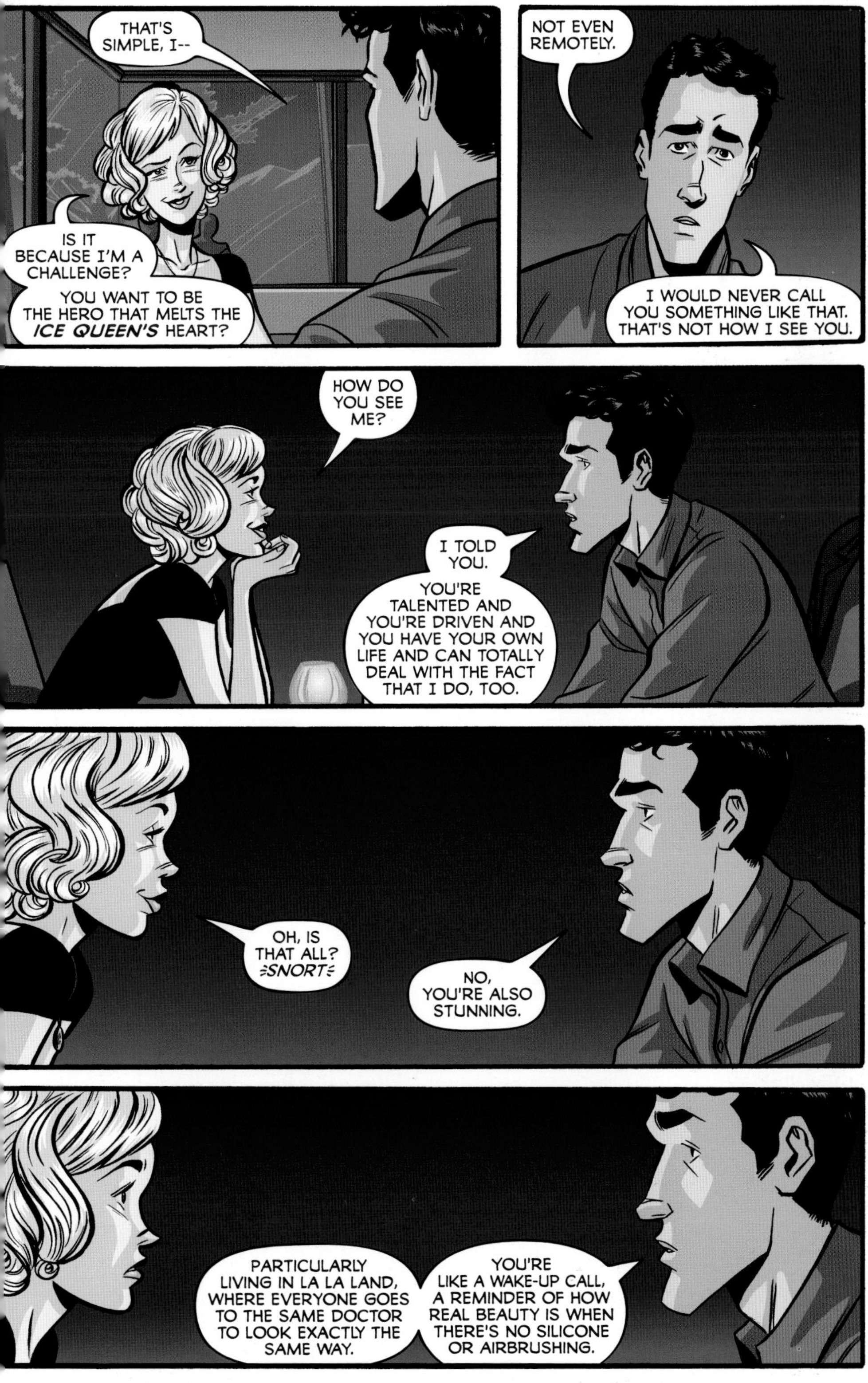
THAT'S SIMPLE, I--
IS IT BECAUSE I'M A CHALLENGE?
YOU WANT TO BE THE HERO THAT MELTS THE *ICE QUEEN'S* HEART?
NOT EVEN REMOTELY.
I WOULD NEVER CALL YOU SOMETHING LIKE THAT. THAT'S NOT HOW I SEE YOU.
HOW DO YOU SEE ME?
I TOLD YOU.
YOU'RE TALENTED AND YOU'RE DRIVEN AND YOU HAVE YOUR OWN LIFE AND CAN TOTALLY DEAL WITH THE FACT THAT I DO, TOO.
OH, IS THAT ALL? *SNORT*
NO, YOU'RE ALSO STUNNING.
YOU'RE LIKE A WAKE-UP CALL, A REMINDER OF HOW REAL BEAUTY IS WHEN THERE'S NO SILICONE OR AIRBRUSHING.
PARTICULARLY LIVING IN LA LA LAND, WHERE EVERYONE GOES TO THE SAME DOCTOR TO LOOK EXACTLY THE SAME WAY.

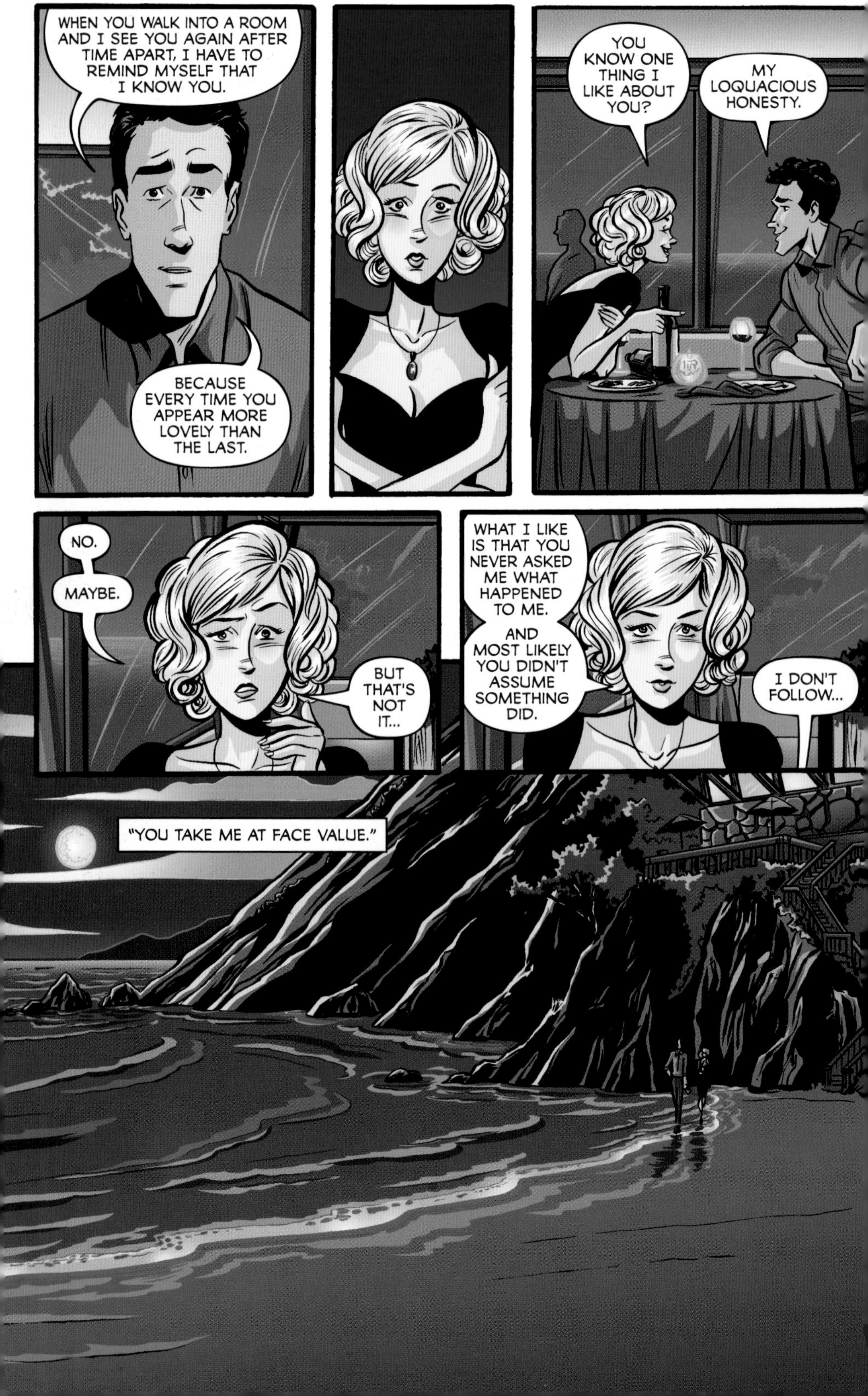
WHEN YOU WALK INTO A ROOM AND I SEE YOU AGAIN AFTER TIME APART, I HAVE TO REMIND MYSELF THAT I KNOW YOU.
BECAUSE EVERY TIME YOU APPEAR MORE LOVELY THAN THE LAST.
YOU KNOW ONE THING I LIKE ABOUT YOU?
MY LOQUACIOUS HONESTY.
NO.
MAYBE.
BUT THAT'S NOT IT...
WHAT I LIKE IS THAT YOU NEVER ASKED ME WHAT HAPPENED TO ME.
AND MOST LIKELY YOU DIDN'T ASSUME SOMETHING DID.
I DON'T FOLLOW...
"YOU TAKE ME AT FACE VALUE."

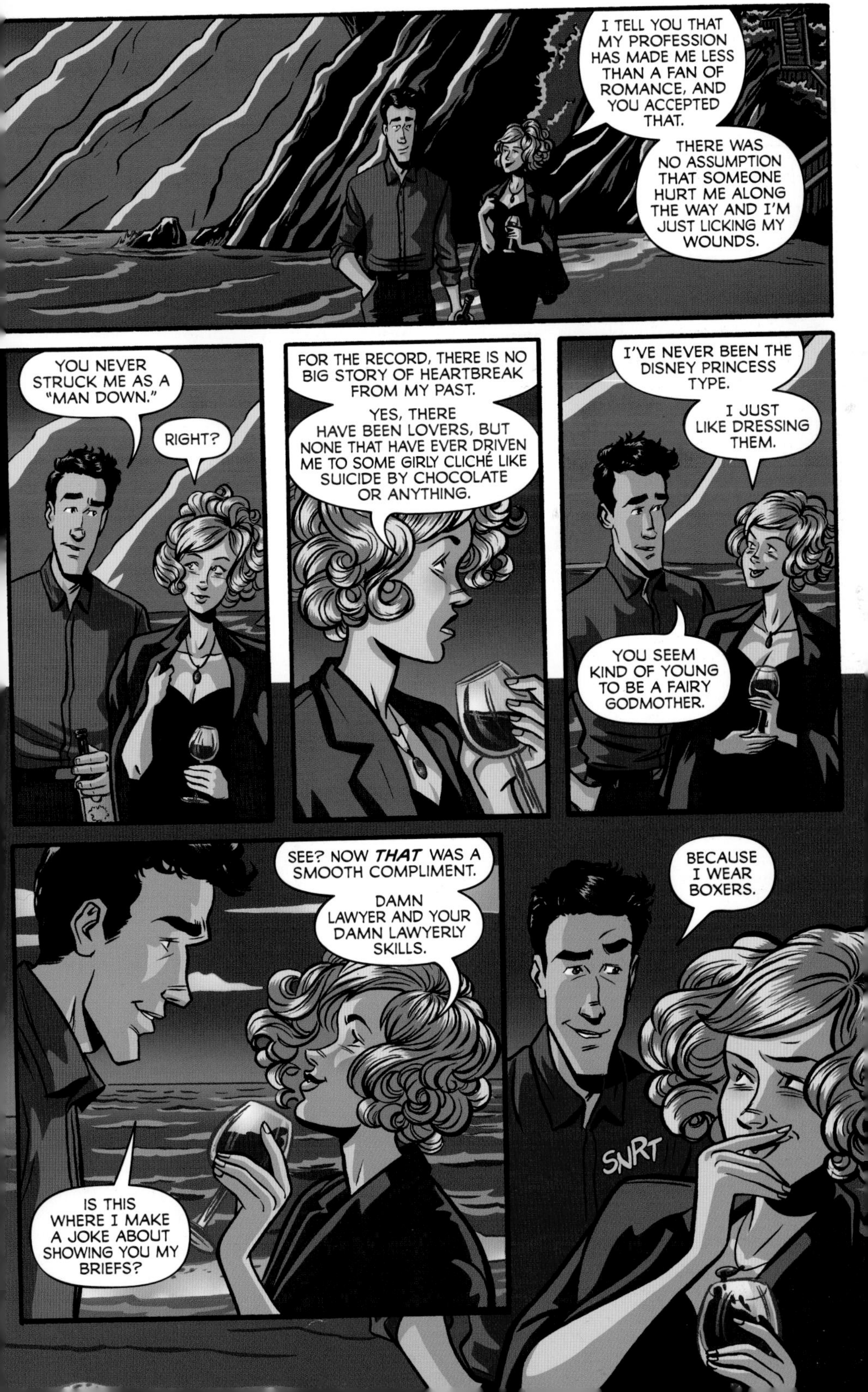
I TELL YOU THAT MY PROFESSION HAS MADE ME LESS THAN A FAN OF ROMANCE, AND YOU ACCEPTED THAT.
THERE WAS NO ASSUMPTION THAT SOMEONE HURT ME ALONG THE WAY AND I'M JUST LICKING MY WOUNDS.
YOU NEVER STRUCK ME AS A "MAN DOWN."
RIGHT?
FOR THE RECORD, THERE IS NO BIG STORY OF HEARTBREAK FROM MY PAST.
YES, THERE HAVE BEEN LOVERS, BUT NONE THAT HAVE EVER DRIVEN ME TO SOME GIRLY CLICHÉ LIKE SUICIDE BY CHOCOLATE OR ANYTHING.
I'VE NEVER BEEN THE DISNEY PRINCESS TYPE.
I JUST LIKE DRESSING THEM.
YOU SEEM KIND OF YOUNG TO BE A FAIRY GODMOTHER.
SEE? NOW *THAT* WAS A SMOOTH COMPLIMENT.
DAMN LAWYER AND YOUR DAMN LAWYERLY SKILLS.
IS THIS WHERE I MAKE A JOKE ABOUT SHOWING YOU MY BRIEFS?
BECAUSE I WEAR BOXERS.
SNRT

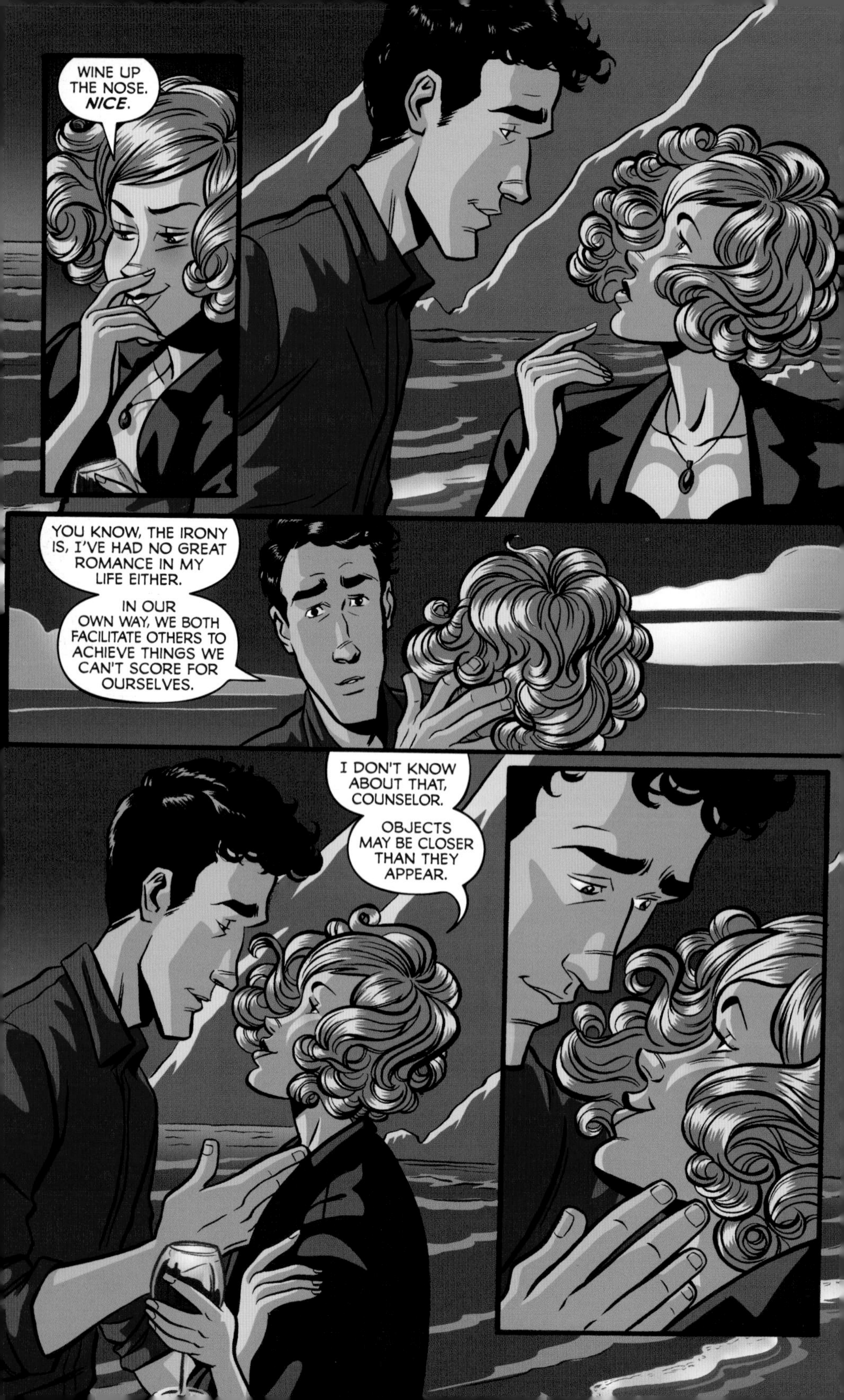
WINE UP THE NOSE. *NICE*.
YOU KNOW, THE IRONY IS, I'VE HAD NO GREAT ROMANCE IN MY LIFE EITHER.
IN OUR OWN WAY, WE BOTH FACILITATE OTHERS TO ACHIEVE THINGS WE CAN'T SCORE FOR OURSELVES.
I DON'T KNOW ABOUT THAT, COUNSELOR.
OBJECTS MAY BE CLOSER THAN THEY APPEAR.

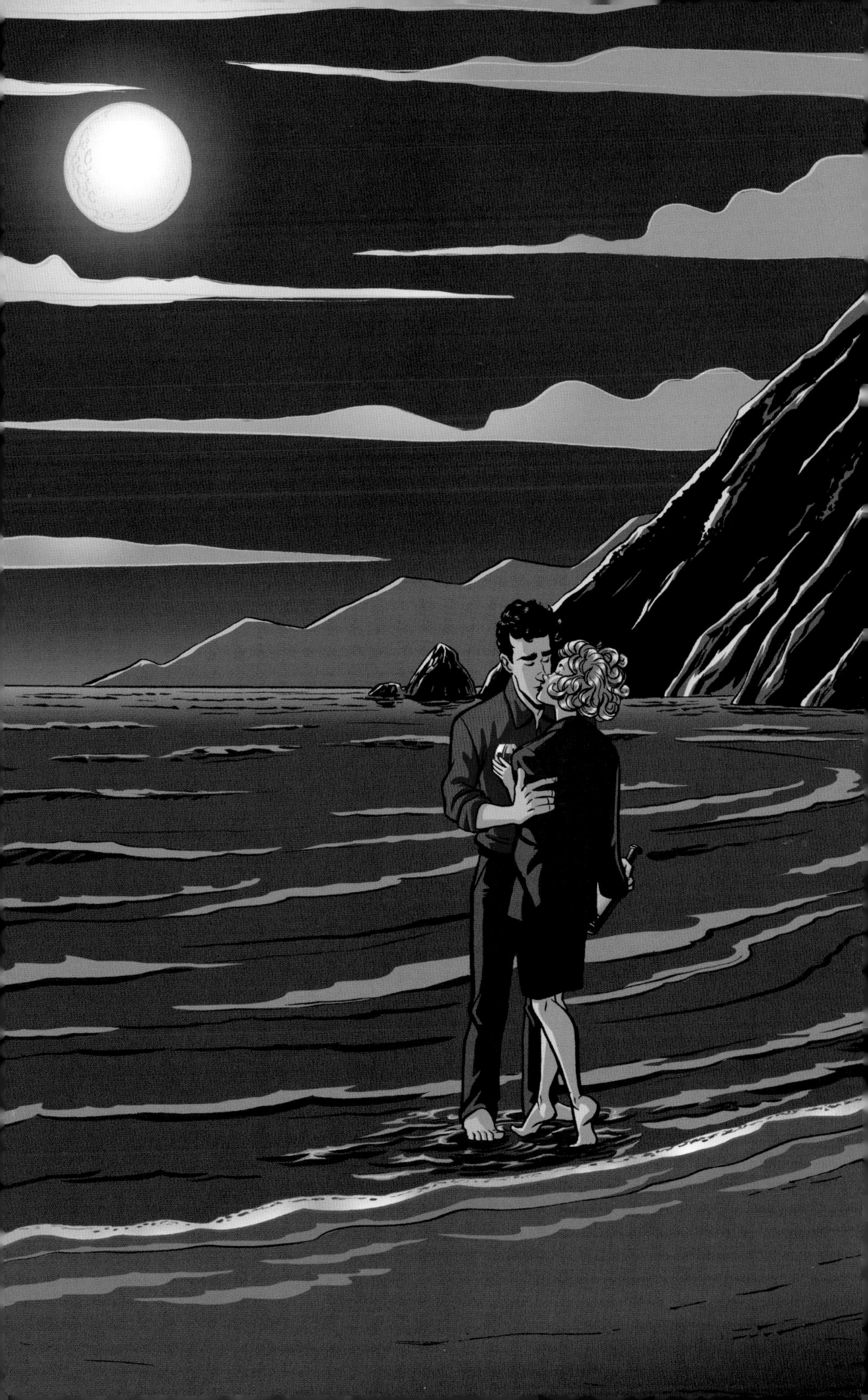

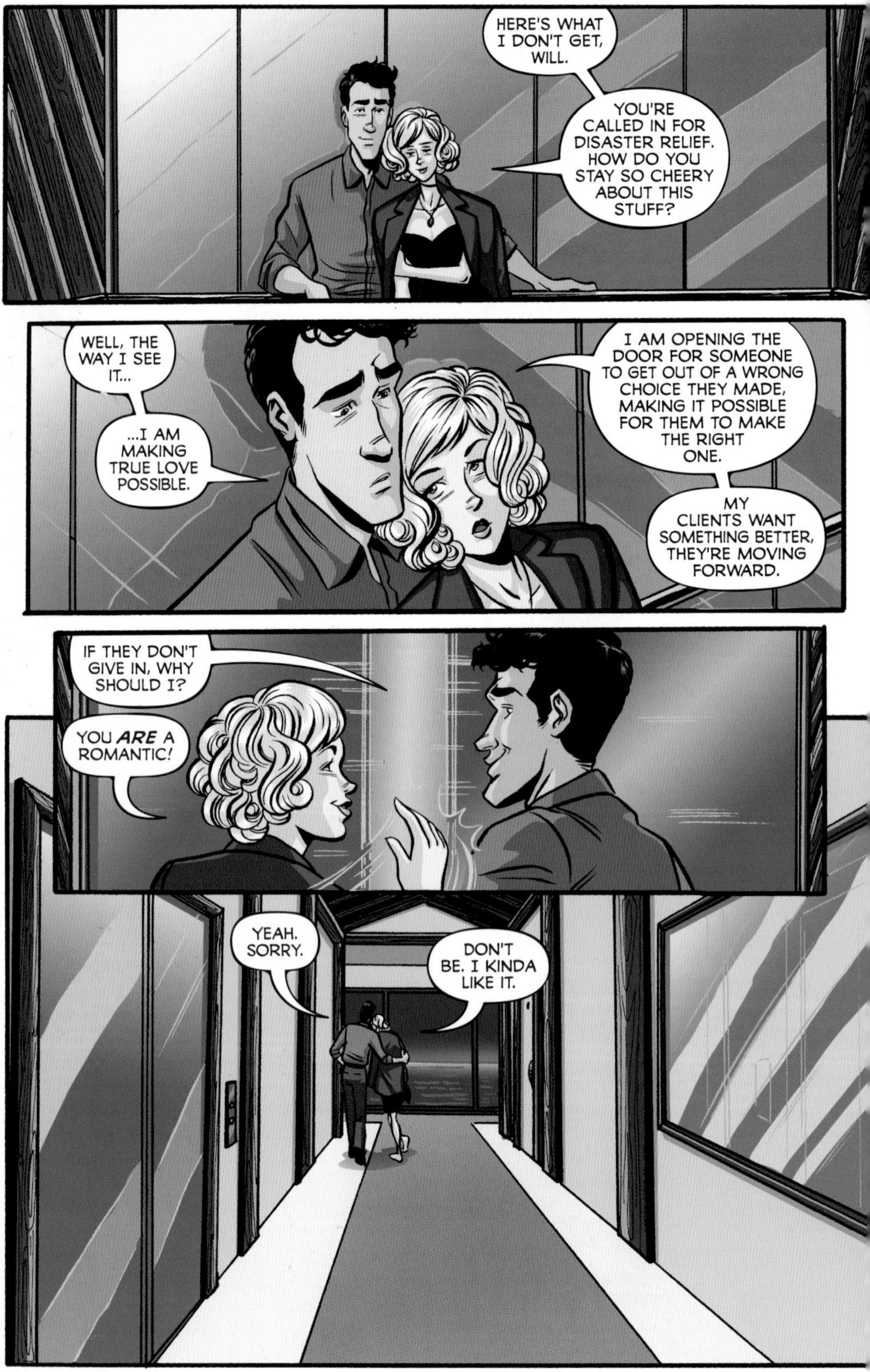
HERE'S WHAT I DON'T GET, WILL.
YOU'RE CALLED IN FOR DISASTER RELIEF. HOW DO YOU STAY SO CHEERY ABOUT THIS STUFF?
WELL, THE WAY I SEE IT...
...I AM MAKING TRUE LOVE POSSIBLE.
I AM OPENING THE DOOR FOR SOMEONE TO GET OUT OF A WRONG CHOICE THEY MADE, MAKING IT POSSIBLE FOR THEM TO MAKE THE RIGHT ONE.
MY CLIENTS WANT SOMETHING BETTER, THEY'RE MOVING FORWARD.
IF THEY DON'T GIVE IN, WHY SHOULD I?
YOU *ARE* A ROMANTIC!
YEAH. SORRY.
DON'T BE. I KINDA LIKE IT.

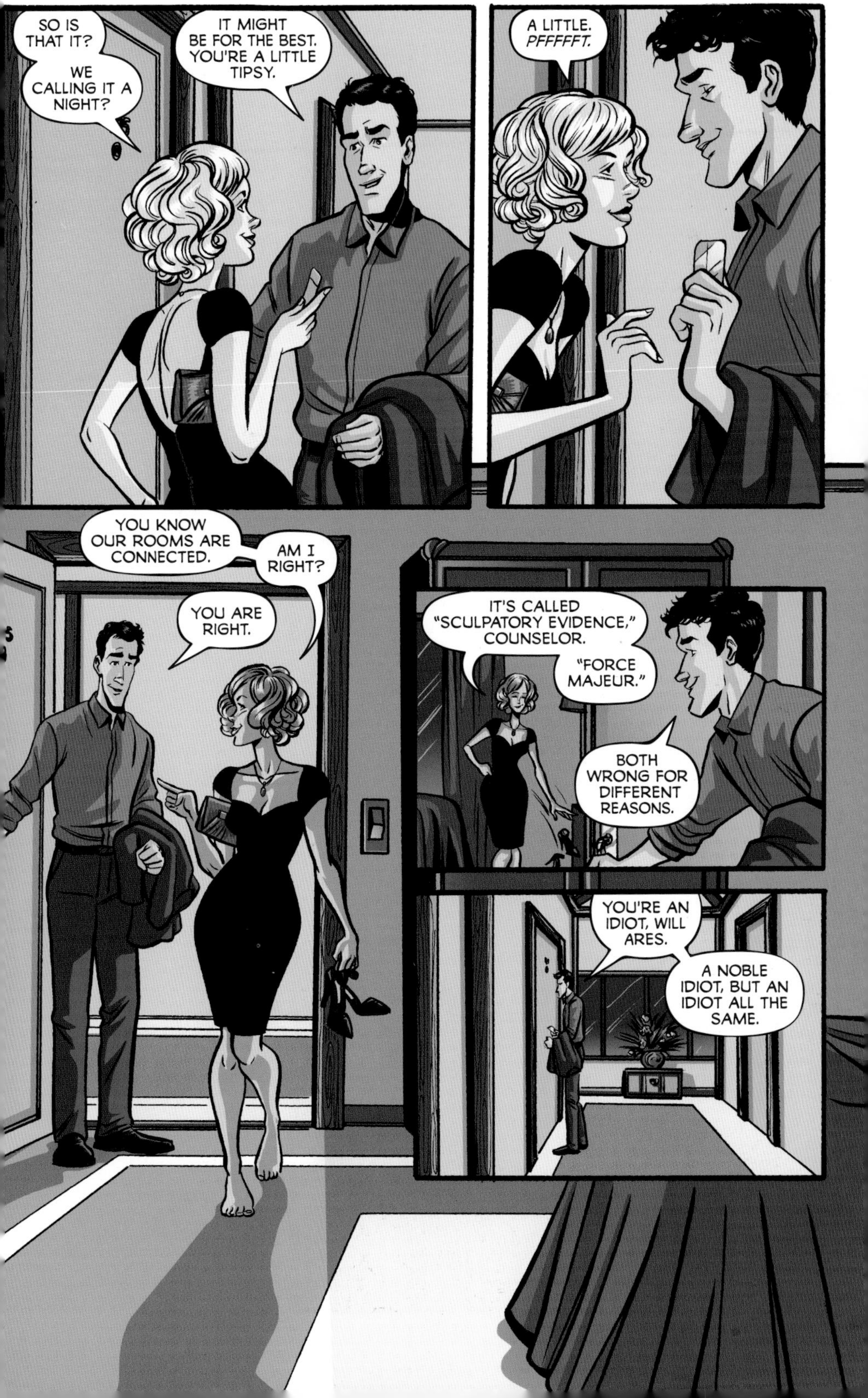
SO IS THAT IT?
WE CALLING IT A NIGHT?
IT MIGHT BE FOR THE BEST. YOU'RE A LITTLE TIPSY.
A LITTLE. *PFFFFFT.*
YOU KNOW OUR ROOMS ARE CONNECTED.
AM I RIGHT?
YOU ARE RIGHT.
IT'S CALLED "SCULPATORY EVIDENCE," COUNSELOR.
"FORCE MAJEUR."
BOTH WRONG FOR DIFFERENT REASONS.
YOU'RE AN IDIOT, WILL ARES.
A NOBLE IDIOT, BUT AN IDIOT ALL THE SAME.

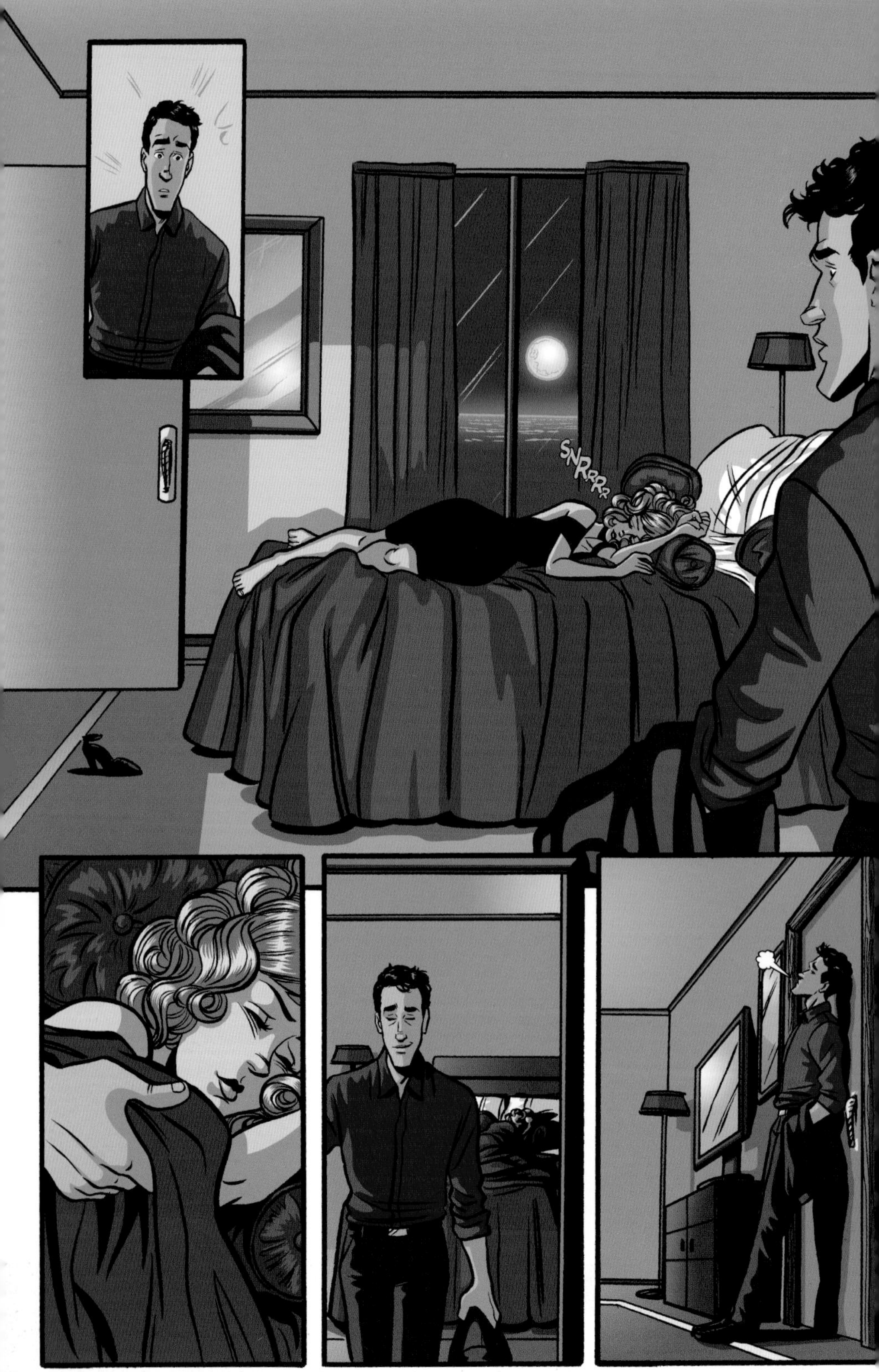
SNRRRR

# CHAPTER SEVEN

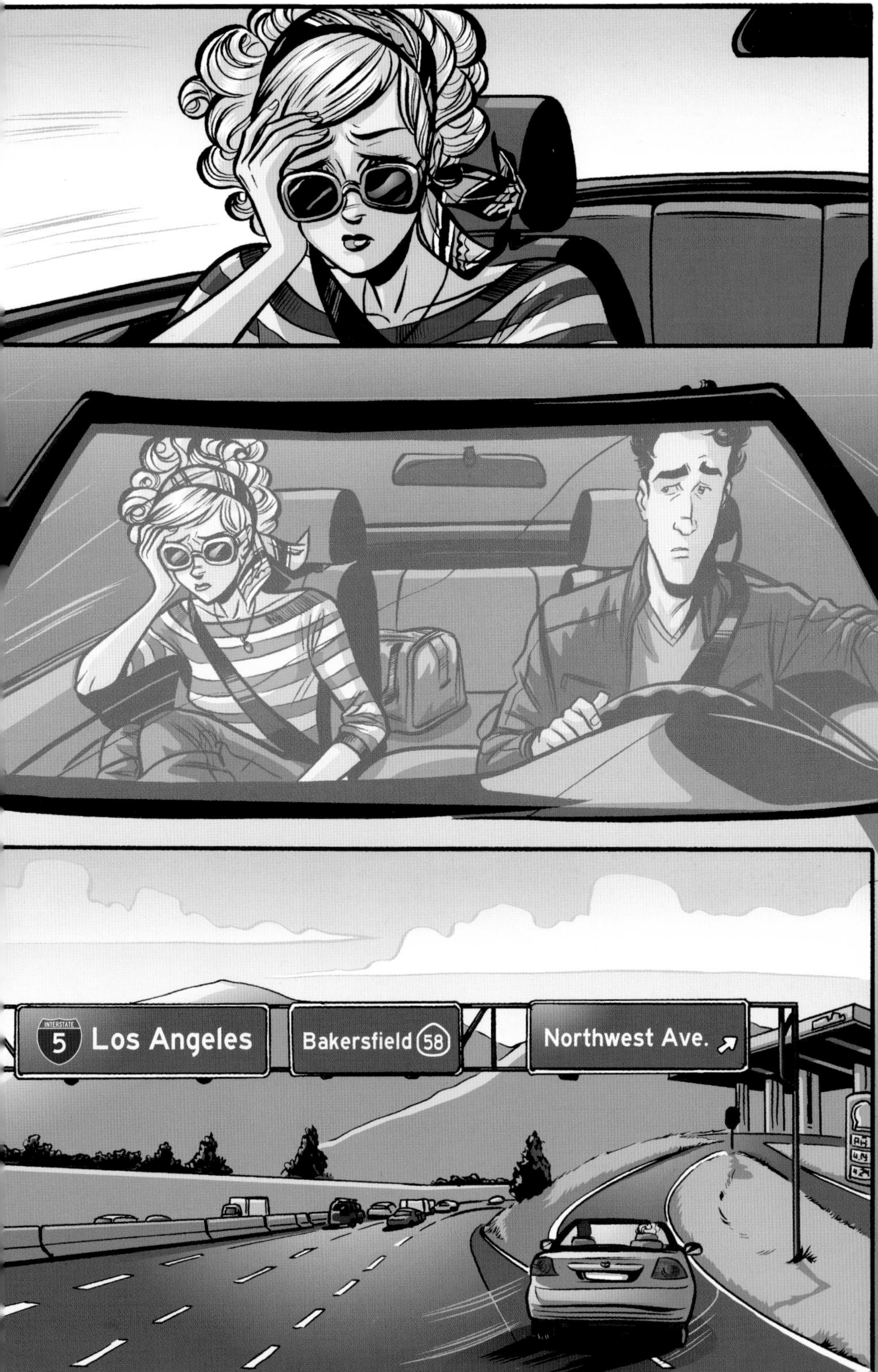

INTERSTATE
5 Los Angeles
Bakersfield 58
Northwest Ave.

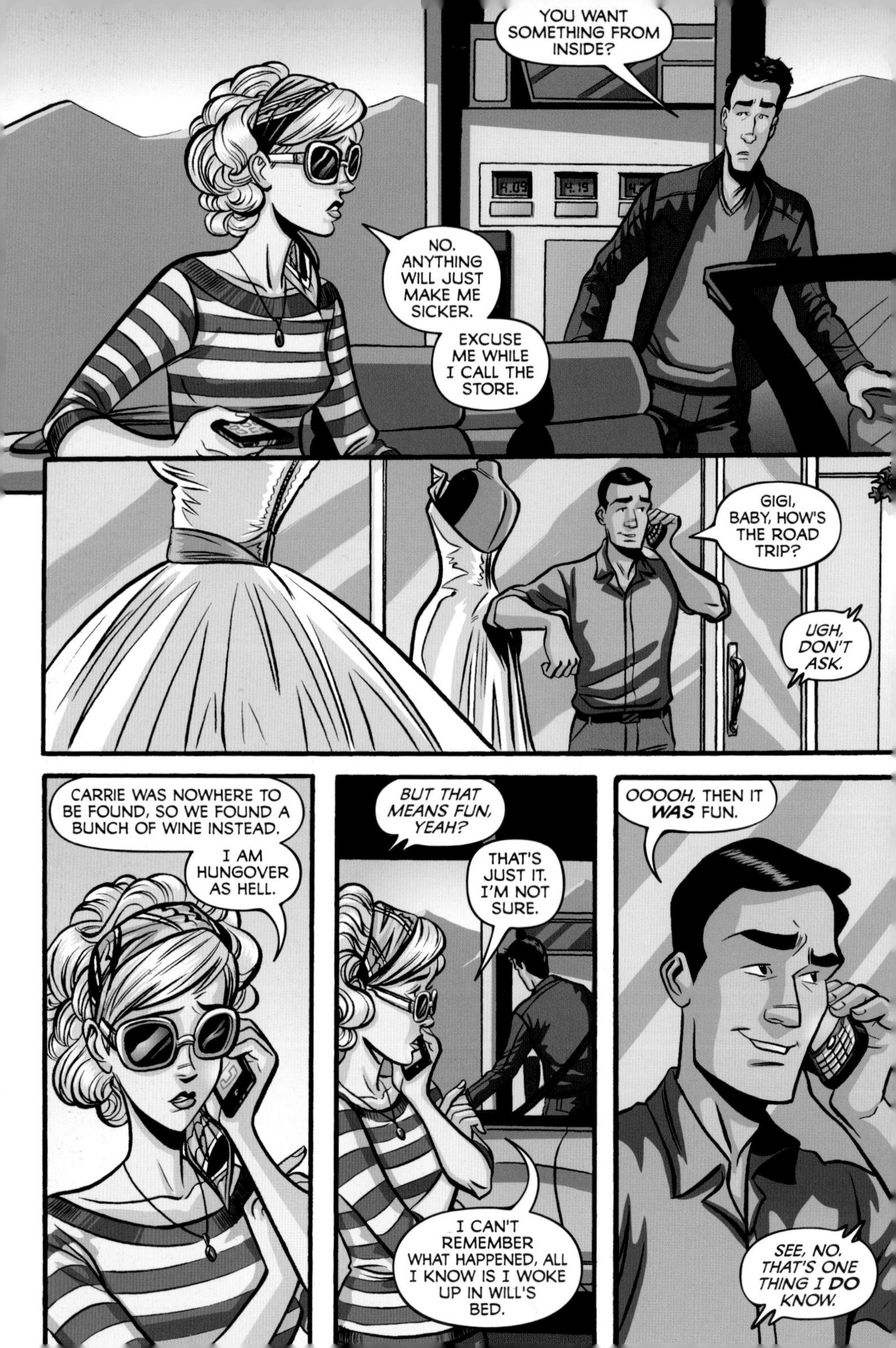

YOU WANT SOMETHING FROM INSIDE?
NO. ANYTHING WILL JUST MAKE ME SICKER.
EXCUSE ME WHILE I CALL THE STORE.
GIGI, BABY, HOW'S THE ROAD TRIP?
*UGH, DON'T ASK.*
CARRIE WAS NOWHERE TO BE FOUND, SO WE FOUND A BUNCH OF WINE INSTEAD.
I AM HUNGOVER AS HELL.
*BUT THAT MEANS FUN, YEAH?*
THAT'S JUST IT. I'M NOT SURE.
I CAN'T REMEMBER WHAT HAPPENED, ALL I KNOW IS I WOKE UP IN WILL'S BED.
*OOOOH,* THEN IT ***WAS*** FUN.
*SEE, NO. THAT'S ONE THING I* ***DO*** *KNOW.*

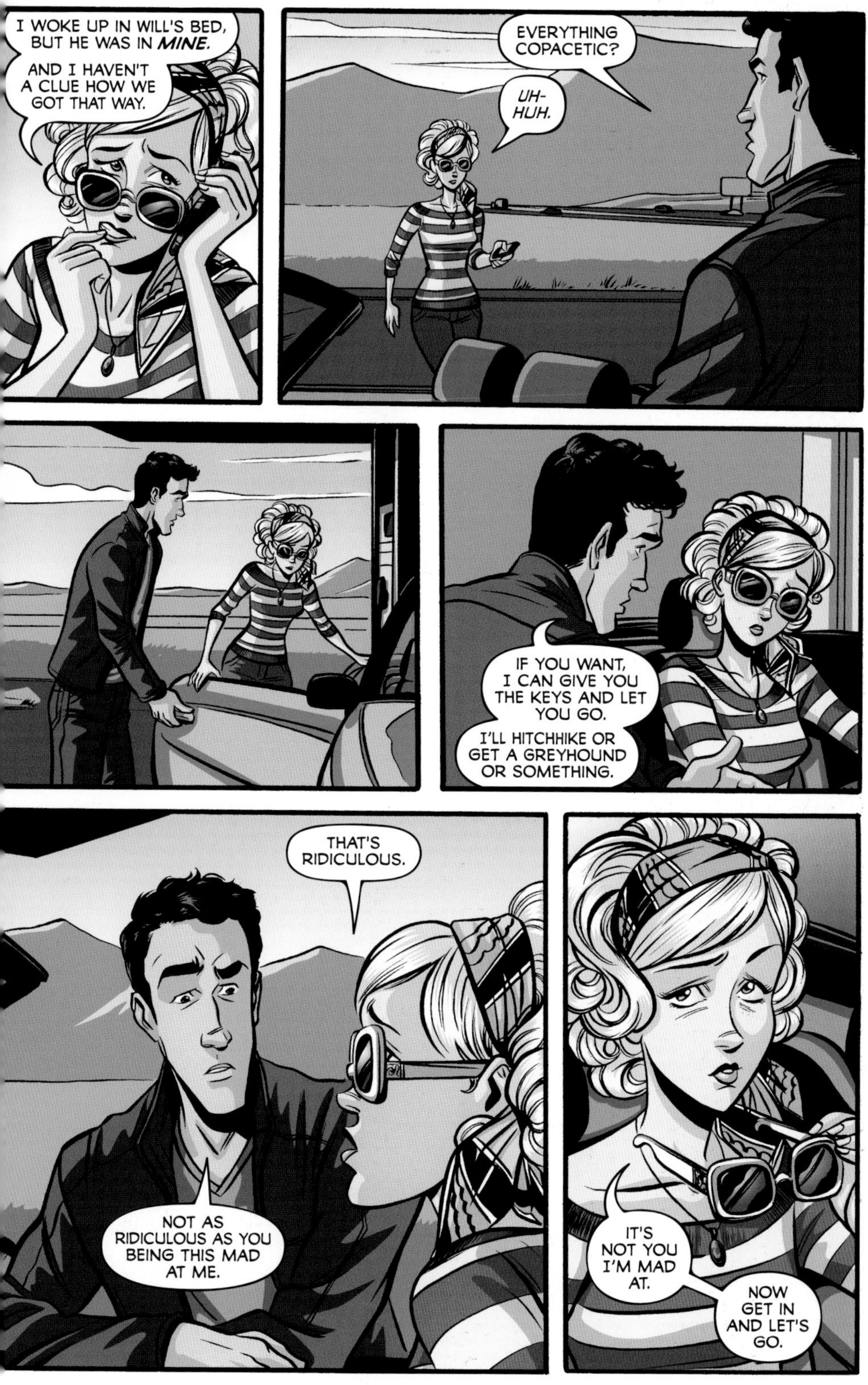

I WOKE UP IN WILL'S BED, BUT HE WAS IN *MINE.*
AND I HAVEN'T A CLUE HOW WE GOT THAT WAY.
EVERYTHING COPACETIC?
*UH-HUH.*
IF YOU WANT, I CAN GIVE YOU THE KEYS AND LET YOU GO.
I'LL HITCHHIKE OR GET A GREYHOUND OR SOMETHING.
THAT'S RIDICULOUS.
NOT AS RIDICULOUS AS YOU BEING THIS MAD AT ME.
IT'S NOT YOU I'M MAD AT.
NOW GET IN AND LET'S GO.

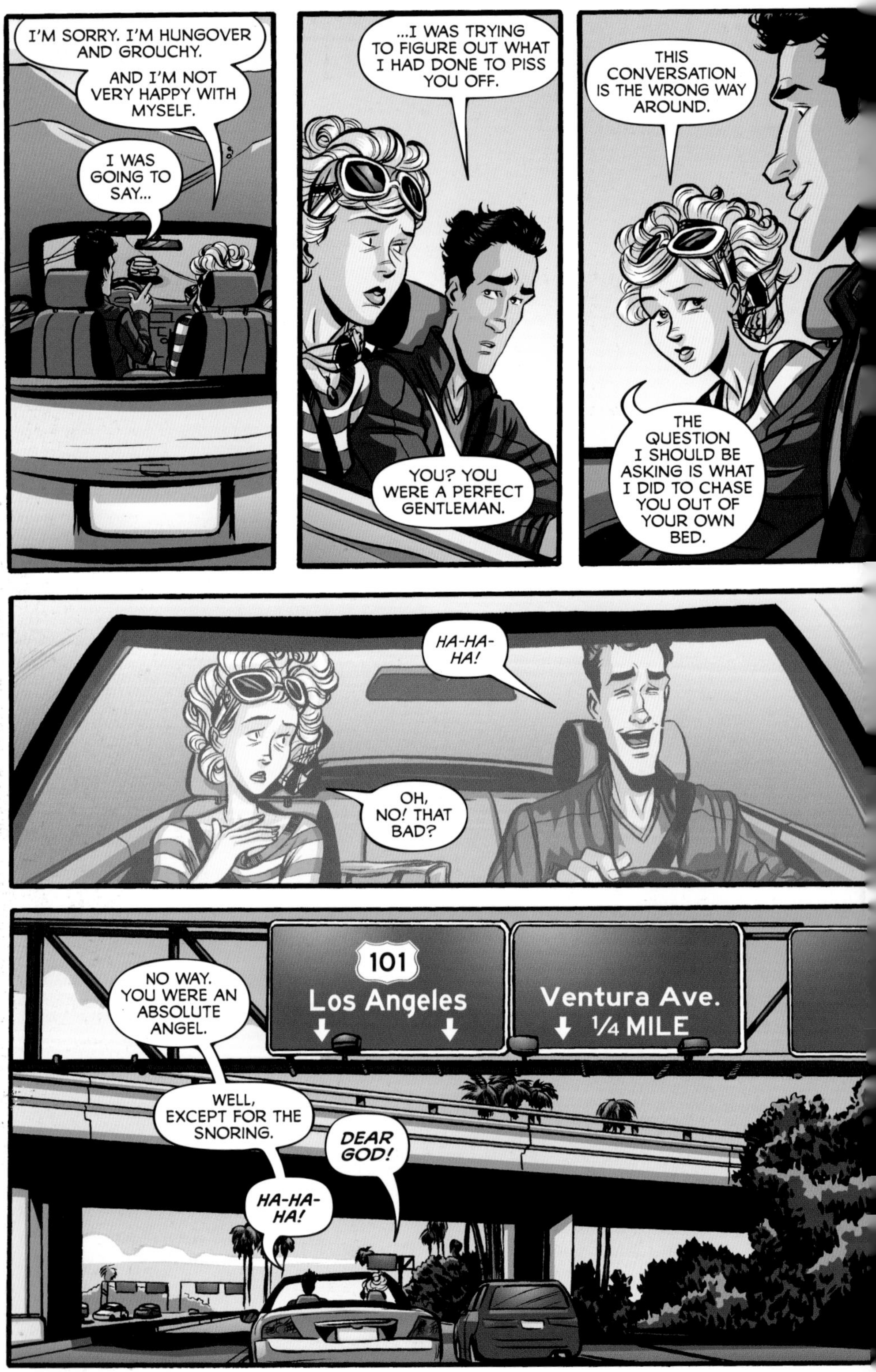
I'M SORRY. I'M HUNGOVER AND GROUCHY.
AND I'M NOT VERY HAPPY WITH MYSELF.
I WAS GOING TO SAY...
...I WAS TRYING TO FIGURE OUT WHAT I HAD DONE TO PISS YOU OFF.
YOU? YOU WERE A PERFECT GENTLEMAN.
THIS CONVERSATION IS THE WRONG WAY AROUND.
THE QUESTION I SHOULD BE ASKING IS WHAT I DID TO CHASE YOU OUT OF YOUR OWN BED.
HA-HA-HA!
OH, NO! THAT BAD?
101
Los Angeles
Ventura Ave.
1/4 MILE
NO WAY. YOU WERE AN ABSOLUTE ANGEL.
WELL, EXCEPT FOR THE SNORING.
DEAR GOD!
HA-HA-HA!

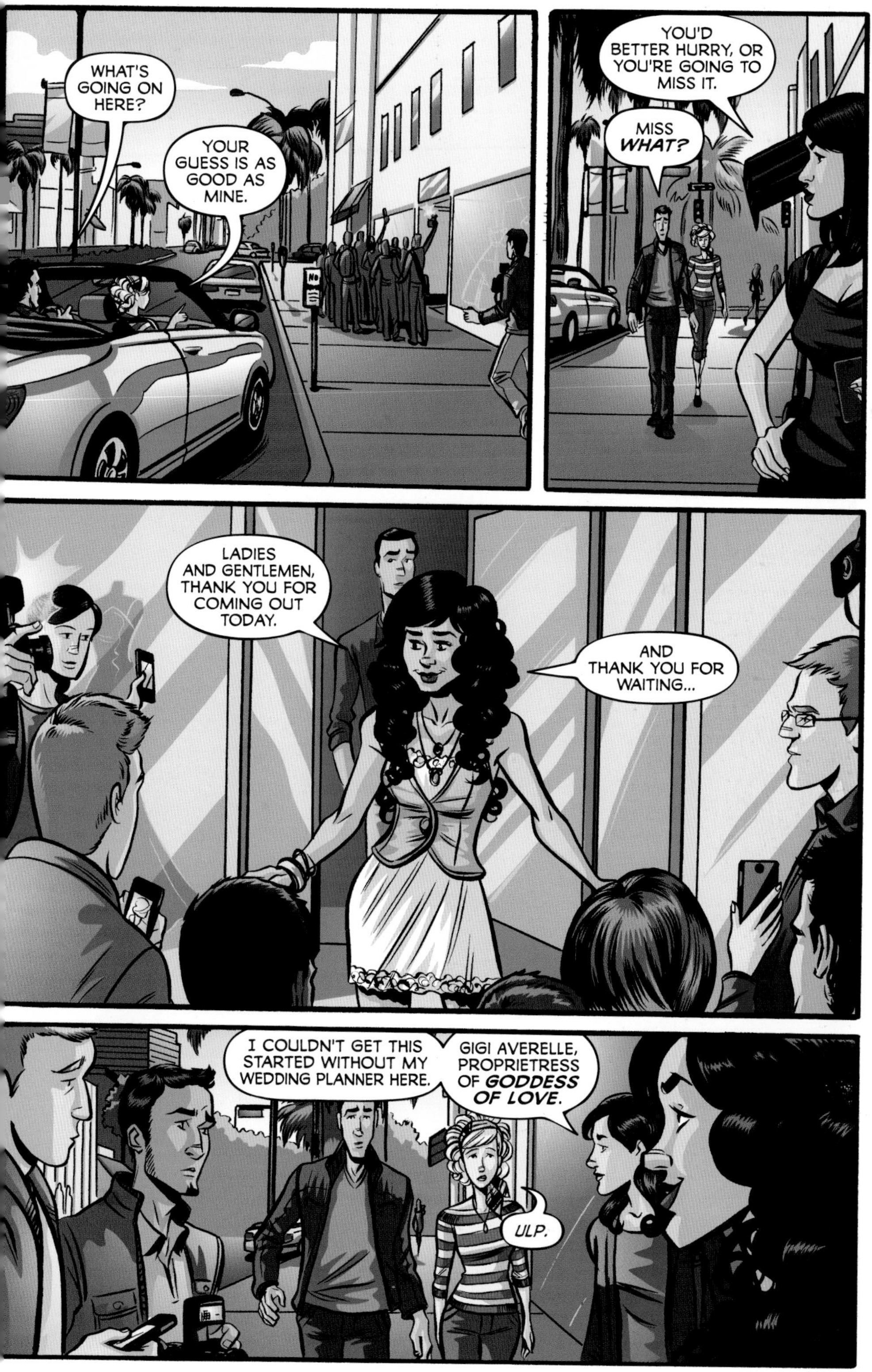
WHAT'S GOING ON HERE?
YOUR GUESS IS AS GOOD AS MINE.
YOU'D BETTER HURRY, OR YOU'RE GOING TO MISS IT.
MISS *WHAT?*
LADIES AND GENTLEMEN, THANK YOU FOR COMING OUT TODAY.
AND THANK YOU FOR WAITING...
I COULDN'T GET THIS STARTED WITHOUT MY WEDDING PLANNER HERE.
GIGI AVERELLE, PROPRIETRESS OF ***GODDESS OF LOVE***.
*ULP.*

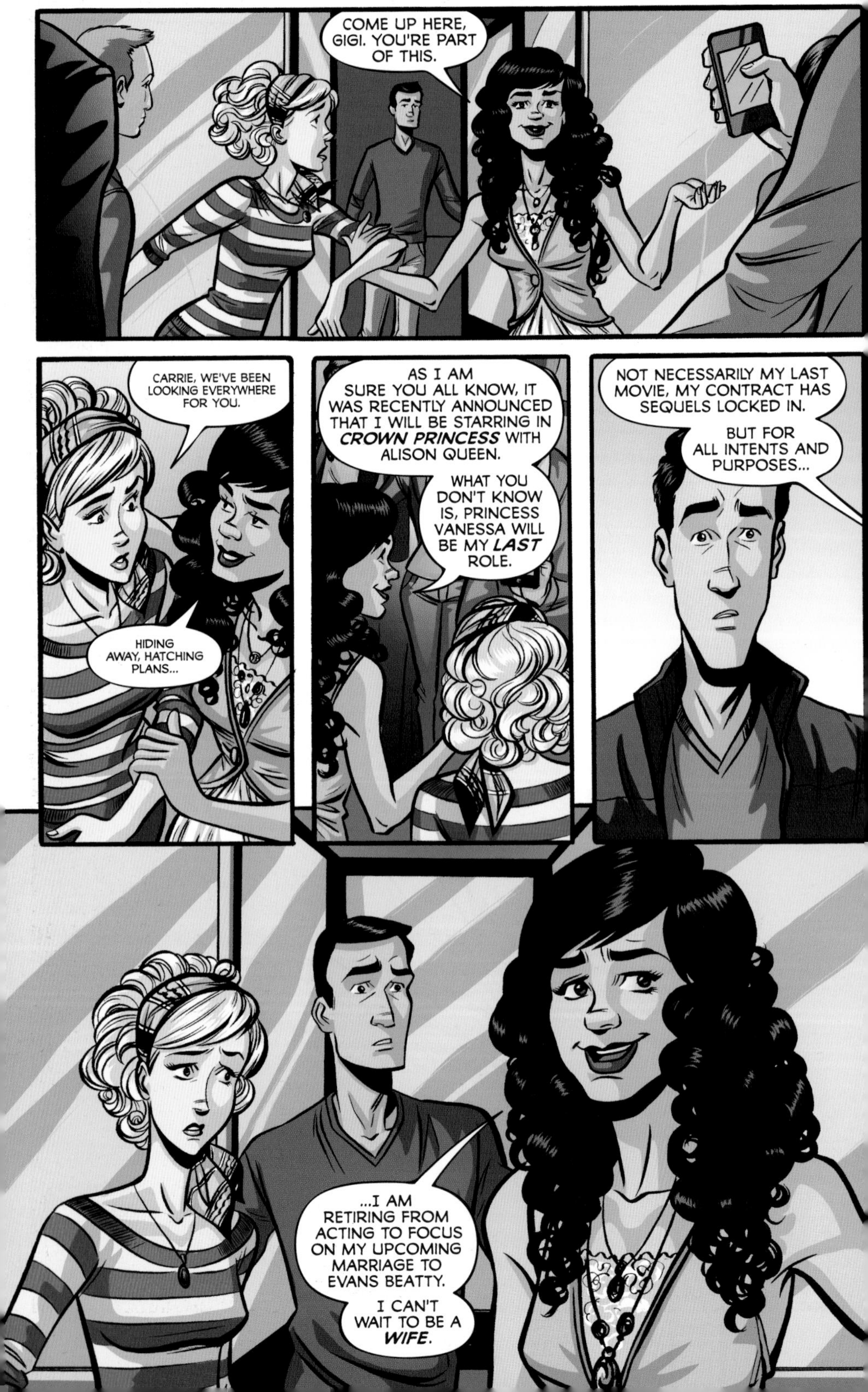

COME UP HERE, GIGI. YOU'RE PART OF THIS.
CARRIE, WE'VE BEEN LOOKING EVERYWHERE FOR YOU.
HIDING AWAY, HATCHING PLANS...
AS I AM SURE YOU ALL KNOW, IT WAS RECENTLY ANNOUNCED THAT I WILL BE STARRING IN *CROWN PRINCESS* WITH ALISON QUEEN.
WHAT YOU DON'T KNOW IS, PRINCESS VANESSA WILL BE MY *LAST* ROLE.
NOT NECESSARILY MY LAST MOVIE, MY CONTRACT HAS SEQUELS LOCKED IN.
BUT FOR ALL INTENTS AND PURPOSES...
...I AM RETIRING FROM ACTING TO FOCUS ON MY UPCOMING MARRIAGE TO EVANS BEATTY.
I CAN'T WAIT TO BE A *WIFE*.

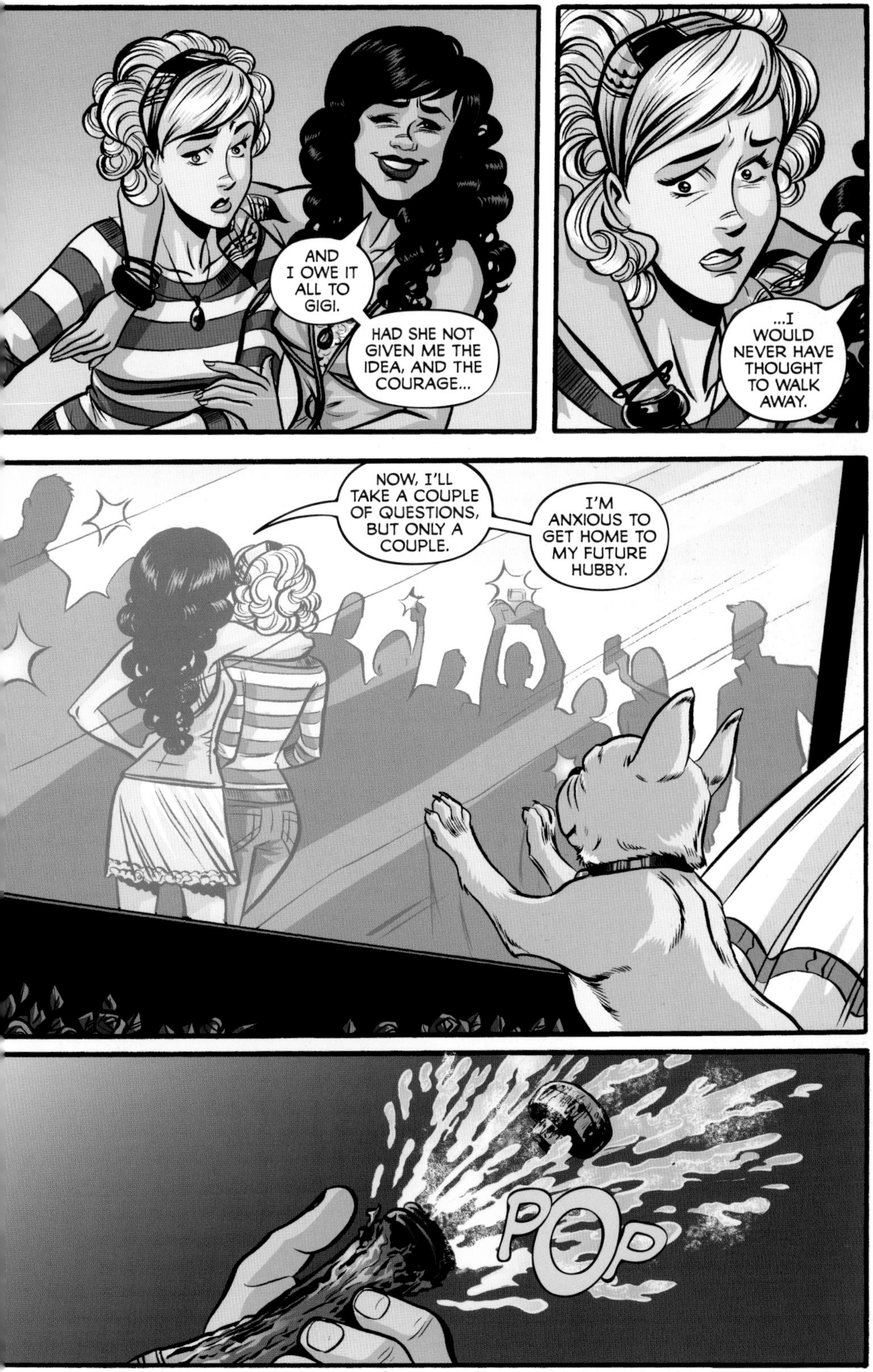
AND I OWE IT ALL TO GIGI.
HAD SHE NOT GIVEN ME THE IDEA, AND THE COURAGE...
...I WOULD NEVER HAVE THOUGHT TO WALK AWAY.
NOW, I'LL TAKE A COUPLE OF QUESTIONS, BUT ONLY A COUPLE.
I'M ANXIOUS TO GET HOME TO MY FUTURE HUBBY.
POP

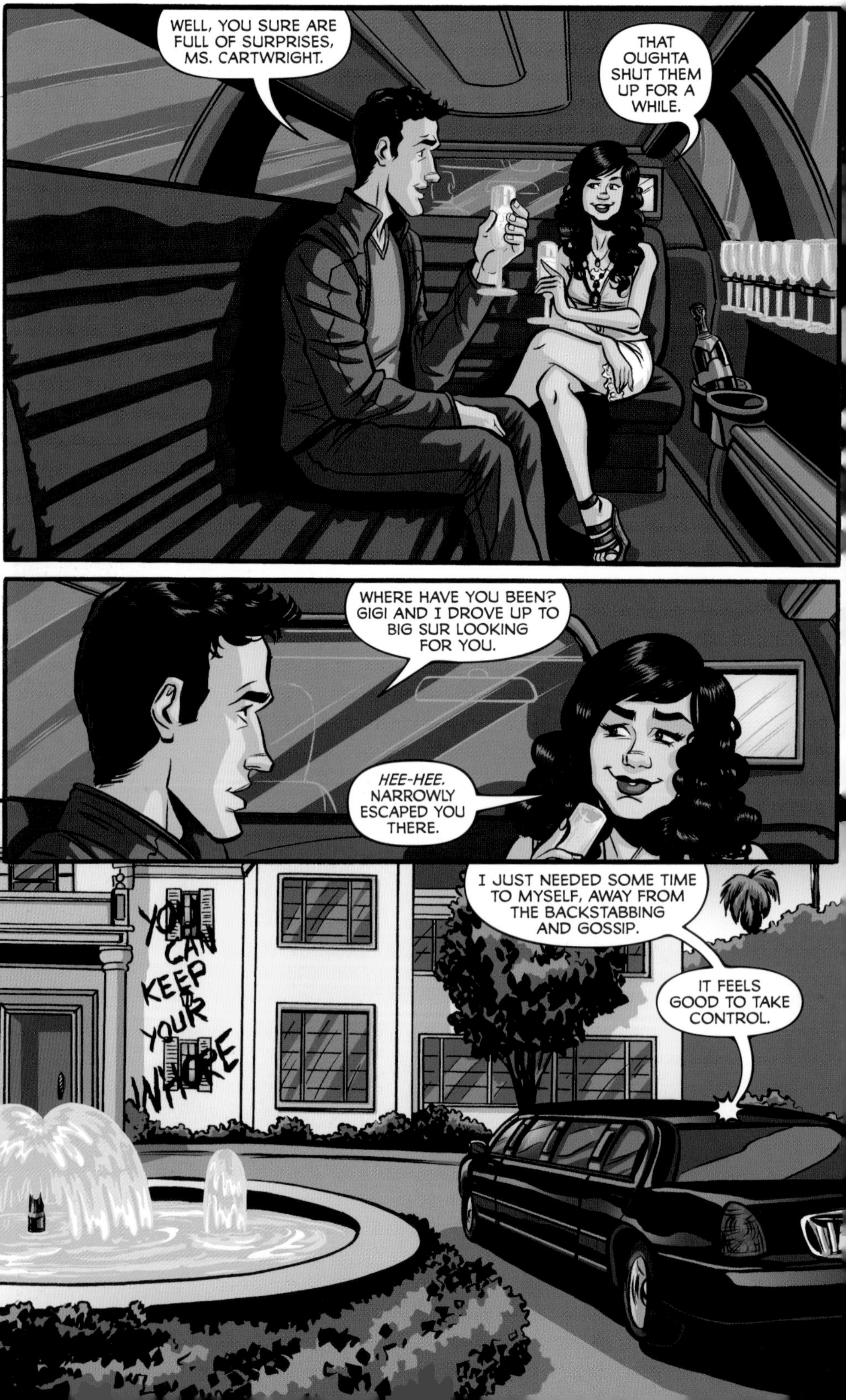
WELL, YOU SURE ARE FULL OF SURPRISES, MS. CARTWRIGHT.
THAT OUGHTA SHUT THEM UP FOR A WHILE.
WHERE HAVE YOU BEEN? GIGI AND I DROVE UP TO BIG SUR LOOKING FOR YOU.
*HEE-HEE.* NARROWLY ESCAPED YOU THERE.
YOU CAN KEEP YOUR
I JUST NEEDED SOME TIME TO MYSELF, AWAY FROM THE BACKSTABBING AND GOSSIP.
IT FEELS GOOD TO TAKE CONTROL.

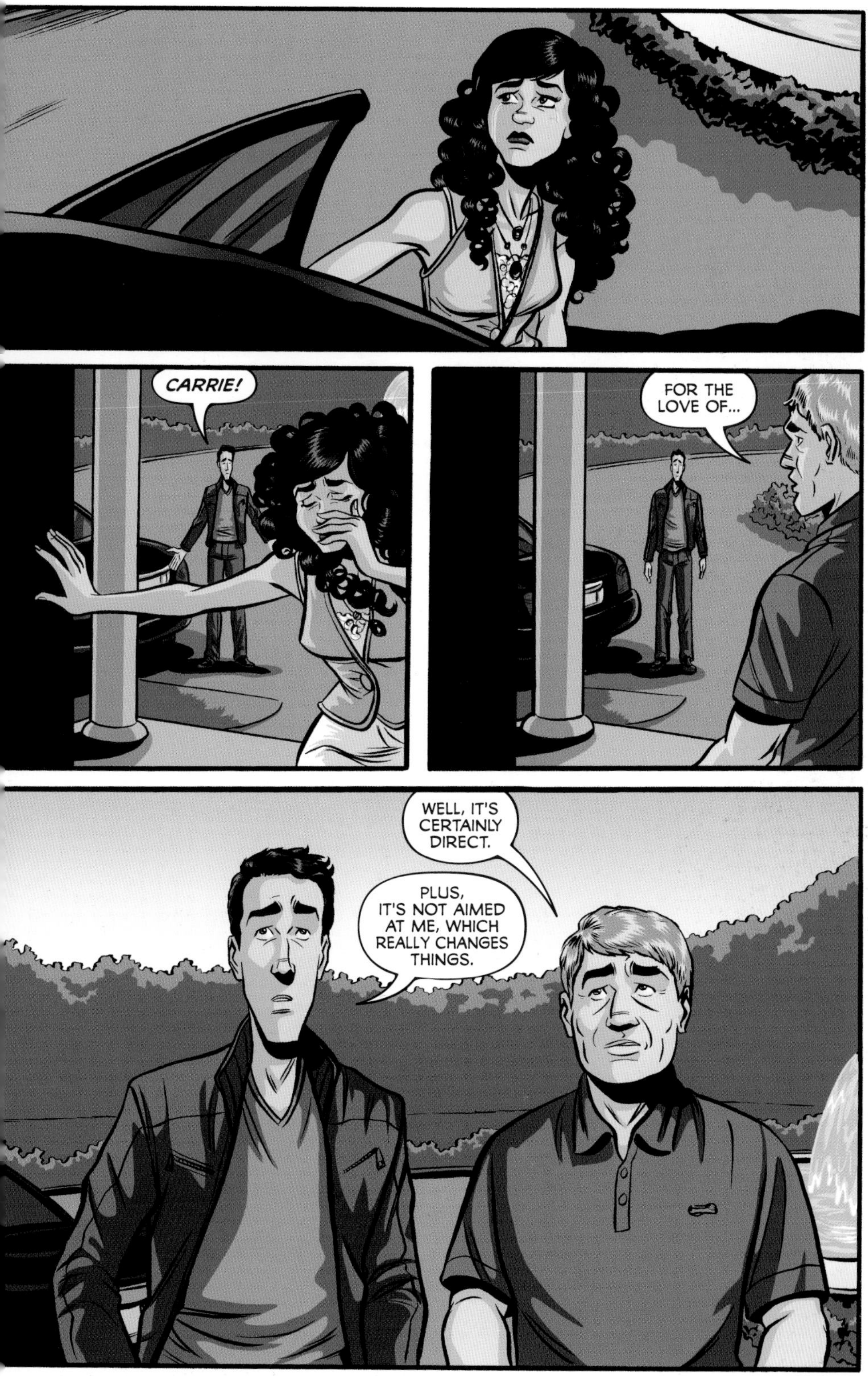
CARRIE!
FOR THE LOVE OF...
WELL, IT'S CERTAINLY DIRECT.
PLUS, IT'S NOT AIMED AT ME, WHICH REALLY CHANGES THINGS.

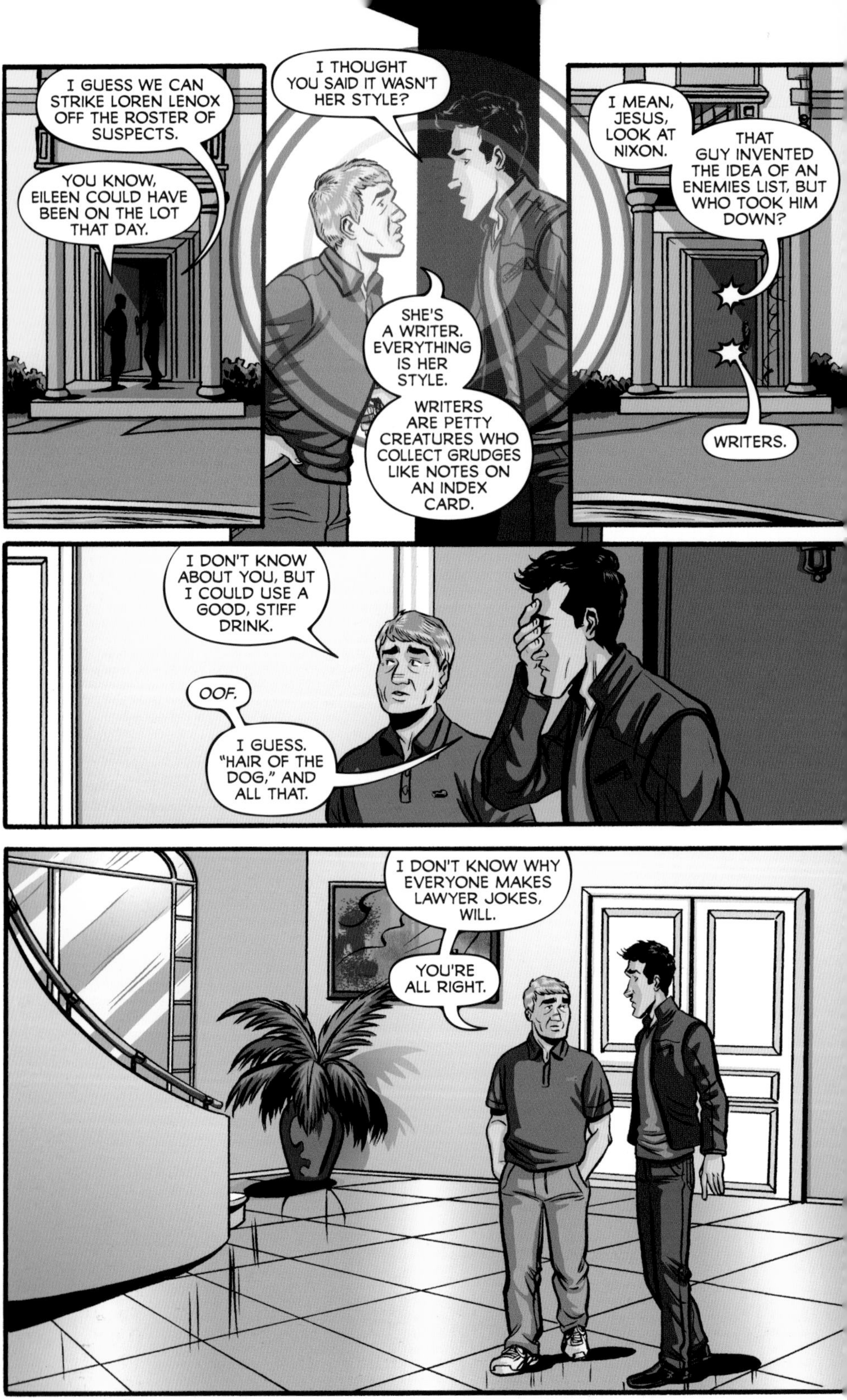
I GUESS WE CAN STRIKE LOREN LENOX OFF THE ROSTER OF SUSPECTS.
YOU KNOW, EILEEN COULD HAVE BEEN ON THE LOT THAT DAY.
I THOUGHT YOU SAID IT WASN'T HER STYLE?
SHE'S A WRITER. EVERYTHING IS HER STYLE.
WRITERS ARE PETTY CREATURES WHO COLLECT GRUDGES LIKE NOTES ON AN INDEX CARD.
I MEAN, JESUS, LOOK AT NIXON.
THAT GUY INVENTED THE IDEA OF AN ENEMIES LIST, BUT WHO TOOK HIM DOWN?
WRITERS.
I DON'T KNOW ABOUT YOU, BUT I COULD USE A GOOD, STIFF DRINK.
*OOF.*
I GUESS. "HAIR OF THE DOG," AND ALL THAT.
I DON'T KNOW WHY EVERYONE MAKES LAWYER JOKES, WILL.
YOU'RE ALL RIGHT.

# CHAPTER EIGHT

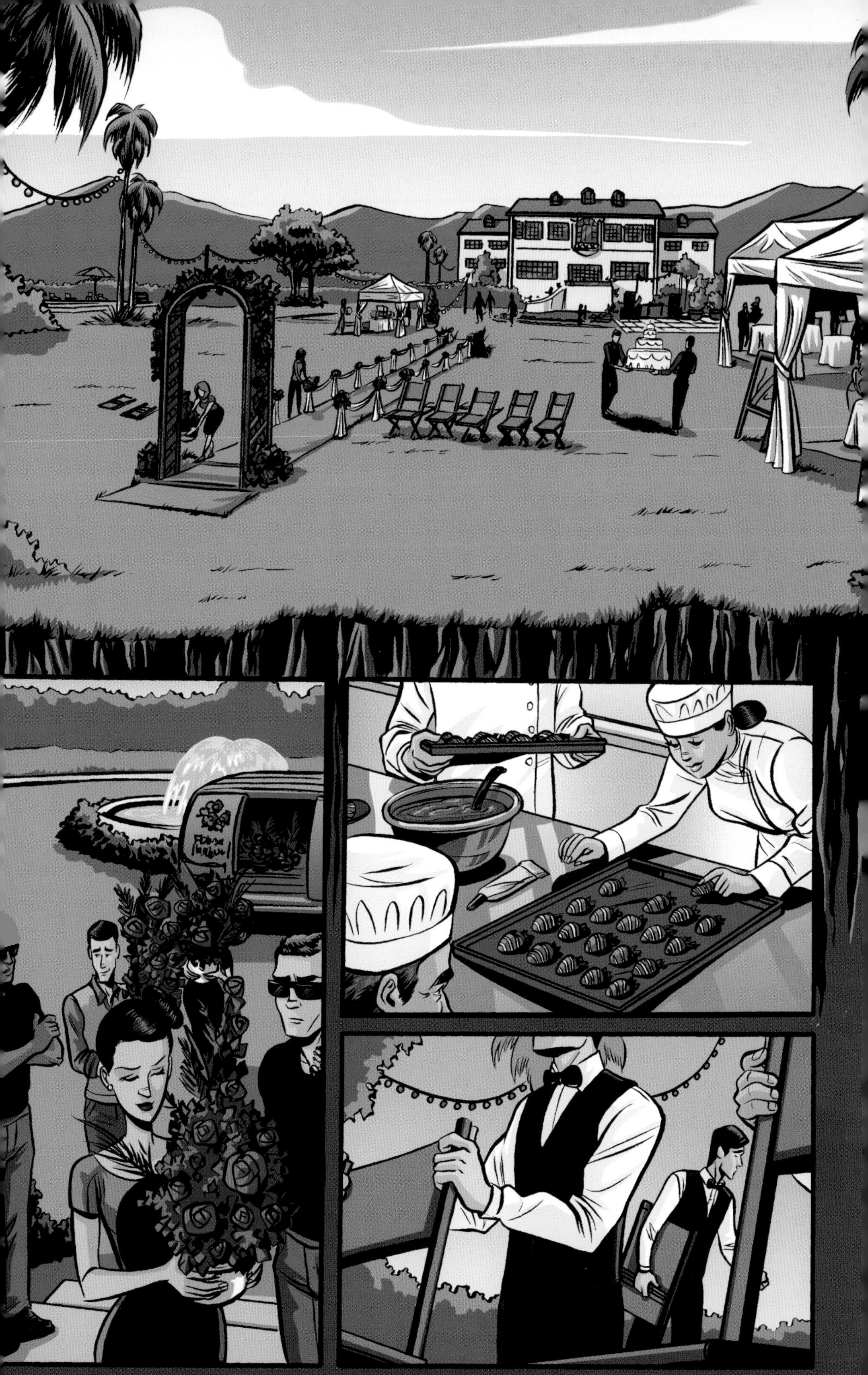

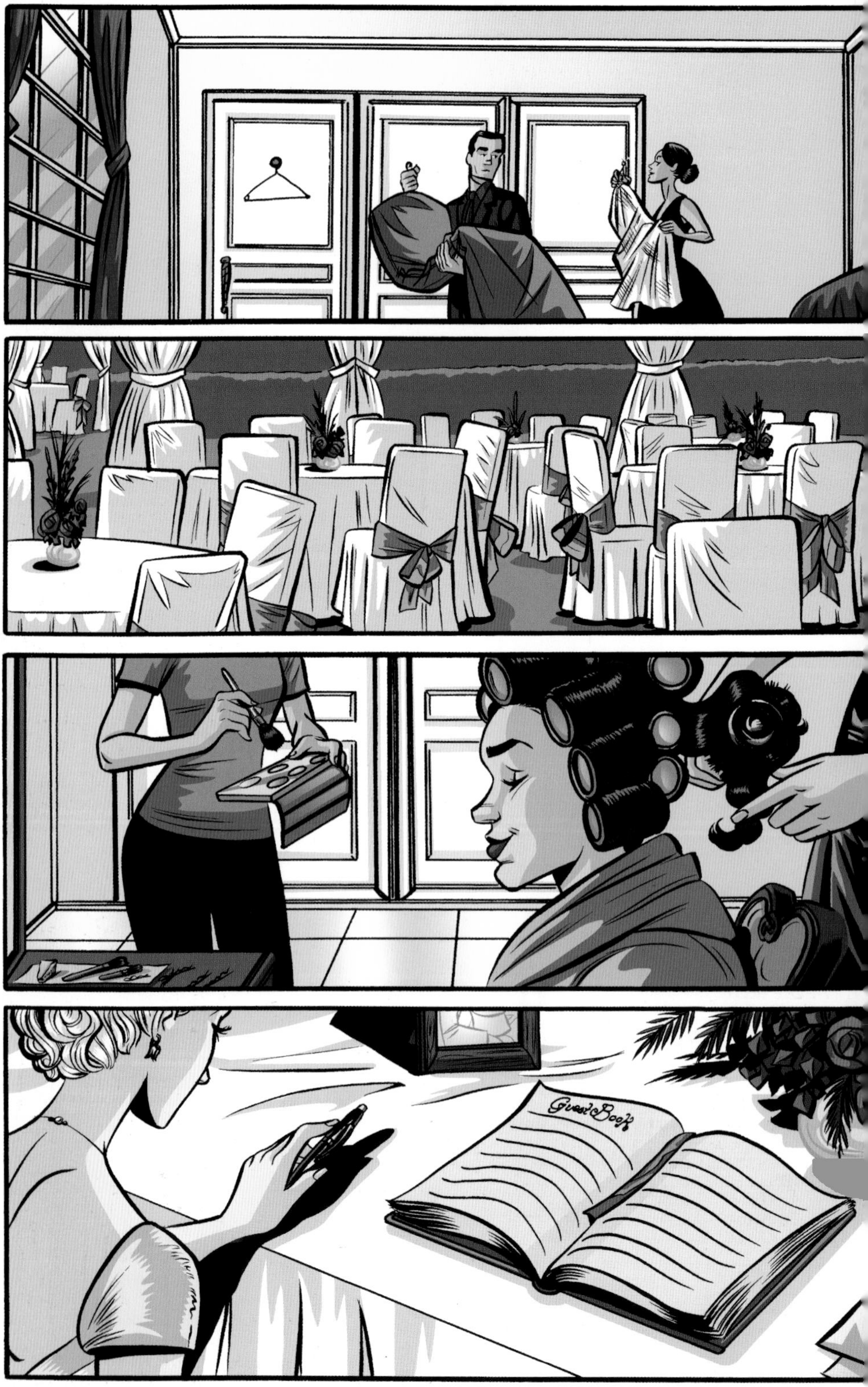
Guest Book

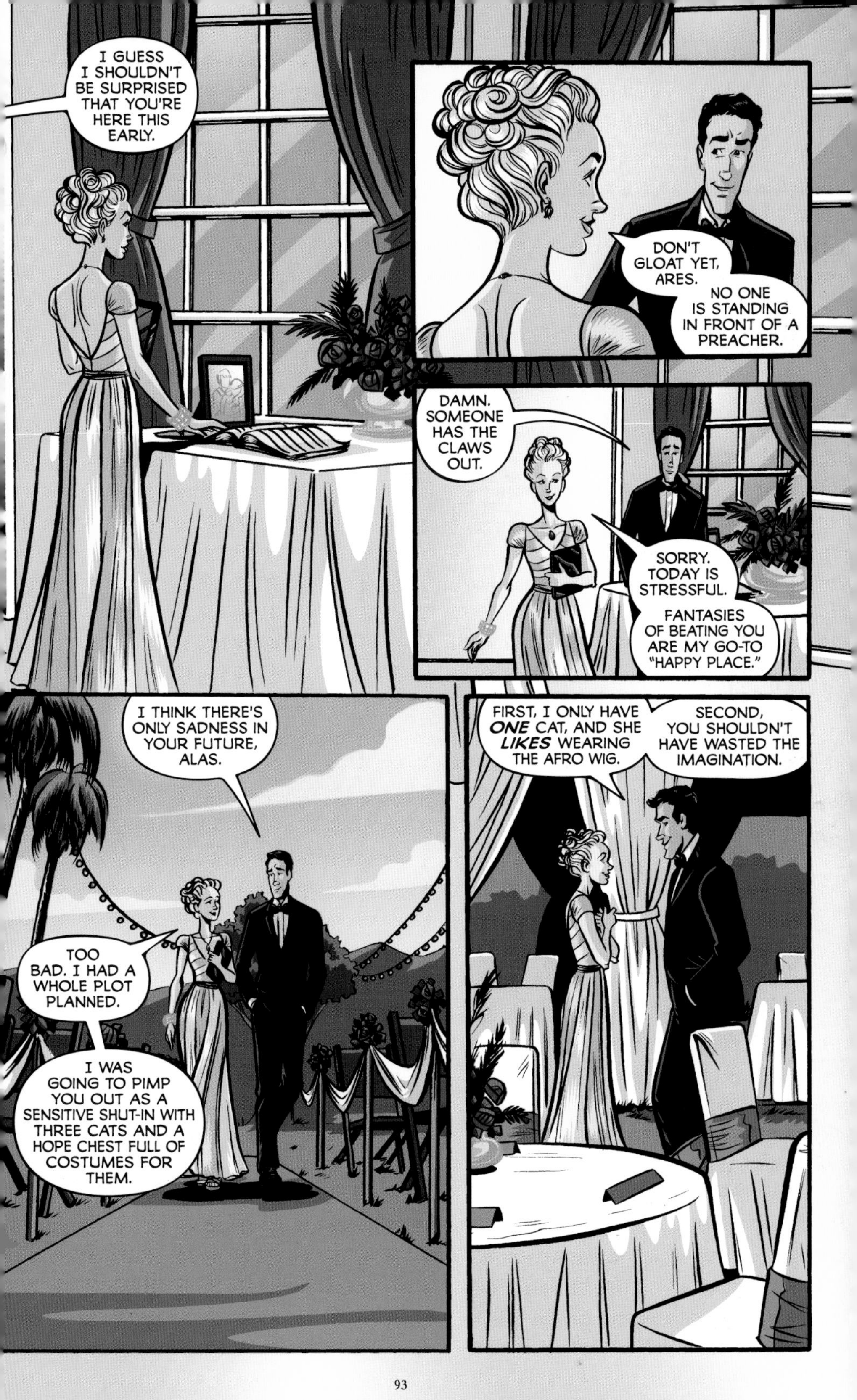
I GUESS I SHOULDN'T BE SURPRISED THAT YOU'RE HERE THIS EARLY.
DON'T GLOAT YET, ARES.
NO ONE IS STANDING IN FRONT OF A PREACHER.
DAMN. SOMEONE HAS THE CLAWS OUT.
SORRY. TODAY IS STRESSFUL.
FANTASIES OF BEATING YOU ARE MY GO-TO "HAPPY PLACE."
I THINK THERE'S ONLY SADNESS IN YOUR FUTURE, ALAS.
TOO BAD. I HAD A WHOLE PLOT PLANNED.
I WAS GOING TO PIMP YOU OUT AS A SENSITIVE SHUT-IN WITH THREE CATS AND A HOPE CHEST FULL OF COSTUMES FOR THEM.
FIRST, I ONLY HAVE ***ONE*** CAT, AND SHE ***LIKES*** WEARING THE AFRO WIG.
SECOND, YOU SHOULDN'T HAVE WASTED THE IMAGINATION.

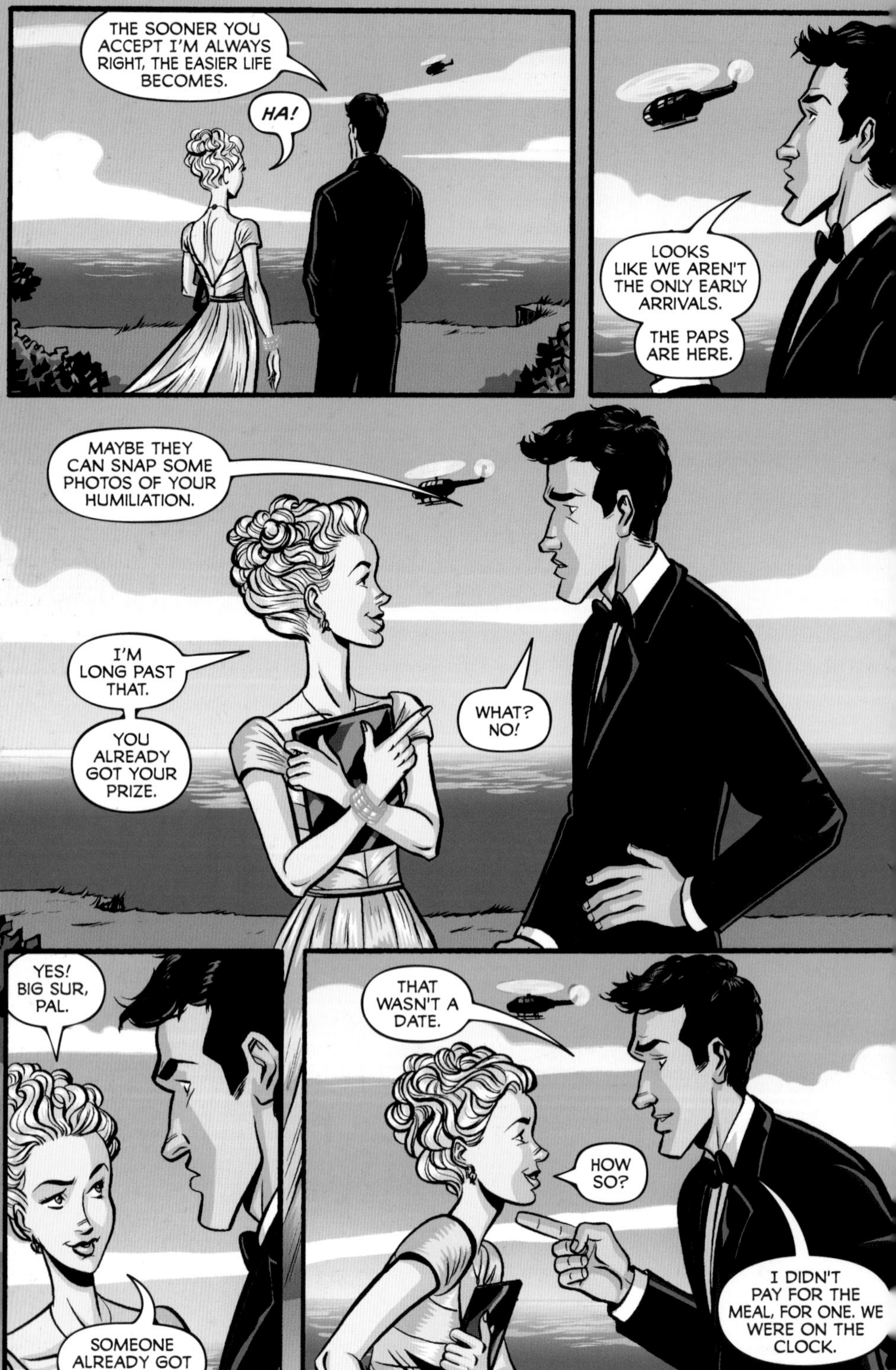
THE SOONER YOU ACCEPT I'M ALWAYS RIGHT, THE EASIER LIFE BECOMES.
HA!
LOOKS LIKE WE AREN'T THE ONLY EARLY ARRIVALS.
THE PAPS ARE HERE.
MAYBE THEY CAN SNAP SOME PHOTOS OF YOUR HUMILIATION.
I'M LONG PAST THAT.
YOU ALREADY GOT YOUR PRIZE.
WHAT? NO!
YES! BIG SUR, PAL.
SOMEONE ALREADY GOT HIS DATE.
THAT WASN'T A DATE.
HOW SO?
I DIDN'T PAY FOR THE MEAL, FOR ONE. WE WERE ON THE CLOCK.

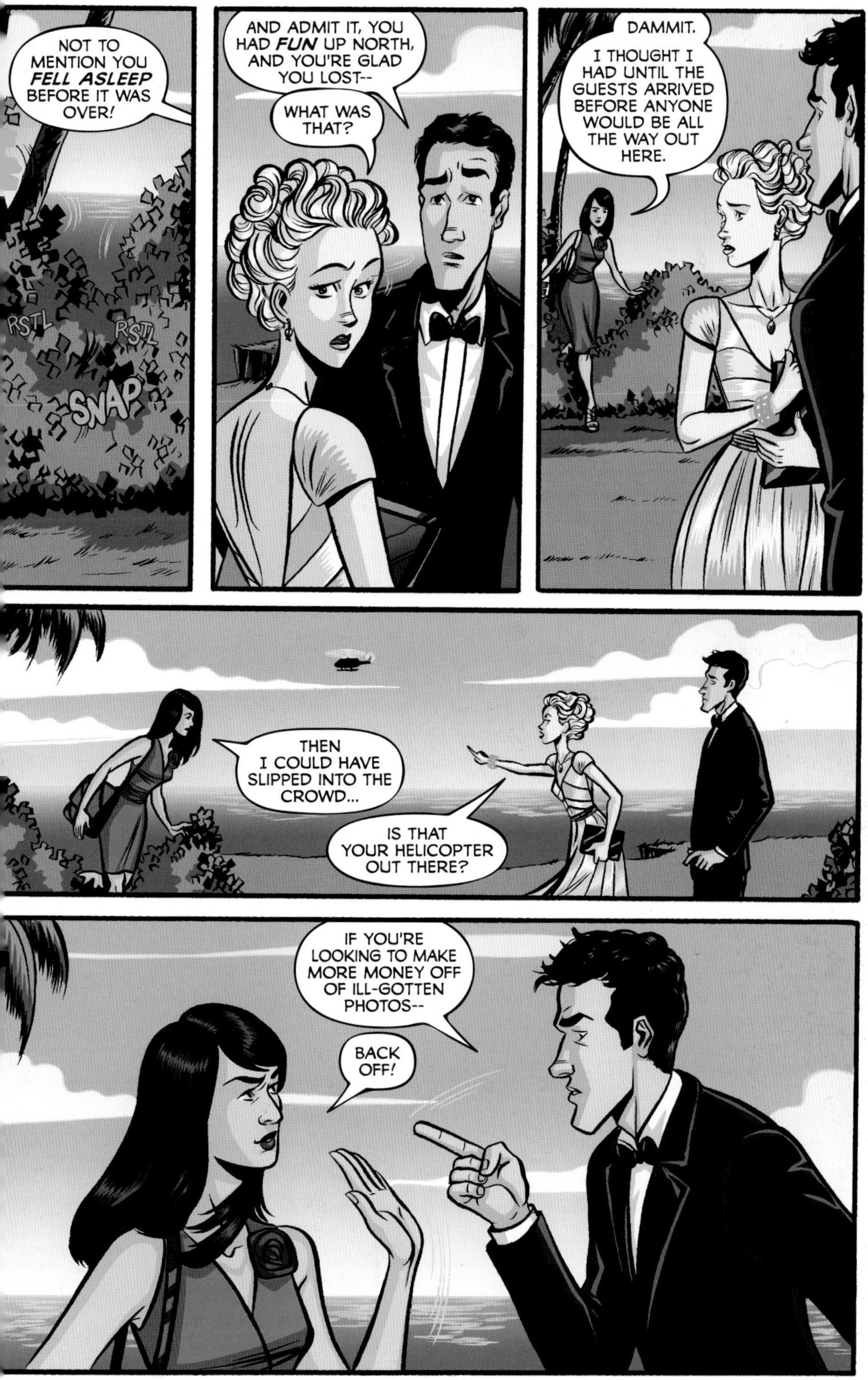
NOT TO MENTION YOU *FELL ASLEEP* BEFORE IT WAS OVER!
RSTL
RSTL
SNAP
AND ADMIT IT, YOU HAD *FUN* UP NORTH, AND YOU'RE GLAD YOU LOST--
WHAT WAS THAT?
DAMMIT.
I THOUGHT I HAD UNTIL THE GUESTS ARRIVED BEFORE ANYONE WOULD BE ALL THE WAY OUT HERE.
THEN I COULD HAVE SLIPPED INTO THE CROWD...
IS THAT YOUR HELICOPTER OUT THERE?
IF YOU'RE LOOKING TO MAKE MORE MONEY OFF OF ILL-GOTTEN PHOTOS--
BACK OFF!

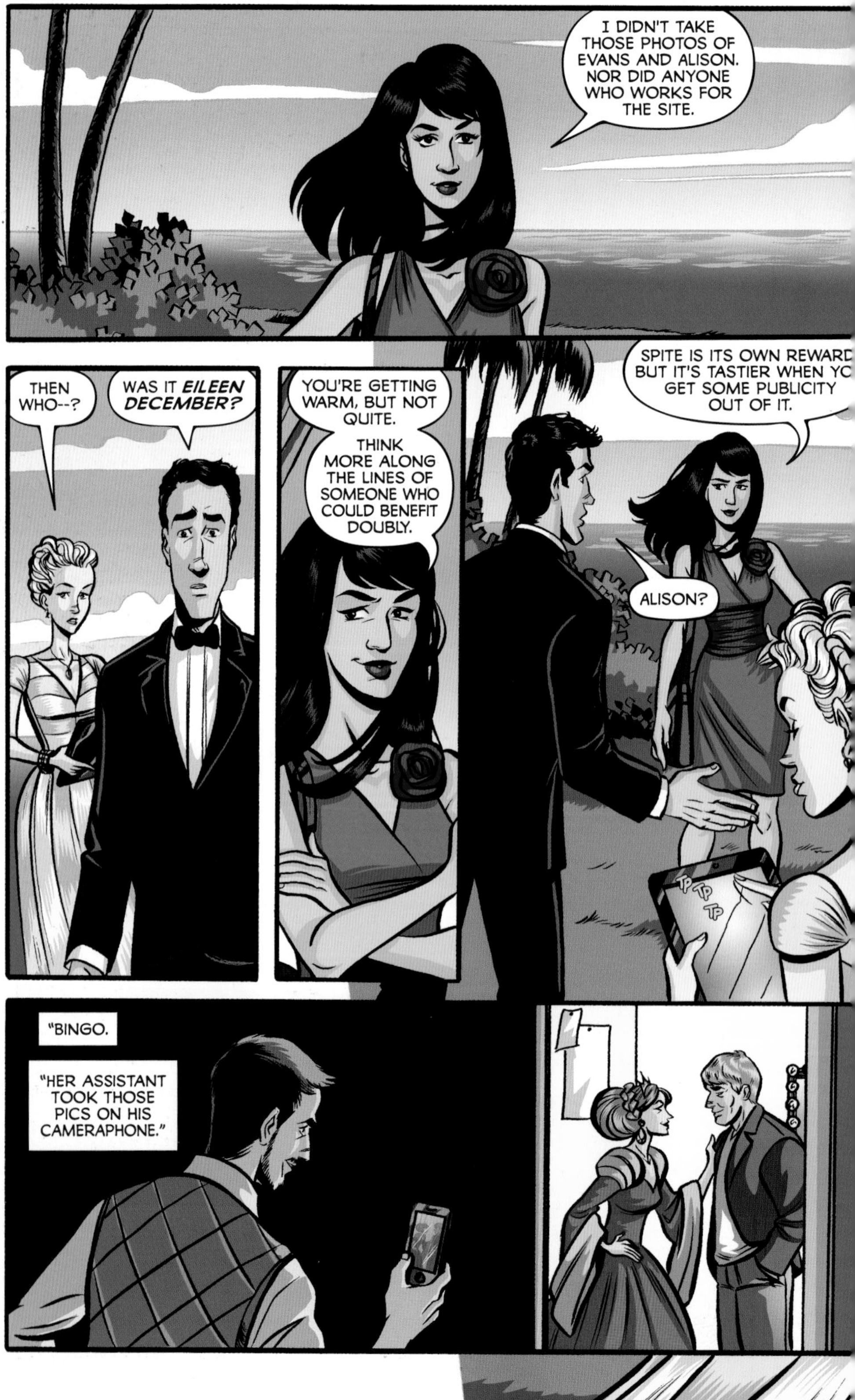
I DIDN'T TAKE THOSE PHOTOS OF EVANS AND ALISON. NOR DID ANYONE WHO WORKS FOR THE SITE.
THEN WHO--?
WAS IT *EILEEN DECEMBER?*
YOU'RE GETTING WARM, BUT NOT QUITE.
THINK MORE ALONG THE LINES OF SOMEONE WHO COULD BENEFIT DOUBLY.
ALISON?
TP TP TP
"BINGO.
"HER ASSISTANT TOOK THOSE PICS ON HIS CAMERAPHONE."

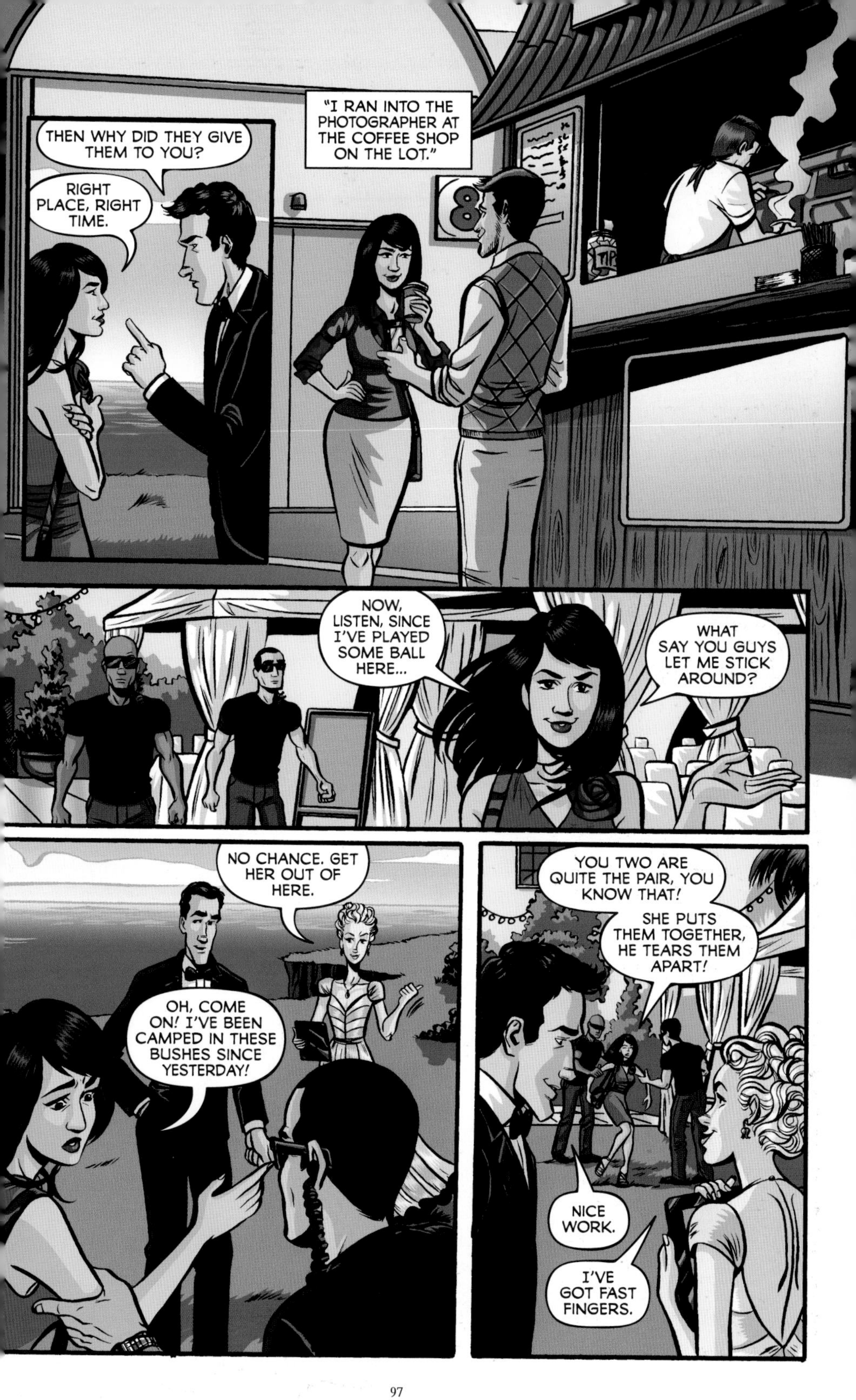
"I RAN INTO THE PHOTOGRAPHER AT THE COFFEE SHOP ON THE LOT."
THEN WHY DID THEY GIVE THEM TO YOU?
RIGHT PLACE, RIGHT TIME.
TIP
NOW, LISTEN, SINCE I'VE PLAYED SOME BALL HERE...
WHAT SAY YOU GUYS LET ME STICK AROUND?
NO CHANCE. GET HER OUT OF HERE.
OH, COME ON! I'VE BEEN CAMPED IN THESE BUSHES SINCE YESTERDAY!
YOU TWO ARE QUITE THE PAIR, YOU KNOW THAT!
SHE PUTS THEM TOGETHER, HE TEARS THEM APART!
NICE WORK.
I'VE GOT FAST FINGERS.

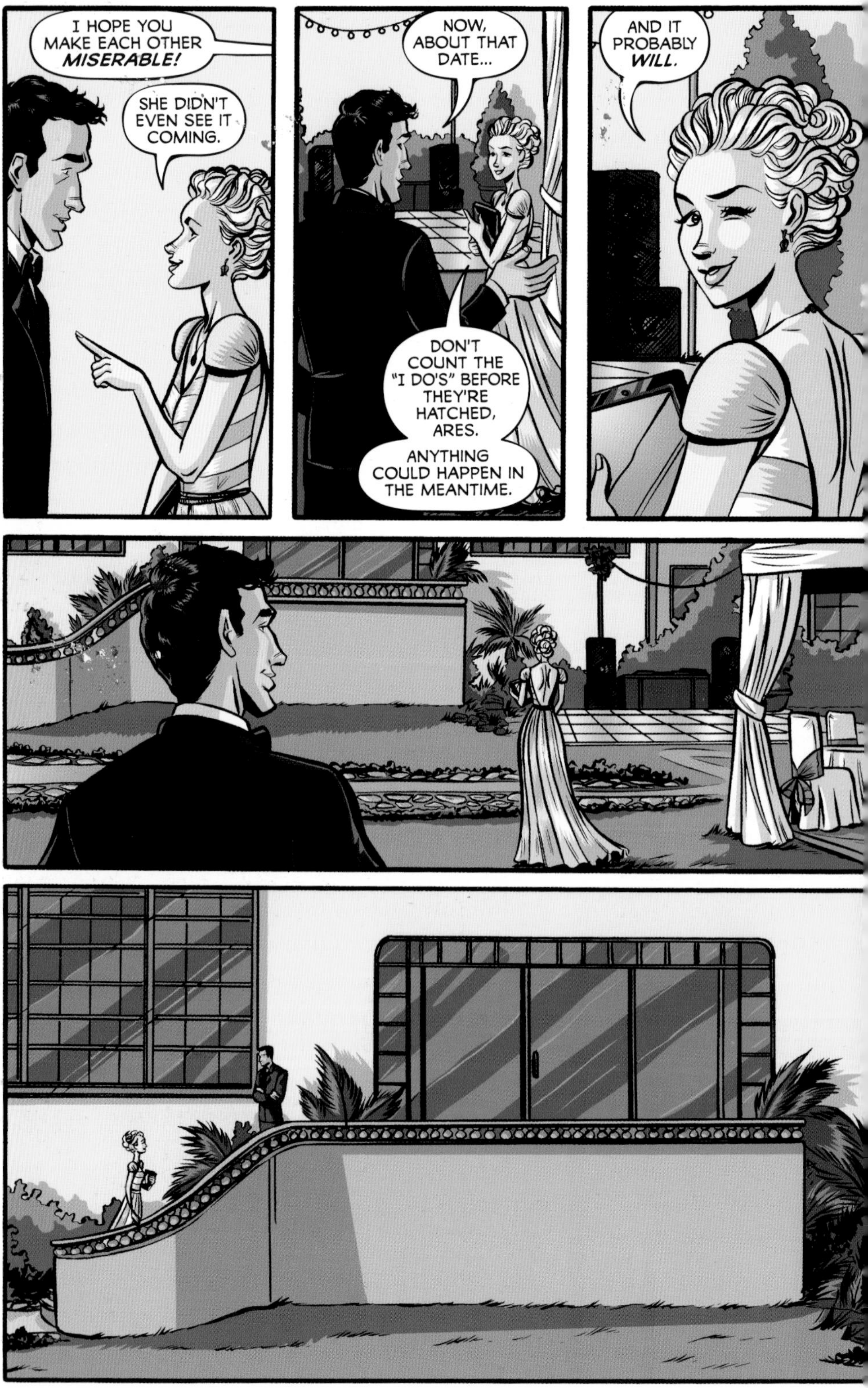
I HOPE YOU MAKE EACH OTHER *MISERABLE!*
SHE DIDN'T EVEN SEE IT COMING.
NOW, ABOUT THAT DATE...
DON'T COUNT THE "I DO'S" BEFORE THEY'RE HATCHED, ARES.
ANYTHING COULD HAPPEN IN THE MEANTIME.
AND IT PROBABLY *WILL.*

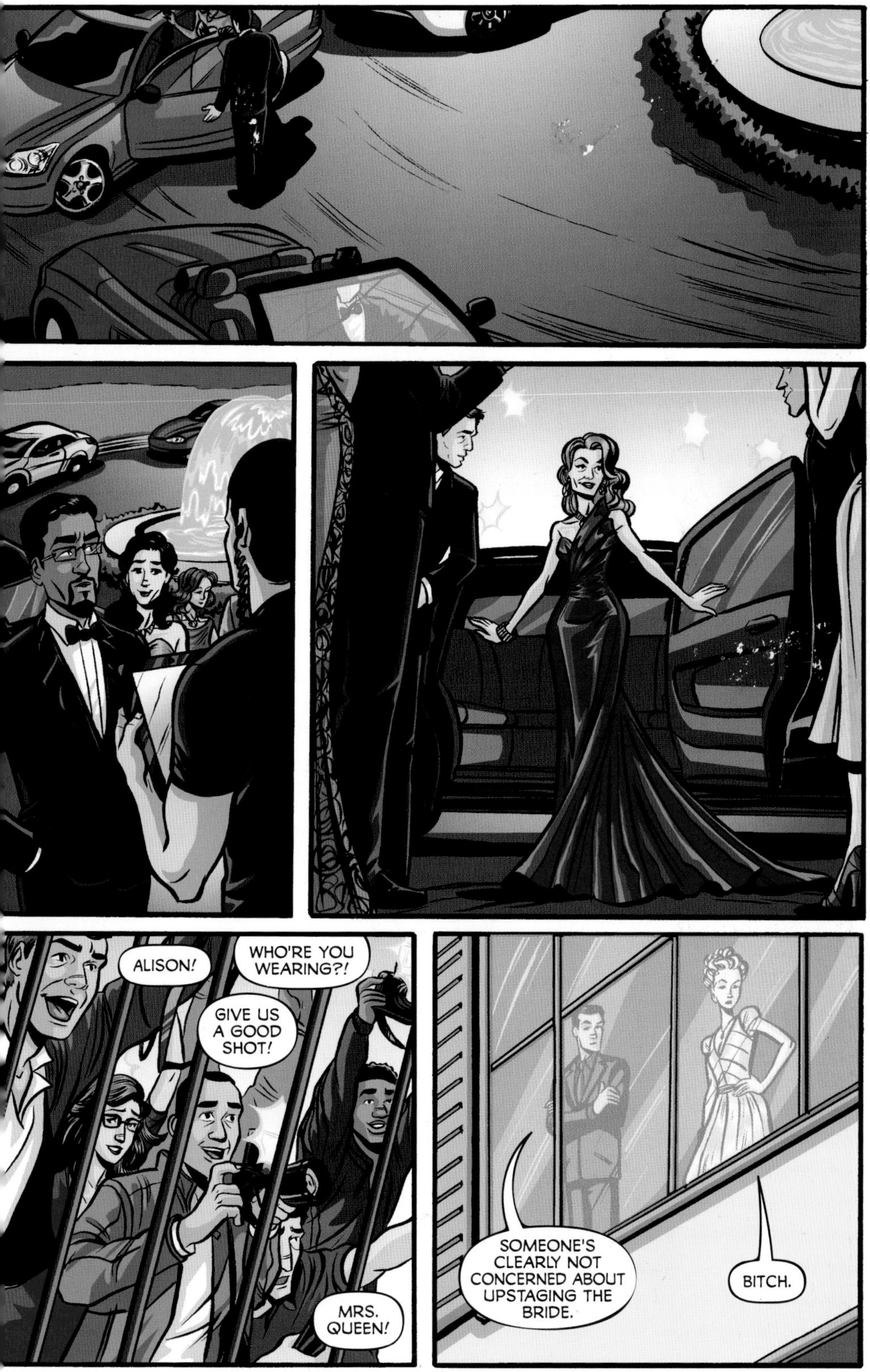
ALISON!
WHO'RE YOU WEARING?!
GIVE US A GOOD SHOT!
MRS. QUEEN!
SOMEONE'S CLEARLY NOT CONCERNED ABOUT UPSTAGING THE BRIDE.
BITCH.

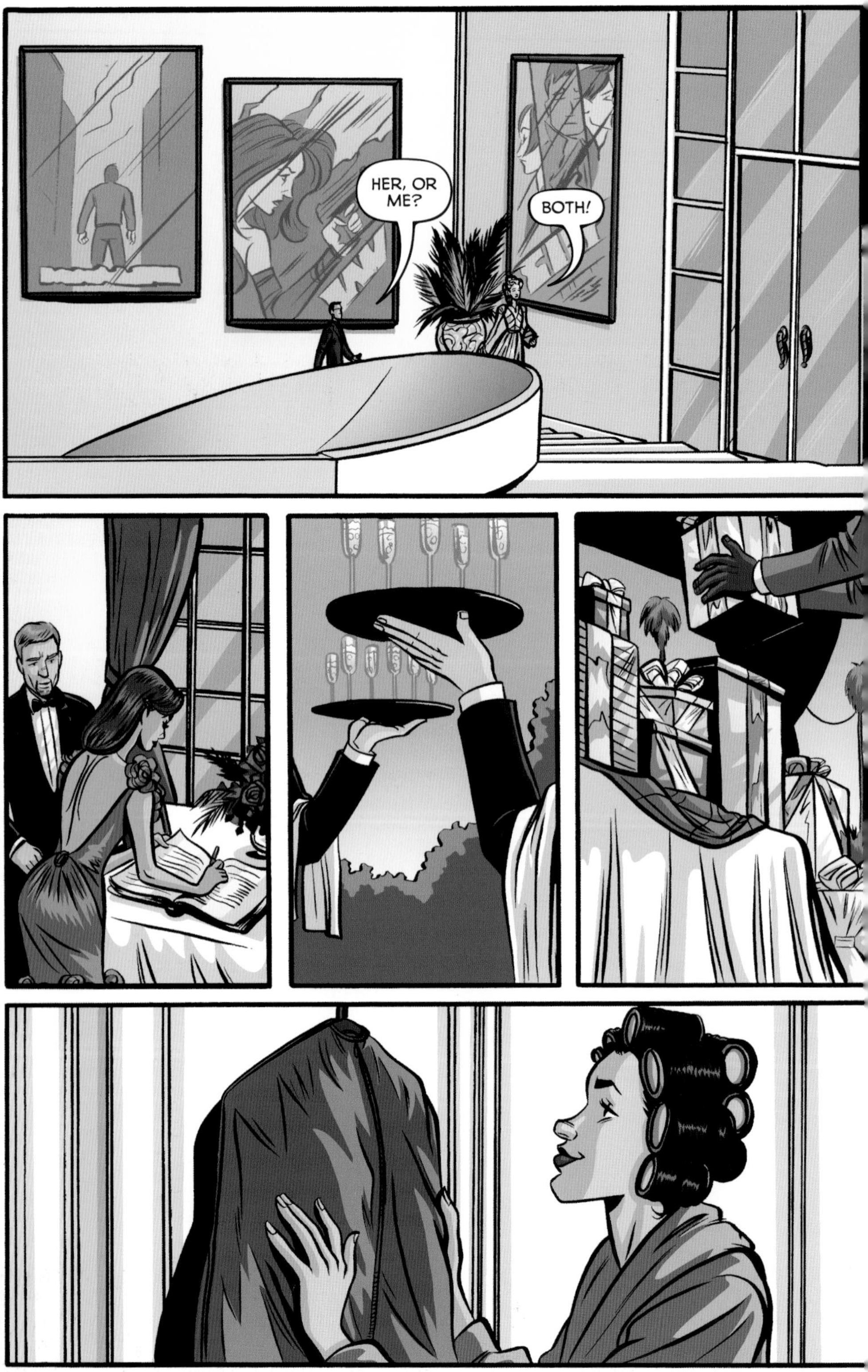
HER, OR ME?
BOTH!

# CHAPTER NINE

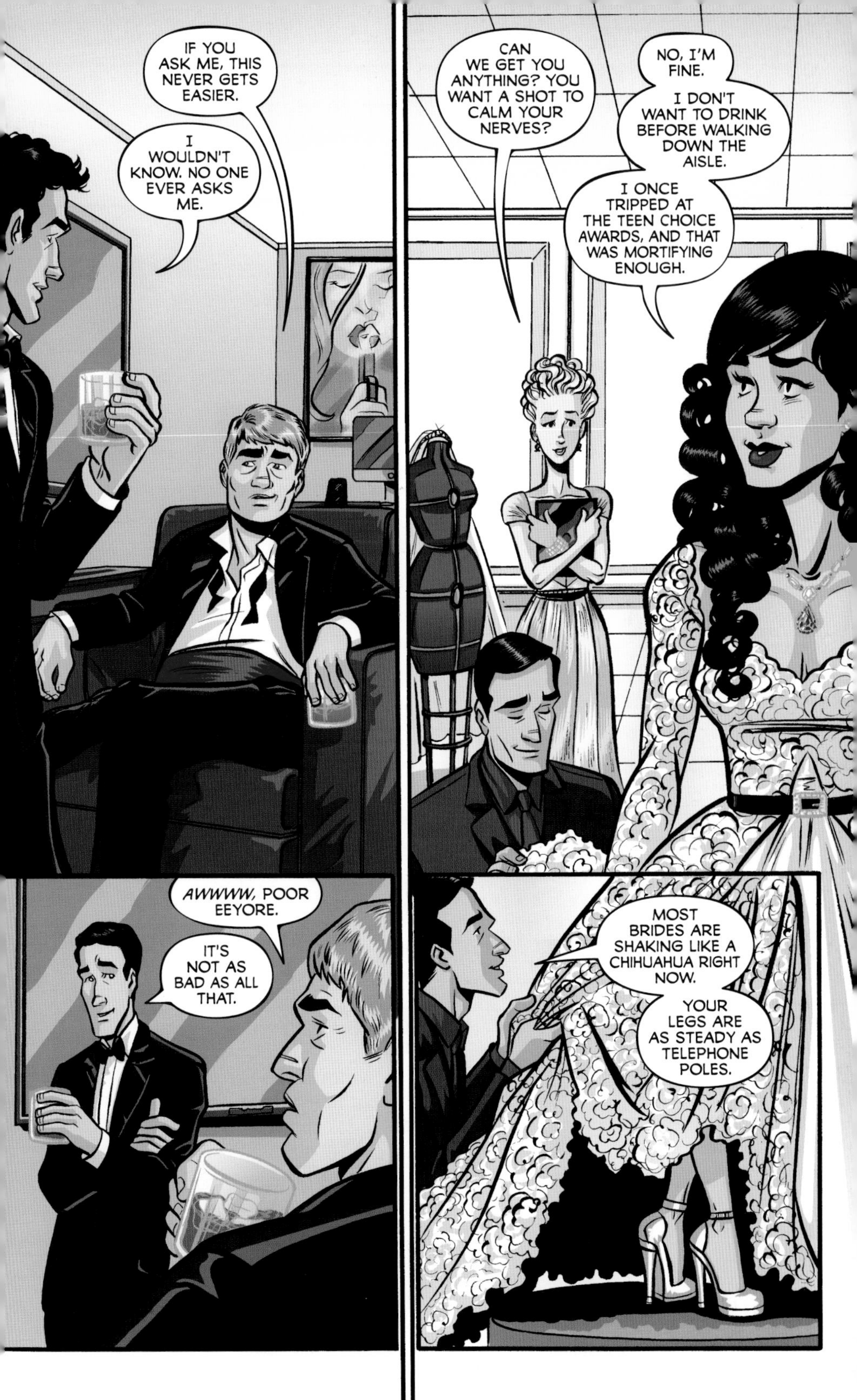
IF YOU ASK ME, THIS NEVER GETS EASIER.
I WOULDN'T KNOW. NO ONE EVER ASKS ME.
CAN WE GET YOU ANYTHING? YOU WANT A SHOT TO CALM YOUR NERVES?
NO, I'M FINE.
I DON'T WANT TO DRINK BEFORE WALKING DOWN THE AISLE.
I ONCE TRIPPED AT THE TEEN CHOICE AWARDS, AND THAT WAS MORTIFYING ENOUGH.
*AWWWW,* POOR EEYORE.
IT'S NOT AS BAD AS ALL THAT.
MOST BRIDES ARE SHAKING LIKE A CHIHUAHUA RIGHT NOW.
YOUR LEGS ARE AS STEADY AS TELEPHONE POLES.

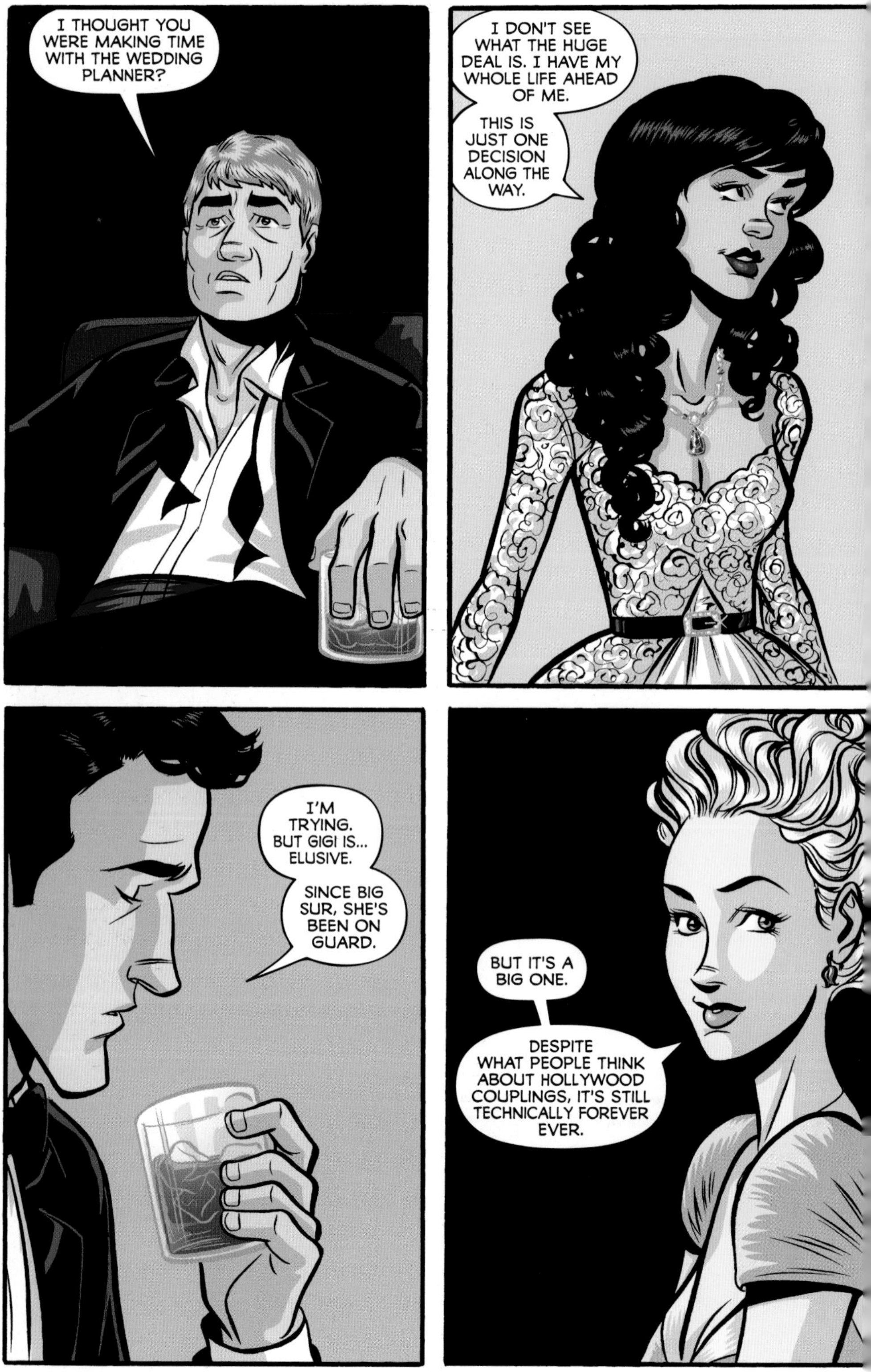
I THOUGHT YOU WERE MAKING TIME WITH THE WEDDING PLANNER?
I DON'T SEE WHAT THE HUGE DEAL IS. I HAVE MY WHOLE LIFE AHEAD OF ME.
THIS IS JUST ONE DECISION ALONG THE WAY.
I'M TRYING. BUT GIGI IS... ELUSIVE.
SINCE BIG SUR, SHE'S BEEN ON GUARD.
BUT IT'S A BIG ONE.
DESPITE WHAT PEOPLE THINK ABOUT HOLLYWOOD COUPLINGS, IT'S STILL TECHNICALLY FOREVER EVER.

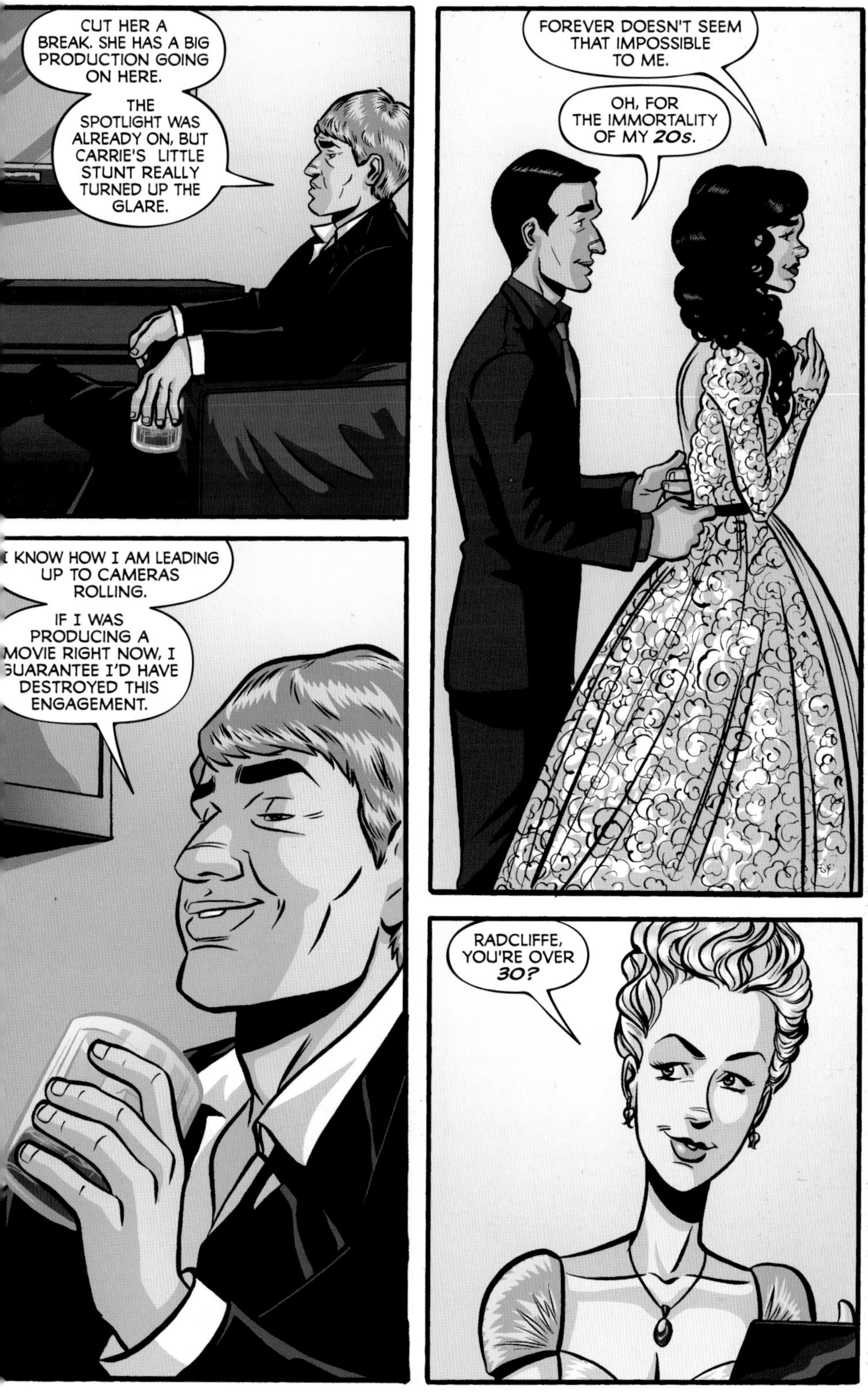
CUT HER A BREAK. SHE HAS A BIG PRODUCTION GOING ON HERE.
THE SPOTLIGHT WAS ALREADY ON, BUT CARRIE'S LITTLE STUNT REALLY TURNED UP THE GLARE.
I KNOW HOW I AM LEADING UP TO CAMERAS ROLLING.
IF I WAS PRODUCING A MOVIE RIGHT NOW, I GUARANTEE I'D HAVE DESTROYED THIS ENGAGEMENT.
FOREVER DOESN'T SEEM THAT IMPOSSIBLE TO ME.
OH, FOR THE IMMORTALITY OF MY *20s*.
RADCLIFFE, YOU'RE OVER *30?*

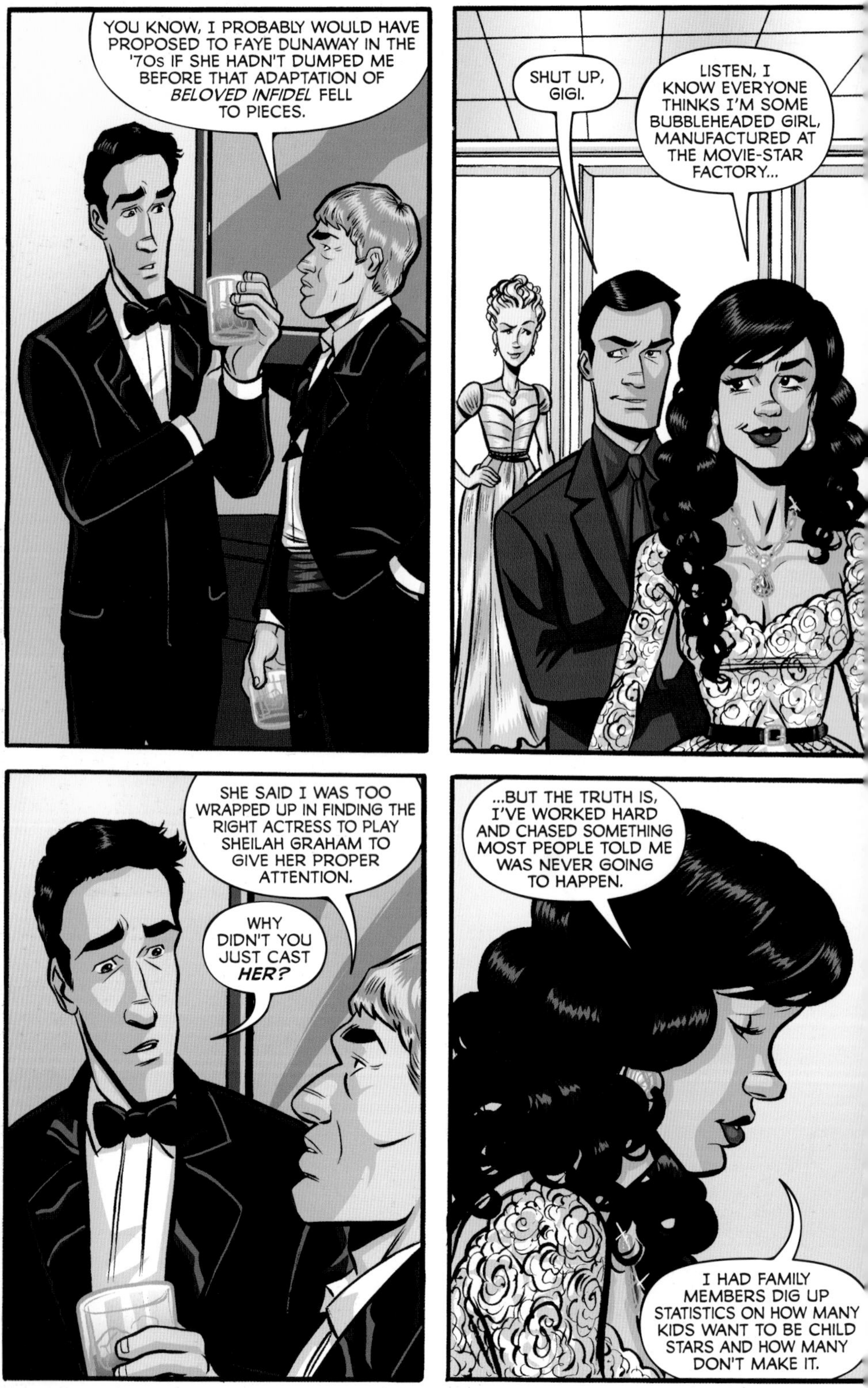

YOU KNOW, I PROBABLY WOULD HAVE PROPOSED TO FAYE DUNAWAY IN THE '70s IF SHE HADN'T DUMPED ME BEFORE THAT ADAPTATION OF *BELOVED INFIDEL* FELL TO PIECES.
SHUT UP, GIGI.
LISTEN, I KNOW EVERYONE THINKS I'M SOME BUBBLEHEADED GIRL, MANUFACTURED AT THE MOVIE-STAR FACTORY...
SHE SAID I WAS TOO WRAPPED UP IN FINDING THE RIGHT ACTRESS TO PLAY SHEILAH GRAHAM TO GIVE HER PROPER ATTENTION.
WHY DIDN'T YOU JUST CAST ***HER?***
...BUT THE TRUTH IS, I'VE WORKED HARD AND CHASED SOMETHING MOST PEOPLE TOLD ME WAS NEVER GOING TO HAPPEN.
I HAD FAMILY MEMBERS DIG UP STATISTICS ON HOW MANY KIDS WANT TO BE CHILD STARS AND HOW MANY DON'T MAKE IT.

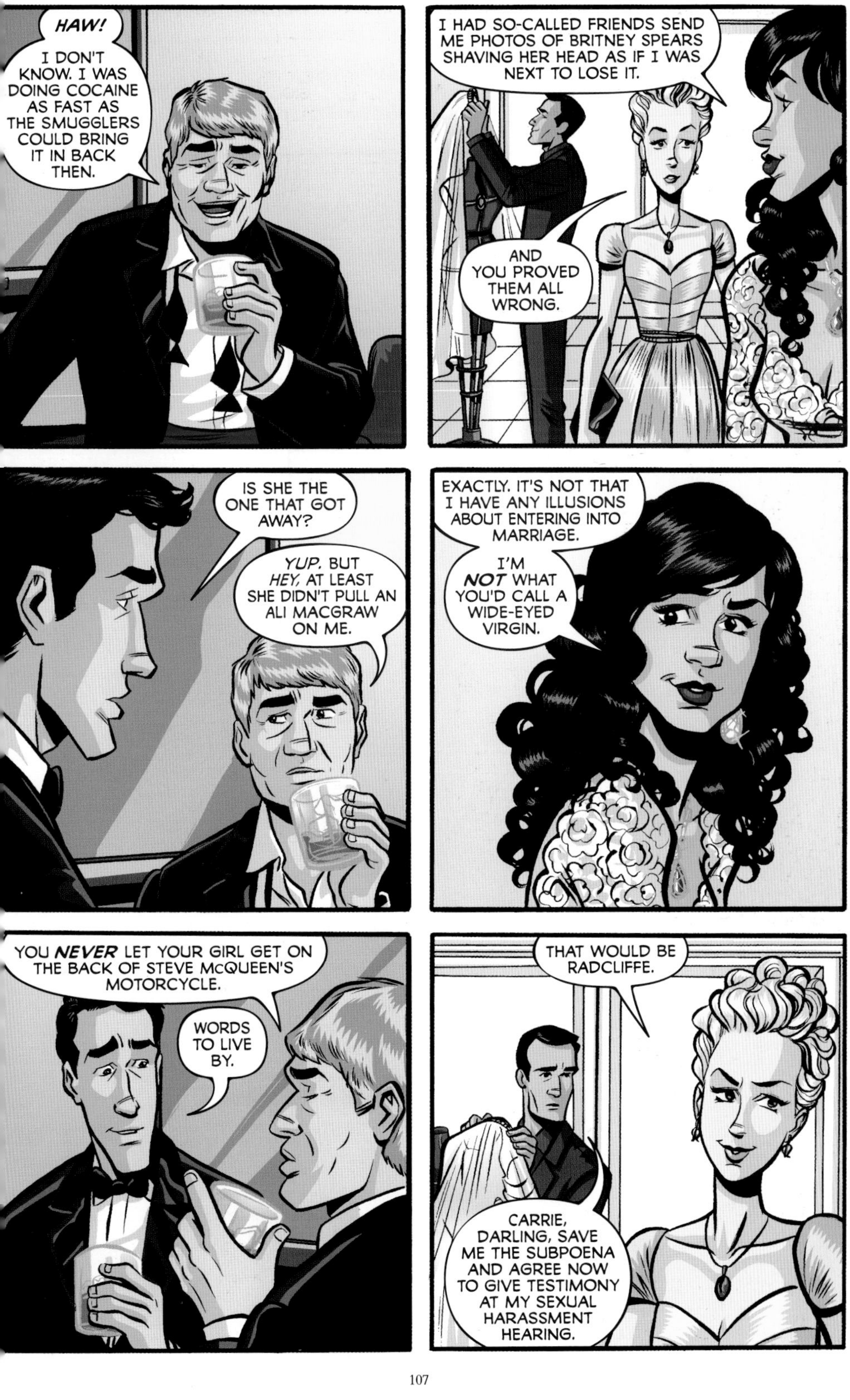
HAW!
I DON'T KNOW. I WAS DOING COCAINE AS FAST AS THE SMUGGLERS COULD BRING IT IN BACK THEN.
I HAD SO-CALLED FRIENDS SEND ME PHOTOS OF BRITNEY SPEARS SHAVING HER HEAD AS IF I WAS NEXT TO LOSE IT.
AND YOU PROVED THEM ALL WRONG.
IS SHE THE ONE THAT GOT AWAY?
YUP. BUT HEY, AT LEAST SHE DIDN'T PULL AN ALI MACGRAW ON ME.
EXACTLY. IT'S NOT THAT I HAVE ANY ILLUSIONS ABOUT ENTERING INTO MARRIAGE.
I'M NOT WHAT YOU'D CALL A WIDE-EYED VIRGIN.
YOU NEVER LET YOUR GIRL GET ON THE BACK OF STEVE McQUEEN'S MOTORCYCLE.
WORDS TO LIVE BY.
THAT WOULD BE RADCLIFFE.
CARRIE, DARLING, SAVE ME THE SUBPOENA AND AGREE NOW TO GIVE TESTIMONY AT MY SEXUAL HARASSMENT HEARING.

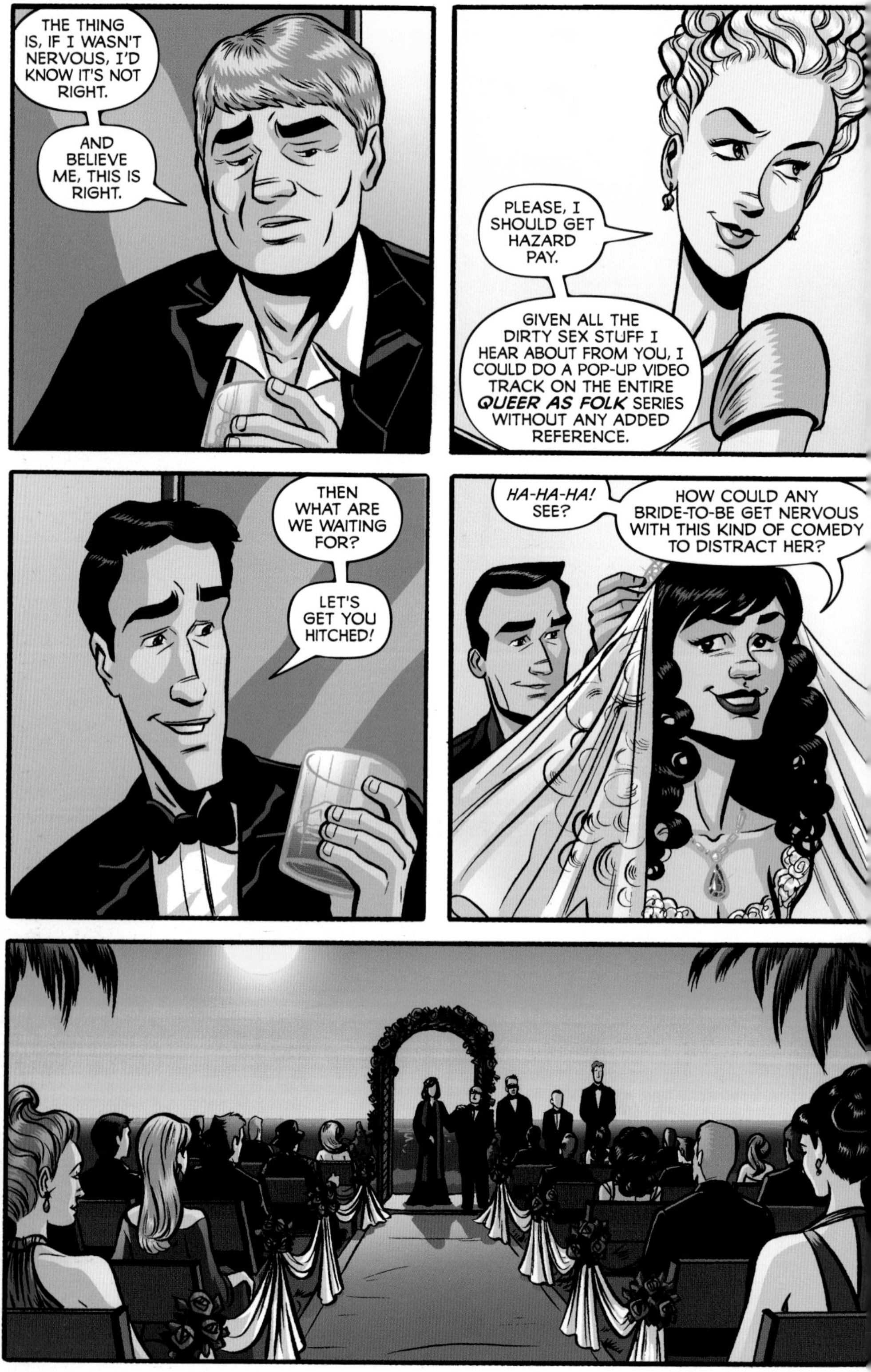
THE THING IS, IF I WASN'T NERVOUS, I'D KNOW IT'S NOT RIGHT.
AND BELIEVE ME, THIS IS RIGHT.
PLEASE, I SHOULD GET HAZARD PAY.
GIVEN ALL THE DIRTY SEX STUFF I HEAR ABOUT FROM YOU, I COULD DO A POP-UP VIDEO TRACK ON THE ENTIRE ***QUEER AS FOLK*** SERIES WITHOUT ANY ADDED REFERENCE.
THEN WHAT ARE WE WAITING FOR?
LET'S GET YOU HITCHED!
*HA-HA-HA!* SEE?
HOW COULD ANY BRIDE-TO-BE GET NERVOUS WITH THIS KIND OF COMEDY TO DISTRACT HER?

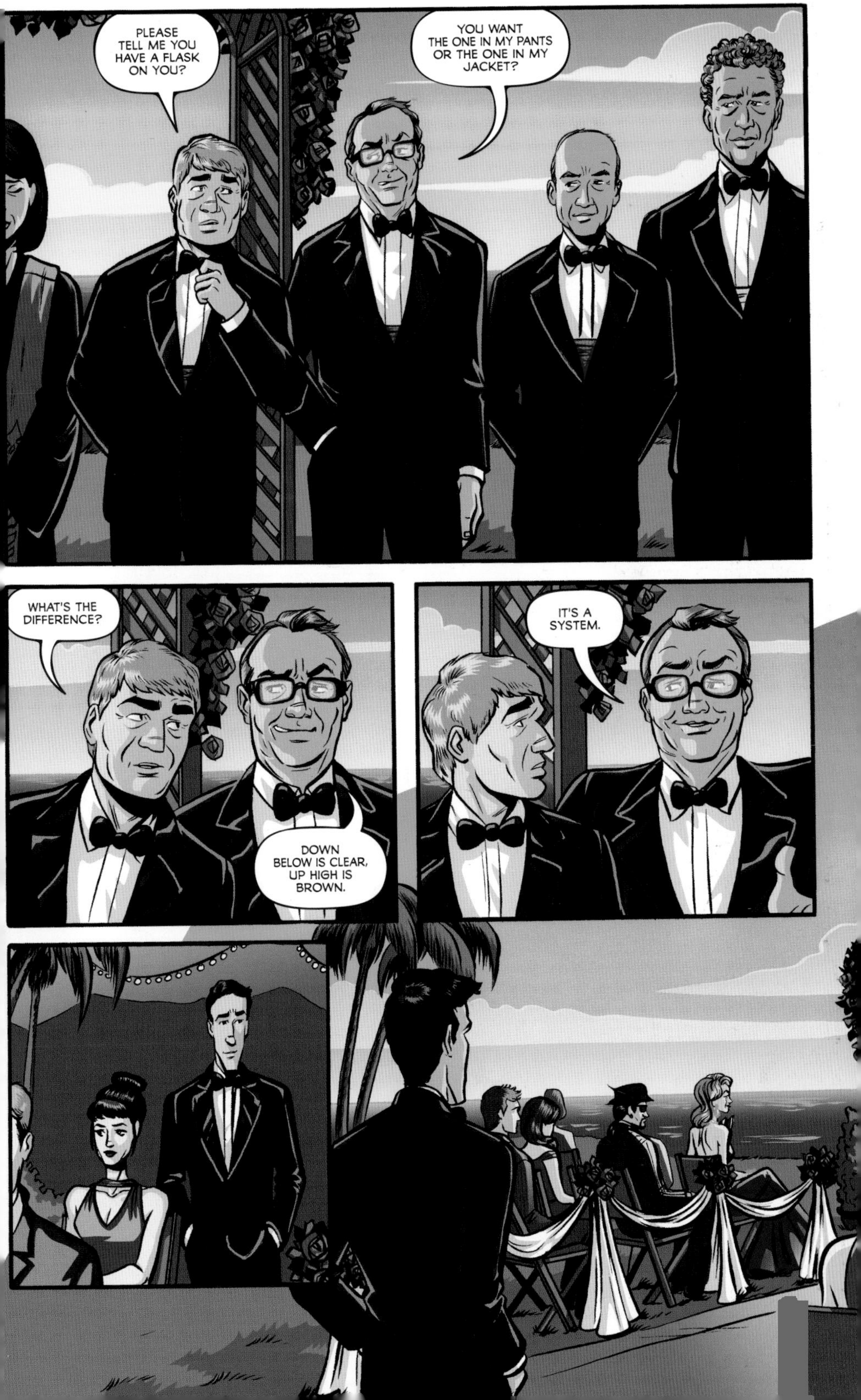
PLEASE TELL ME YOU HAVE A FLASK ON YOU?
YOU WANT THE ONE IN MY PANTS OR THE ONE IN MY JACKET?
WHAT'S THE DIFFERENCE?
DOWN BELOW IS CLEAR, UP HIGH IS BROWN.
IT'S A SYSTEM.

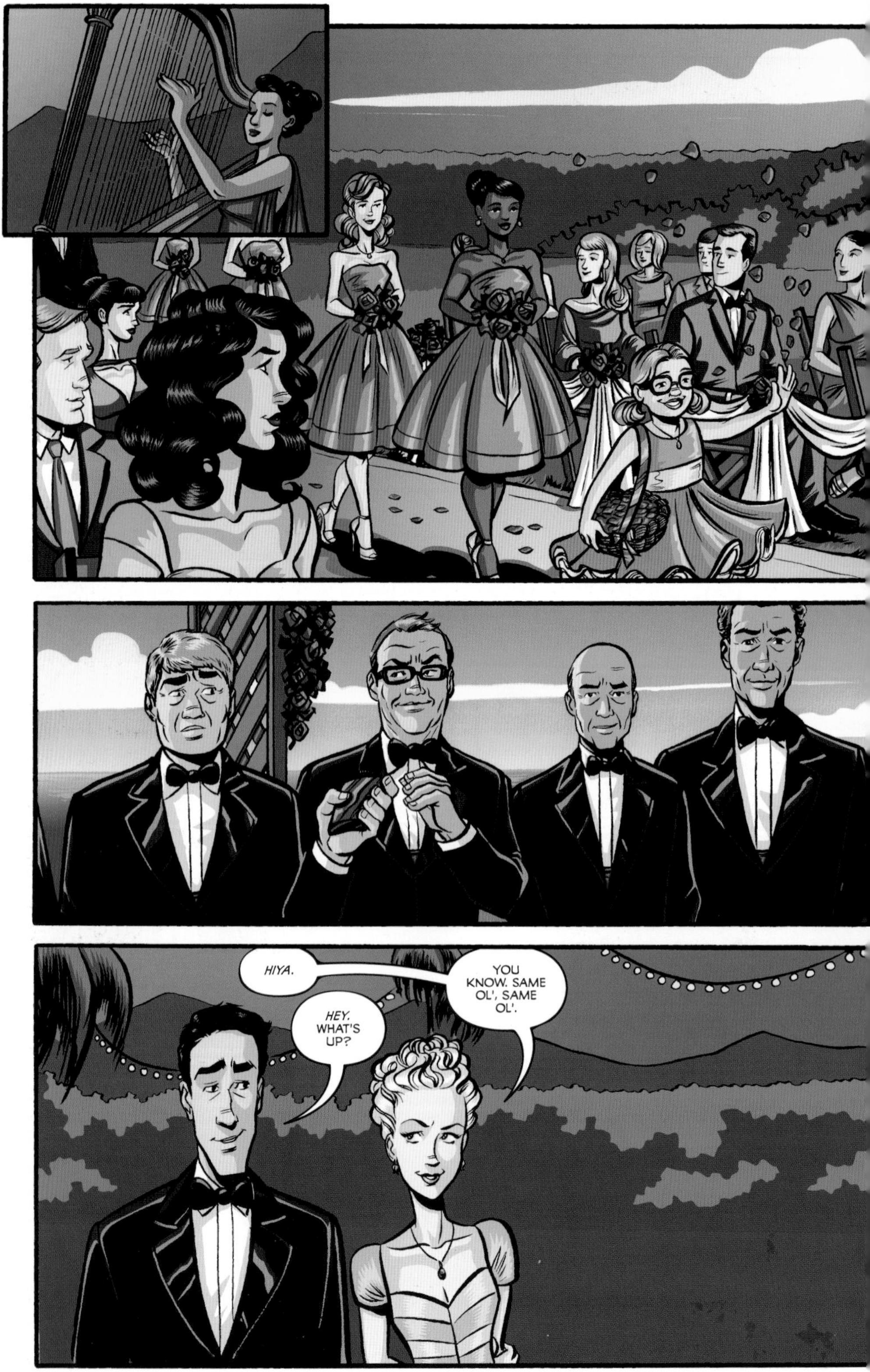
HIYA.
HEY. WHAT'S UP?
YOU KNOW. SAME OL', SAME OL'.

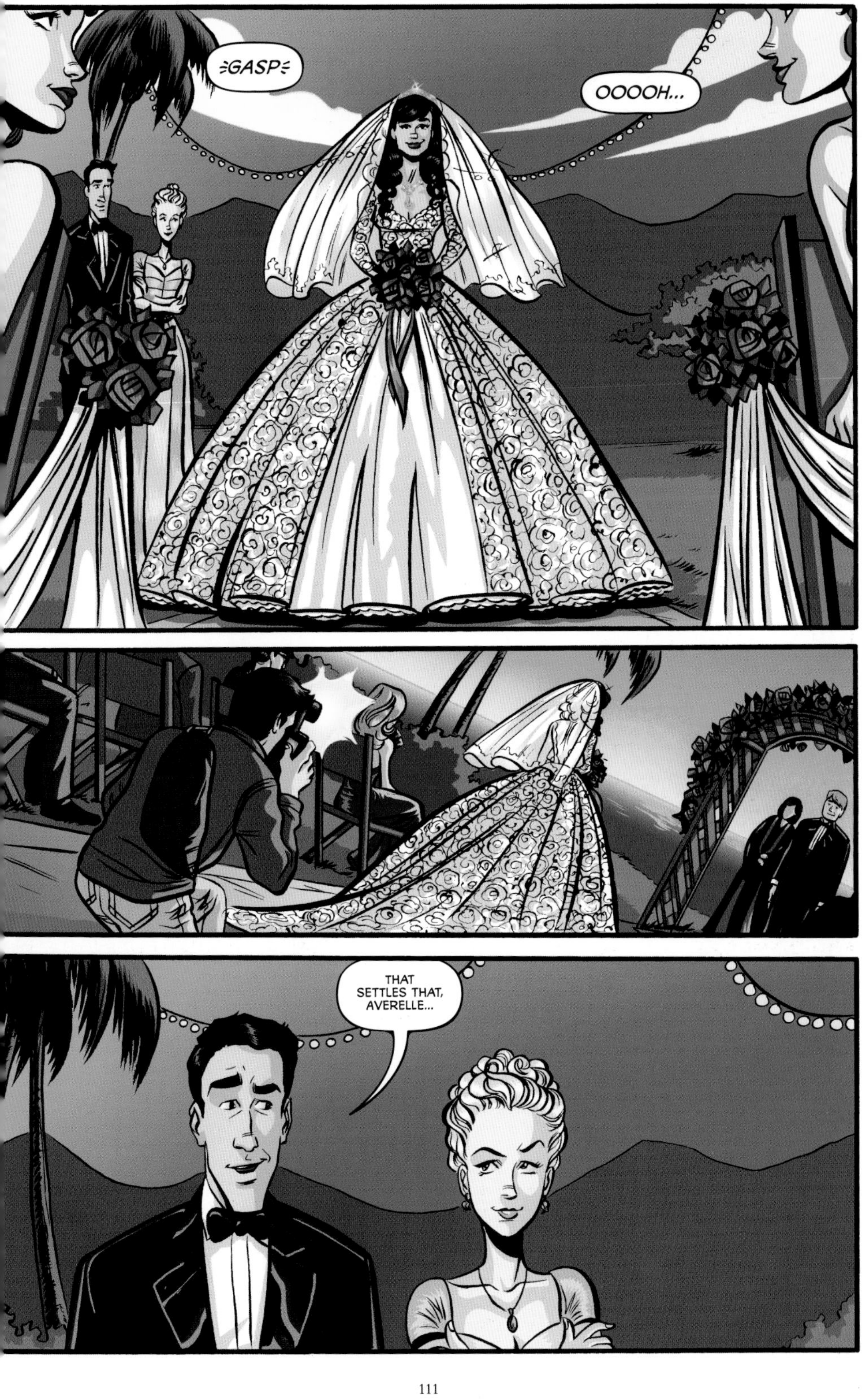
GASP
OOOOH...
THAT SETTLES THAT, AVERELLE...

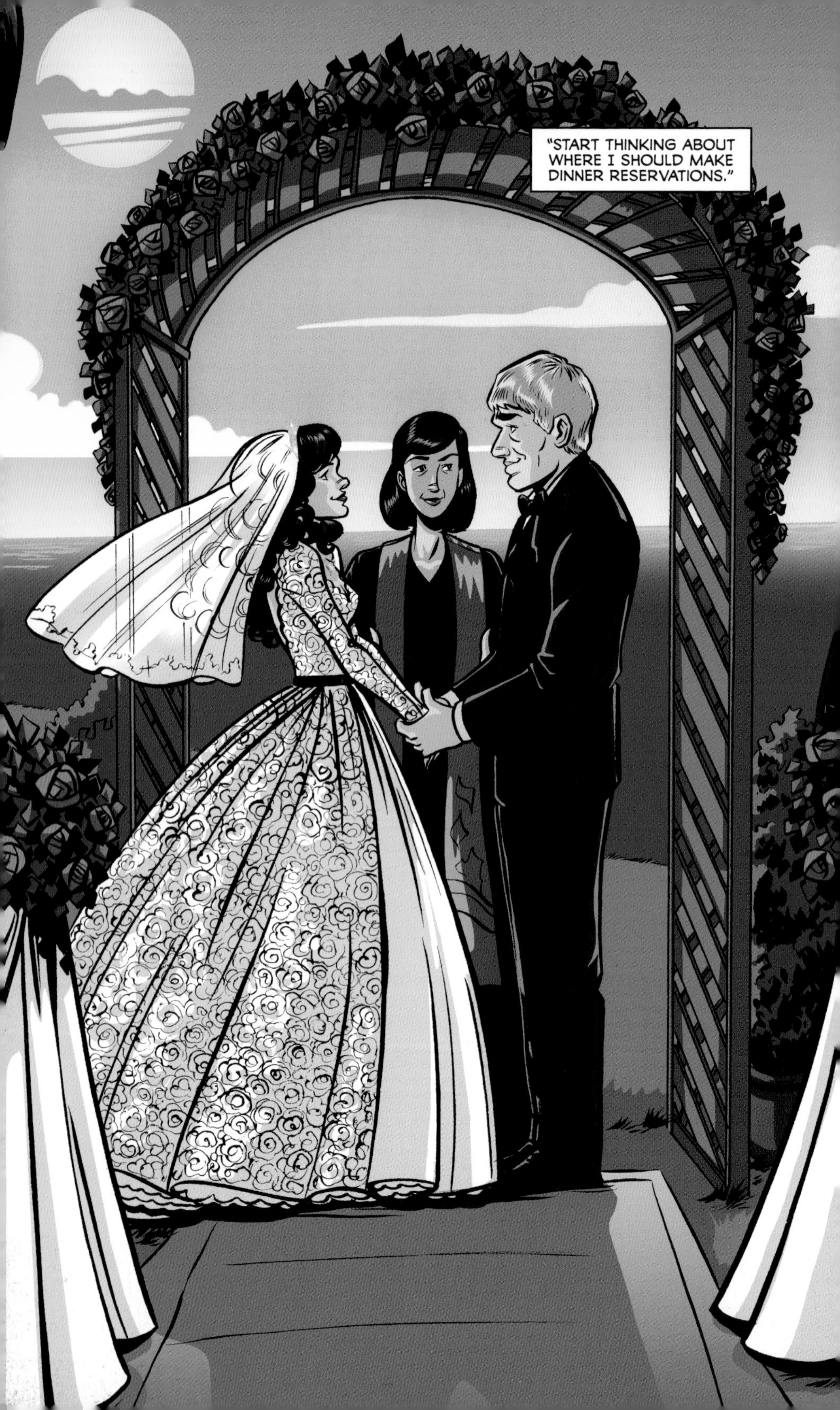
"START THINKING ABOUT WHERE I SHOULD MAKE DINNER RESERVATIONS."

# CHAPTER TEN

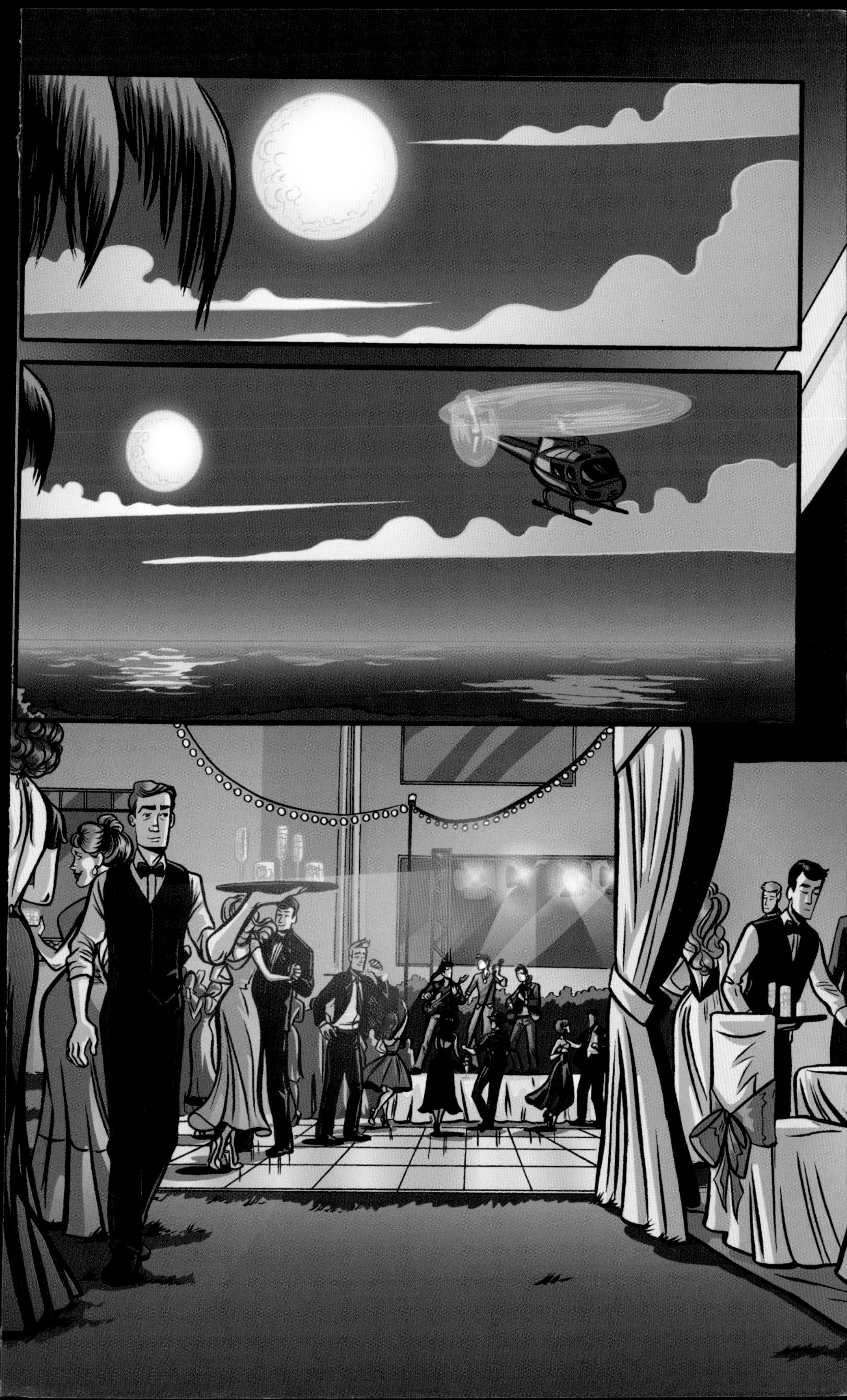

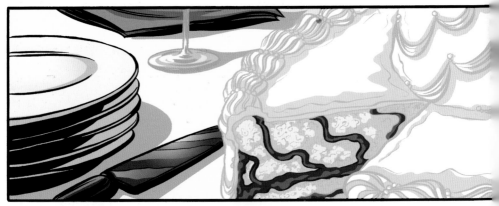

THE DIVORCE ATTORNEY GOING STAG AT A WEDDING.

HOW IRONIC.

FAIR COMMENTARY. BUT WHERE'S YOUR DATE, ALISON?

LOOK AROUND YOU, DEAR BOY.

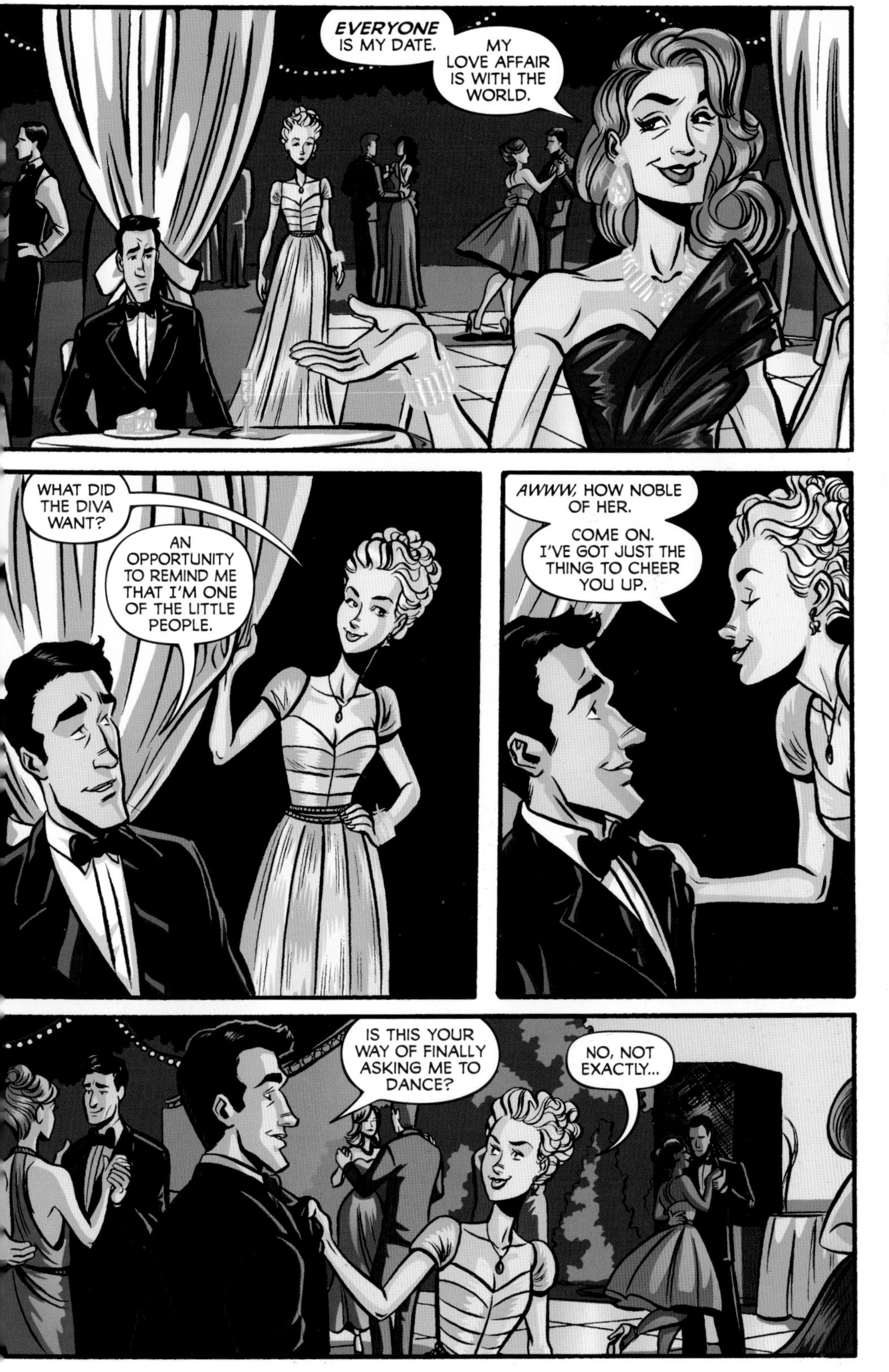
EVERYONE IS MY DATE.
MY LOVE AFFAIR IS WITH THE WORLD.
WHAT DID THE DIVA WANT?
AN OPPORTUNITY TO REMIND ME THAT I'M ONE OF THE LITTLE PEOPLE.
AWWW, HOW NOBLE OF HER.
COME ON. I'VE GOT JUST THE THING TO CHEER YOU UP.
IS THIS YOUR WAY OF FINALLY ASKING ME TO DANCE?
NO, NOT EXACTLY...

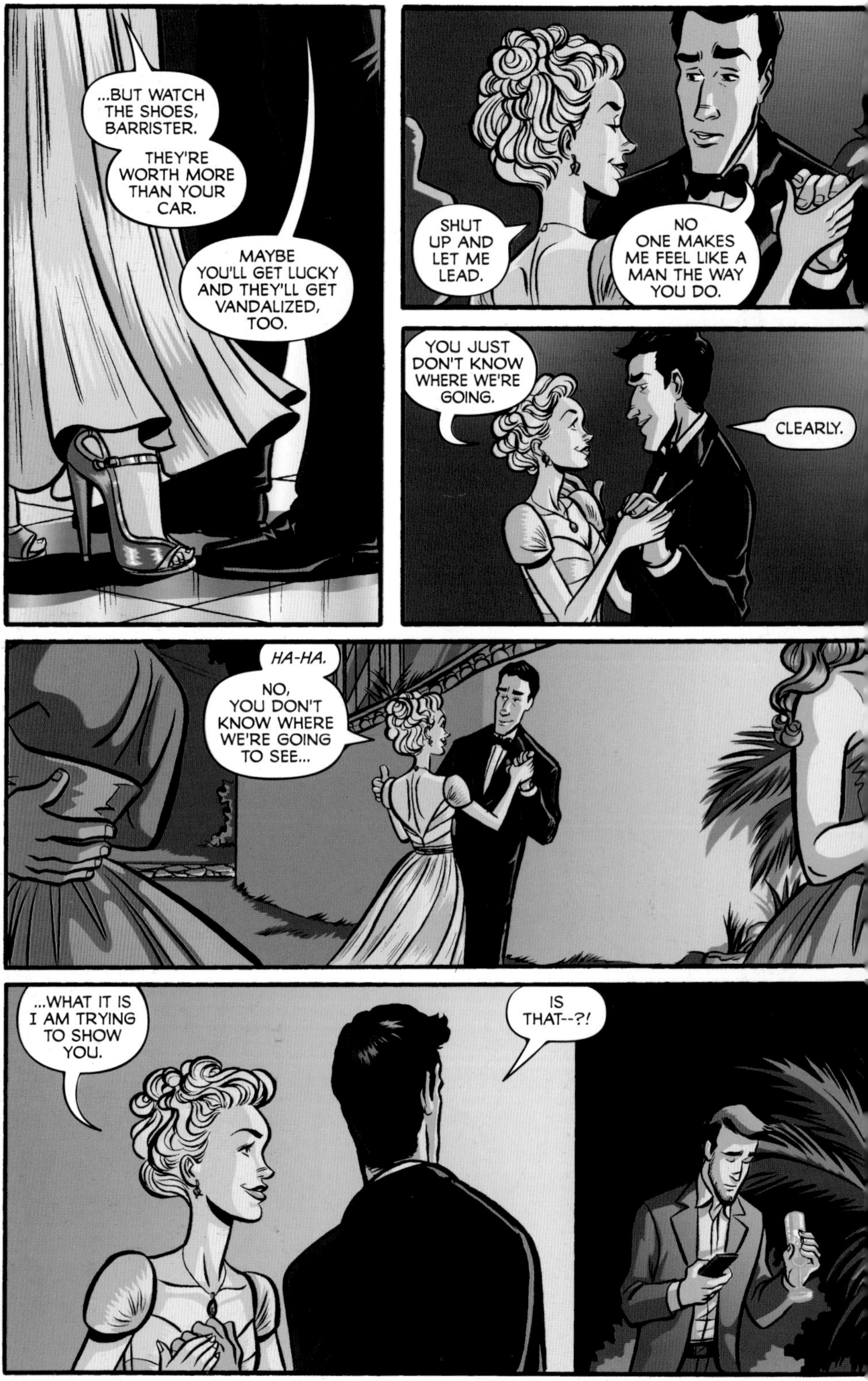

...BUT WATCH THE SHOES, BARRISTER.
THEY'RE WORTH MORE THAN YOUR CAR.
MAYBE YOU'LL GET LUCKY AND THEY'LL GET VANDALIZED, TOO.
SHUT UP AND LET ME LEAD.
NO ONE MAKES ME FEEL LIKE A MAN THE WAY YOU DO.
YOU JUST DON'T KNOW WHERE WE'RE GOING.
CLEARLY.
HA-HA.
NO, YOU DON'T KNOW WHERE WE'RE GOING TO SEE...
...WHAT IT IS I AM TRYING TO SHOW YOU.
IS THAT--?!

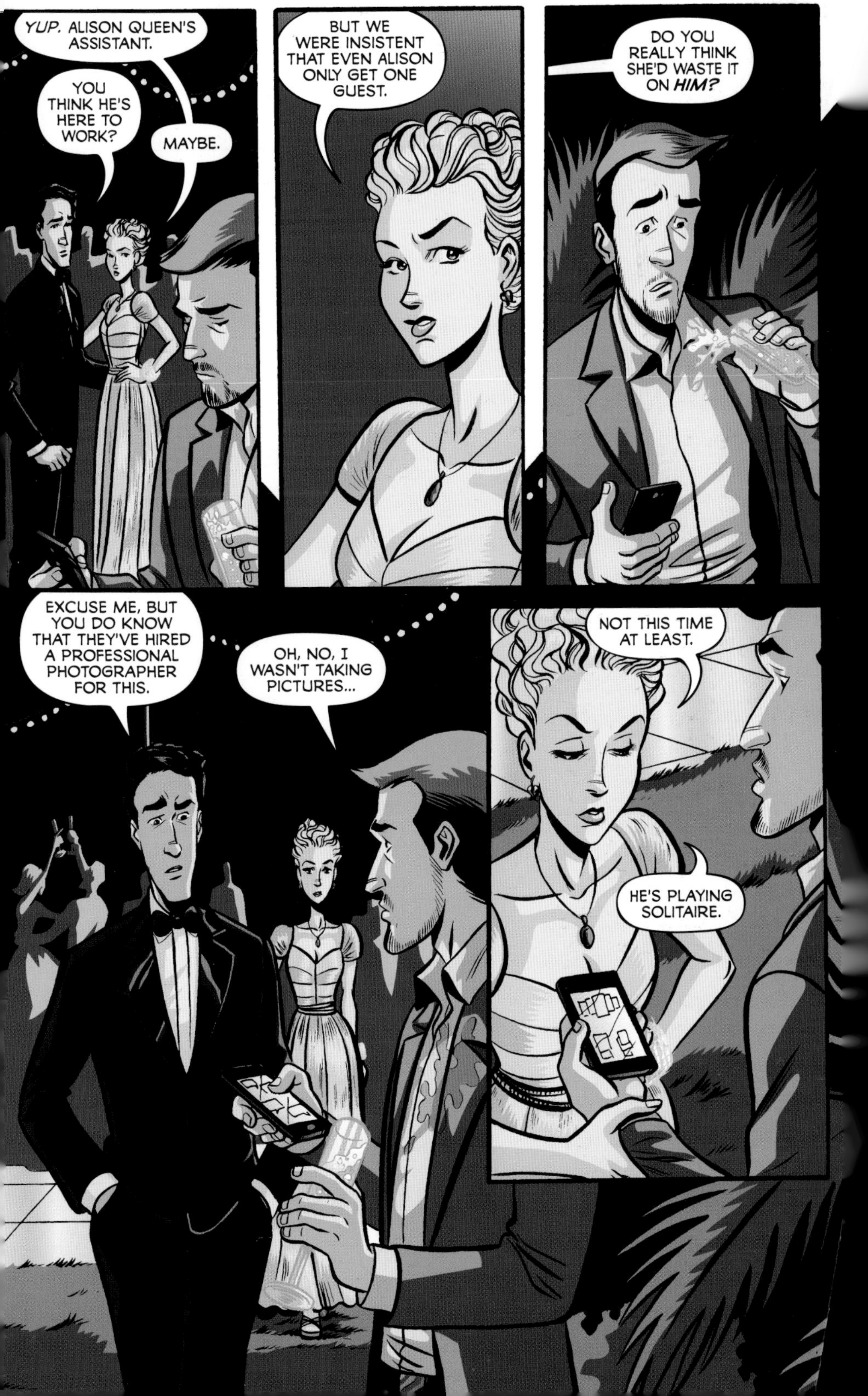
*YUP.* ALISON QUEEN'S ASSISTANT.
YOU THINK HE'S HERE TO WORK?
MAYBE.
BUT WE WERE INSISTENT THAT EVEN ALISON ONLY GET ONE GUEST.
DO YOU REALLY THINK SHE'D WASTE IT ON ***HIM?***
EXCUSE ME, BUT YOU DO KNOW THAT THEY'VE HIRED A PROFESSIONAL PHOTOGRAPHER FOR THIS.
OH, NO, I WASN'T TAKING PICTURES...
NOT THIS TIME AT LEAST.
HE'S PLAYING SOLITAIRE.

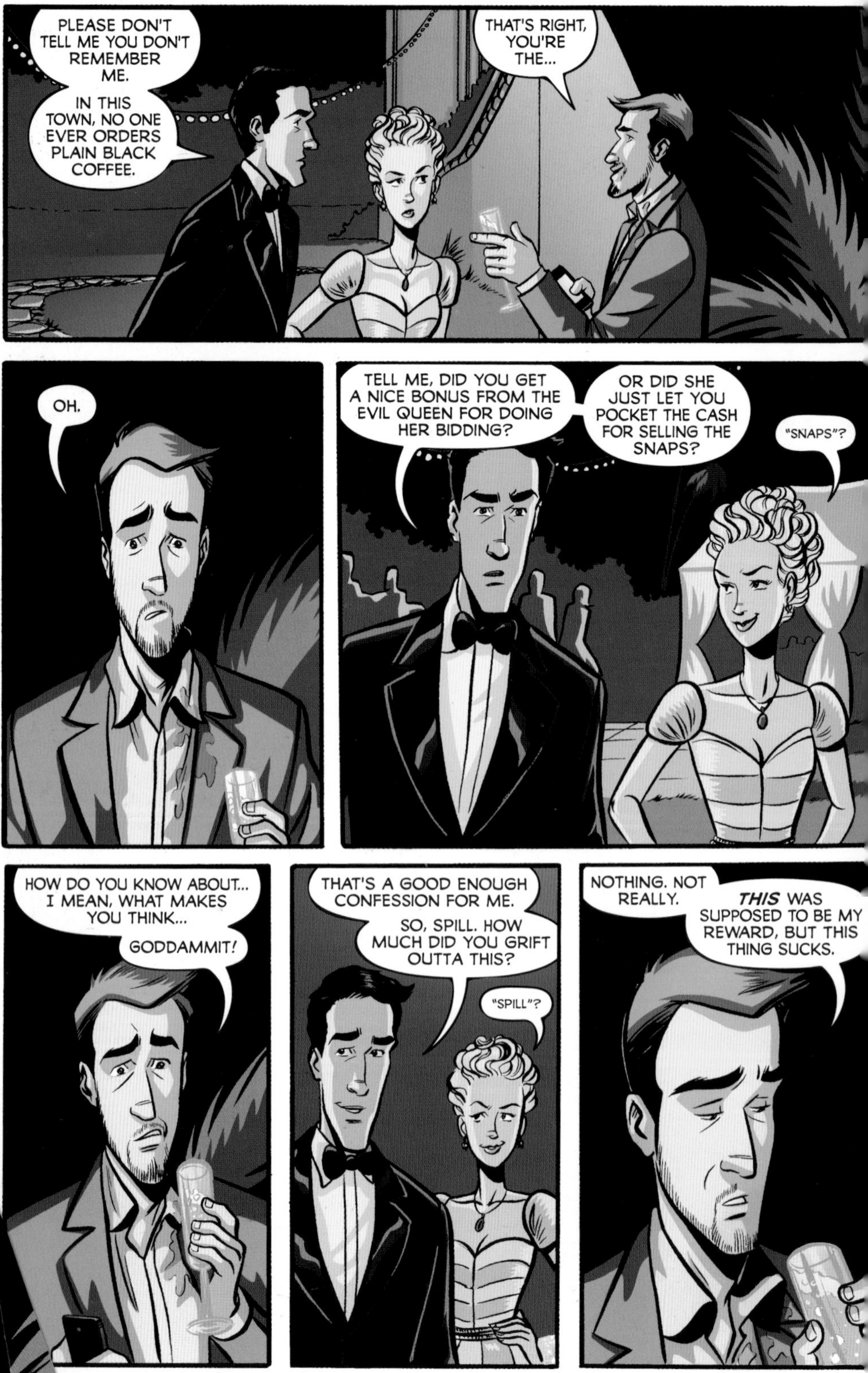
PLEASE DON'T TELL ME YOU DON'T REMEMBER ME.
IN THIS TOWN, NO ONE EVER ORDERS PLAIN BLACK COFFEE.
THAT'S RIGHT, YOU'RE THE...
OH.
TELL ME, DID YOU GET A NICE BONUS FROM THE EVIL QUEEN FOR DOING HER BIDDING?
OR DID SHE JUST LET YOU POCKET THE CASH FOR SELLING THE SNAPS?
"SNAPS"?
HOW DO YOU KNOW ABOUT... I MEAN, WHAT MAKES YOU THINK...
GODDAMMIT!
THAT'S A GOOD ENOUGH CONFESSION FOR ME.
SO, SPILL. HOW MUCH DID YOU GRIFT OUTTA THIS?
"SPILL"?
NOTHING. NOT REALLY.
THIS WAS SUPPOSED TO BE MY REWARD, BUT THIS THING SUCKS.

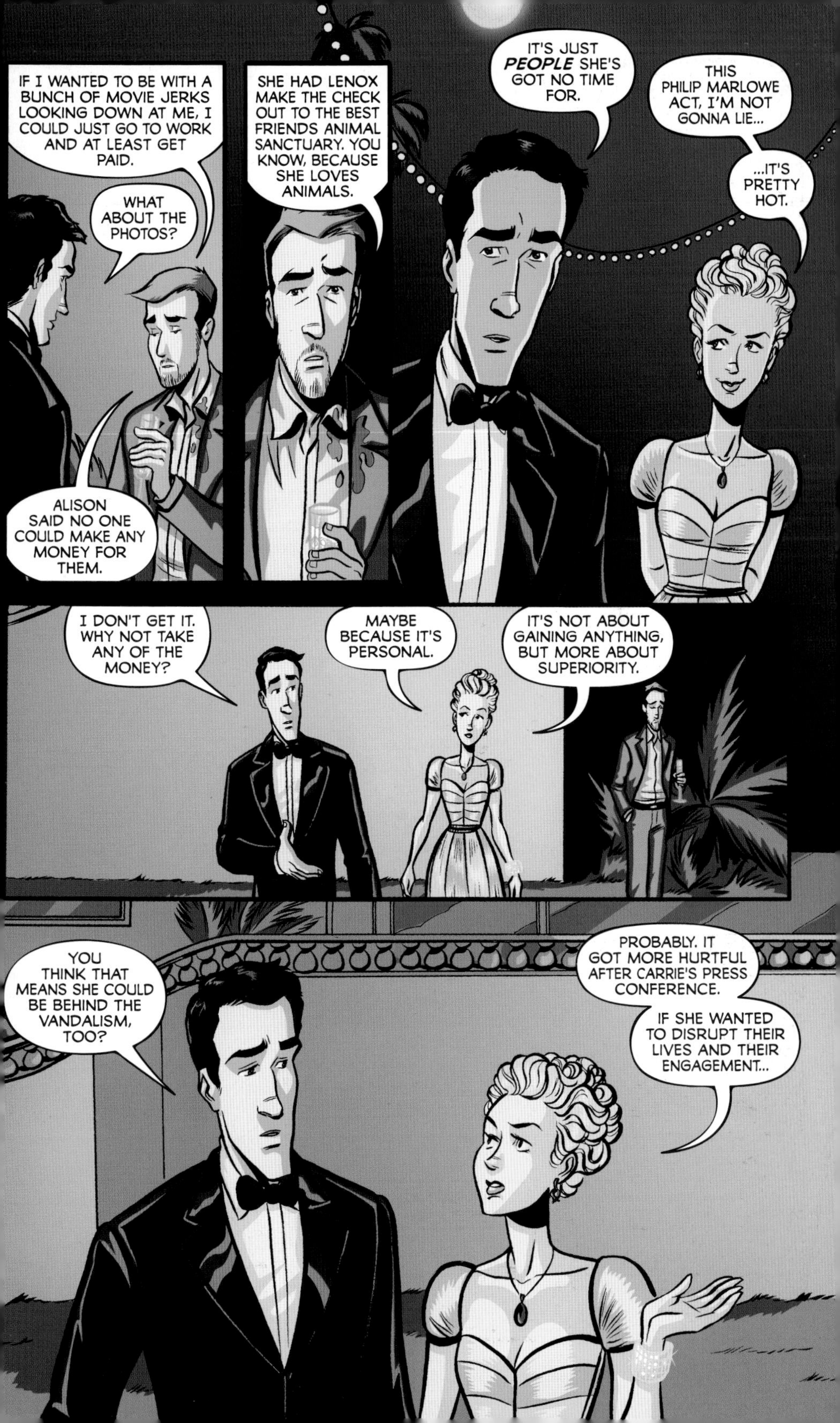
IF I WANTED TO BE WITH A BUNCH OF MOVIE JERKS LOOKING DOWN AT ME, I COULD JUST GO TO WORK AND AT LEAST GET PAID.
WHAT ABOUT THE PHOTOS?
ALISON SAID NO ONE COULD MAKE ANY MONEY FOR THEM.
SHE HAD LENOX MAKE THE CHECK OUT TO THE BEST FRIENDS ANIMAL SANCTUARY. YOU KNOW, BECAUSE SHE LOVES ANIMALS.
IT'S JUST *PEOPLE* SHE'S GOT NO TIME FOR.
THIS PHILIP MARLOWE ACT, I'M NOT GONNA LIE...
...IT'S PRETTY HOT.
I DON'T GET IT. WHY NOT TAKE ANY OF THE MONEY?
MAYBE BECAUSE IT'S PERSONAL.
IT'S NOT ABOUT GAINING ANYTHING, BUT MORE ABOUT SUPERIORITY.
YOU THINK THAT MEANS SHE COULD BE BEHIND THE VANDALISM, TOO?
PROBABLY. IT GOT MORE HURTFUL AFTER CARRIE'S PRESS CONFERENCE.
IF SHE WANTED TO DISRUPT THEIR LIVES AND THEIR ENGAGEMENT...

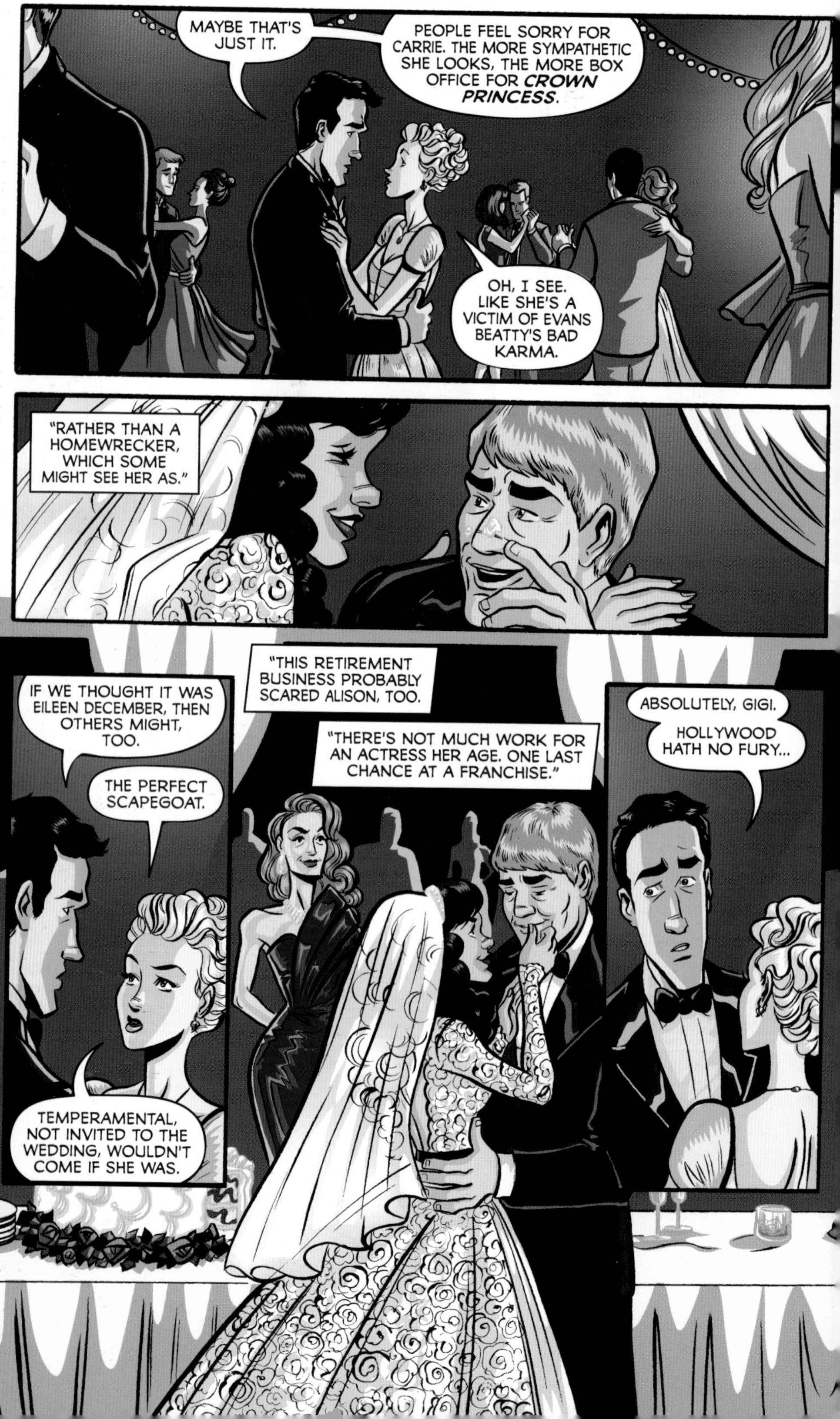

MAYBE THAT'S JUST IT.
PEOPLE FEEL SORRY FOR CARRIE. THE MORE SYMPATHETIC SHE LOOKS, THE MORE BOX OFFICE FOR *CROWN PRINCESS*.
OH, I SEE. LIKE SHE'S A VICTIM OF EVANS BEATTY'S BAD KARMA.
"RATHER THAN A HOMEWRECKER, WHICH SOME MIGHT SEE HER AS."
IF WE THOUGHT IT WAS EILEEN DECEMBER, THEN OTHERS MIGHT, TOO.
THE PERFECT SCAPEGOAT.
TEMPERAMENTAL, NOT INVITED TO THE WEDDING, WOULDN'T COME IF SHE WAS.
"THIS RETIREMENT BUSINESS PROBABLY SCARED ALISON, TOO.
"THERE'S NOT MUCH WORK FOR AN ACTRESS HER AGE. ONE LAST CHANCE AT A FRANCHISE."
ABSOLUTELY, GIGI.
HOLLYWOOD HATH NO FURY...

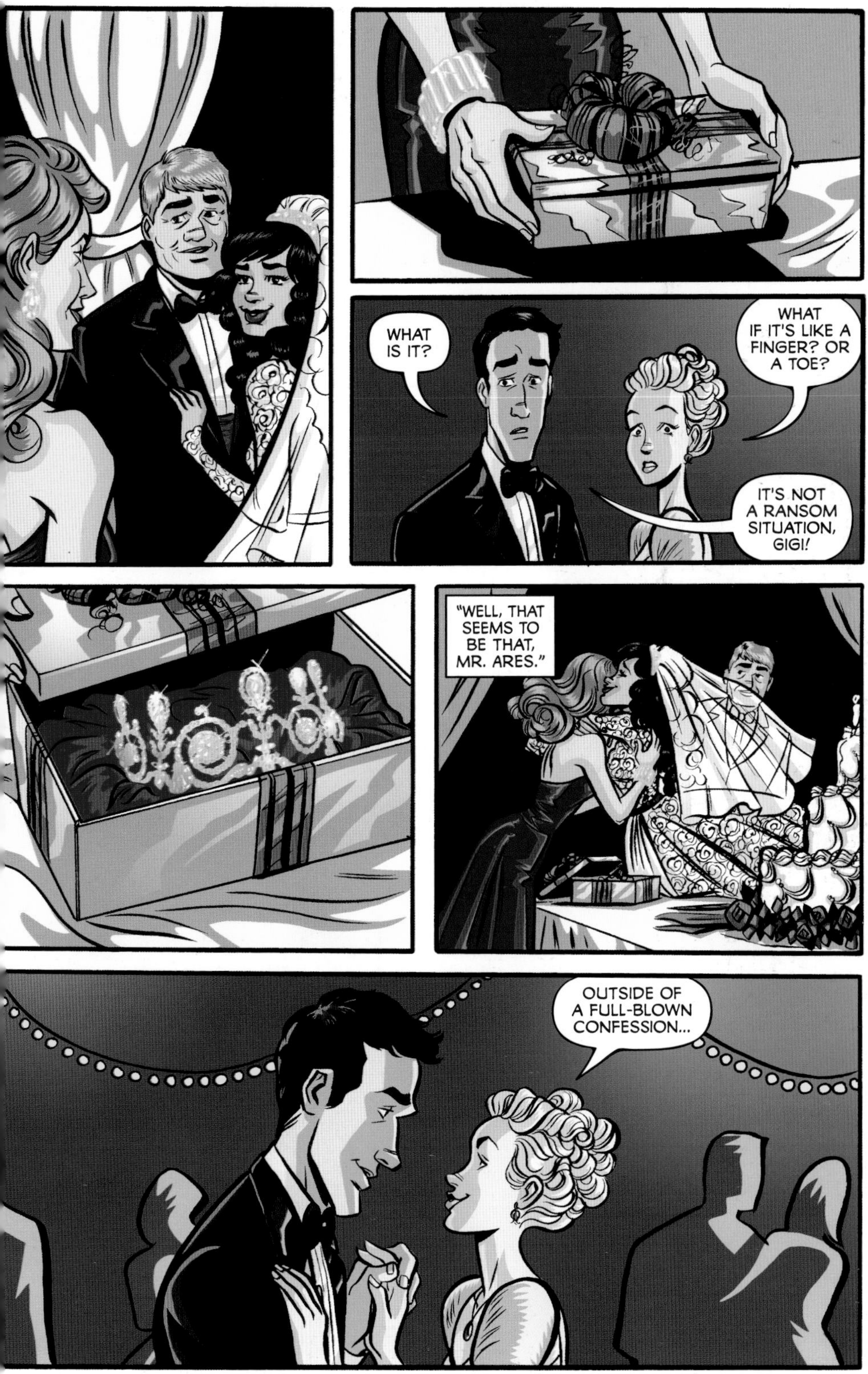
WHAT IS IT?
WHAT IF IT'S LIKE A FINGER? OR A TOE?
IT'S NOT A RANSOM SITUATION, GIGI!
"WELL, THAT SEEMS TO BE THAT, MR. ARES."
OUTSIDE OF A FULL-BLOWN CONFESSION...

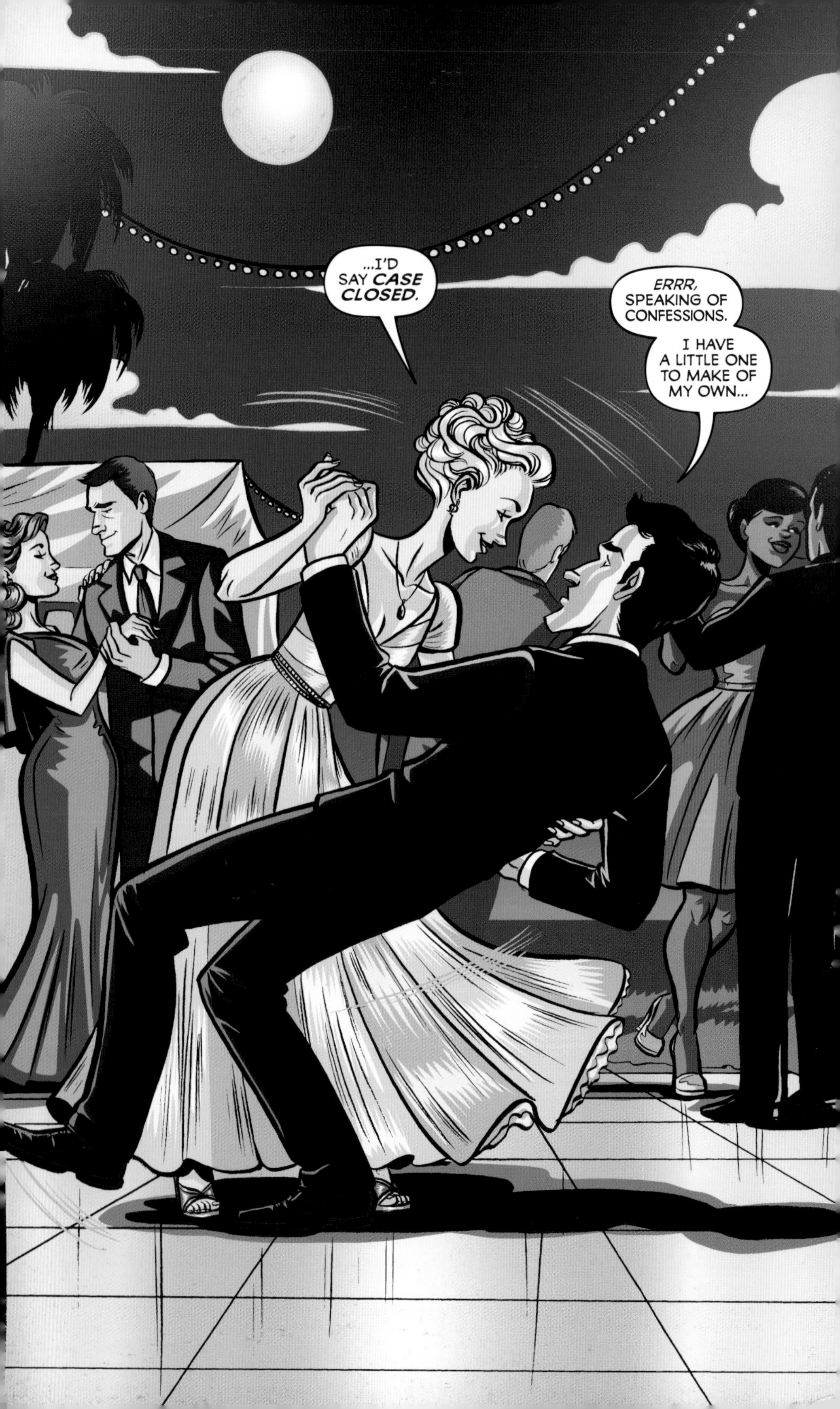

...I'D SAY *CASE CLOSED.*
*ERRR,* SPEAKING OF CONFESSIONS.
I HAVE A LITTLE ONE TO MAKE OF MY OWN...

# CHAPTER ELEVEN

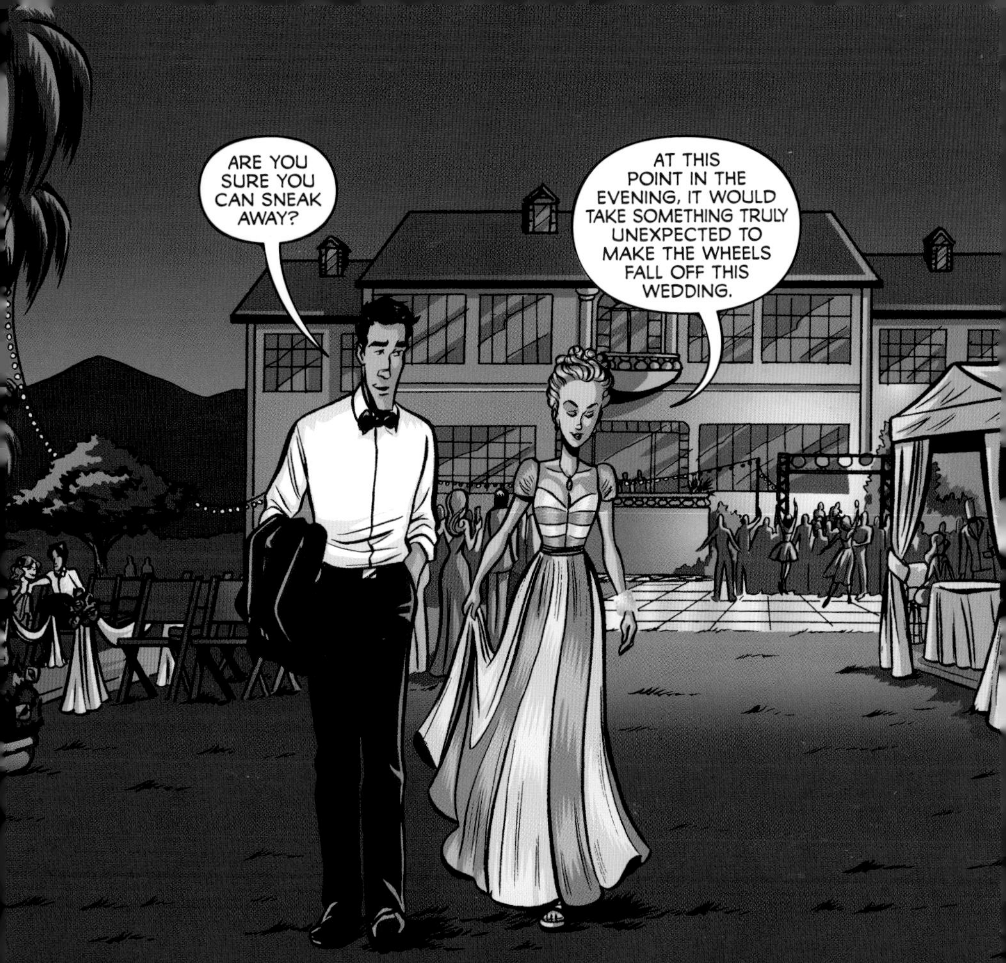
ARE YOU SURE YOU CAN SNEAK AWAY?
AT THIS POINT IN THE EVENING, IT WOULD TAKE SOMETHING TRULY UNEXPECTED TO MAKE THE WHEELS FALL OFF THIS WEDDING.

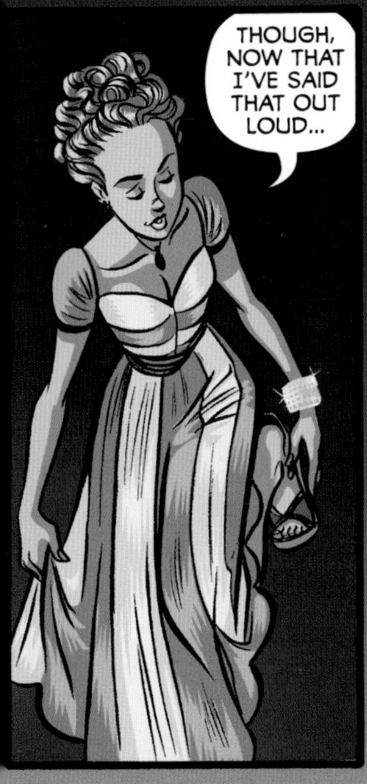
THOUGH, NOW THAT I'VE SAID THAT OUT LOUD...

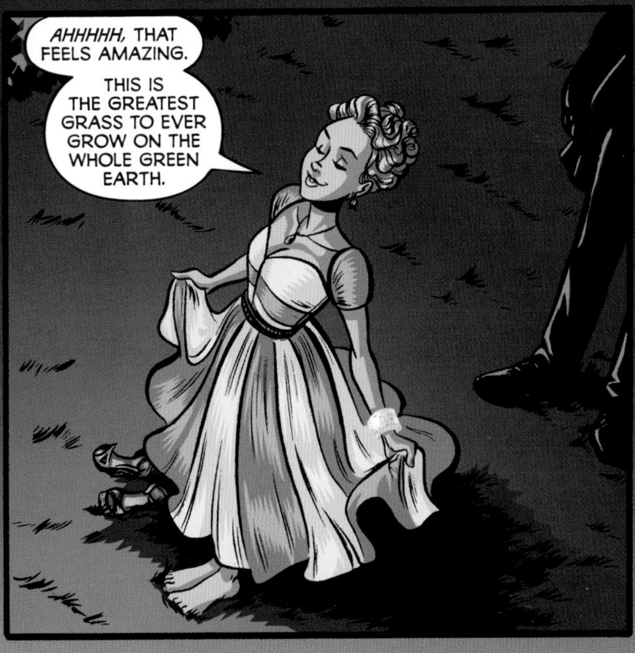
*AHHHHH,* THAT FEELS AMAZING.
THIS IS THE GREATEST GRASS TO EVER GROW ON THE WHOLE GREEN EARTH.

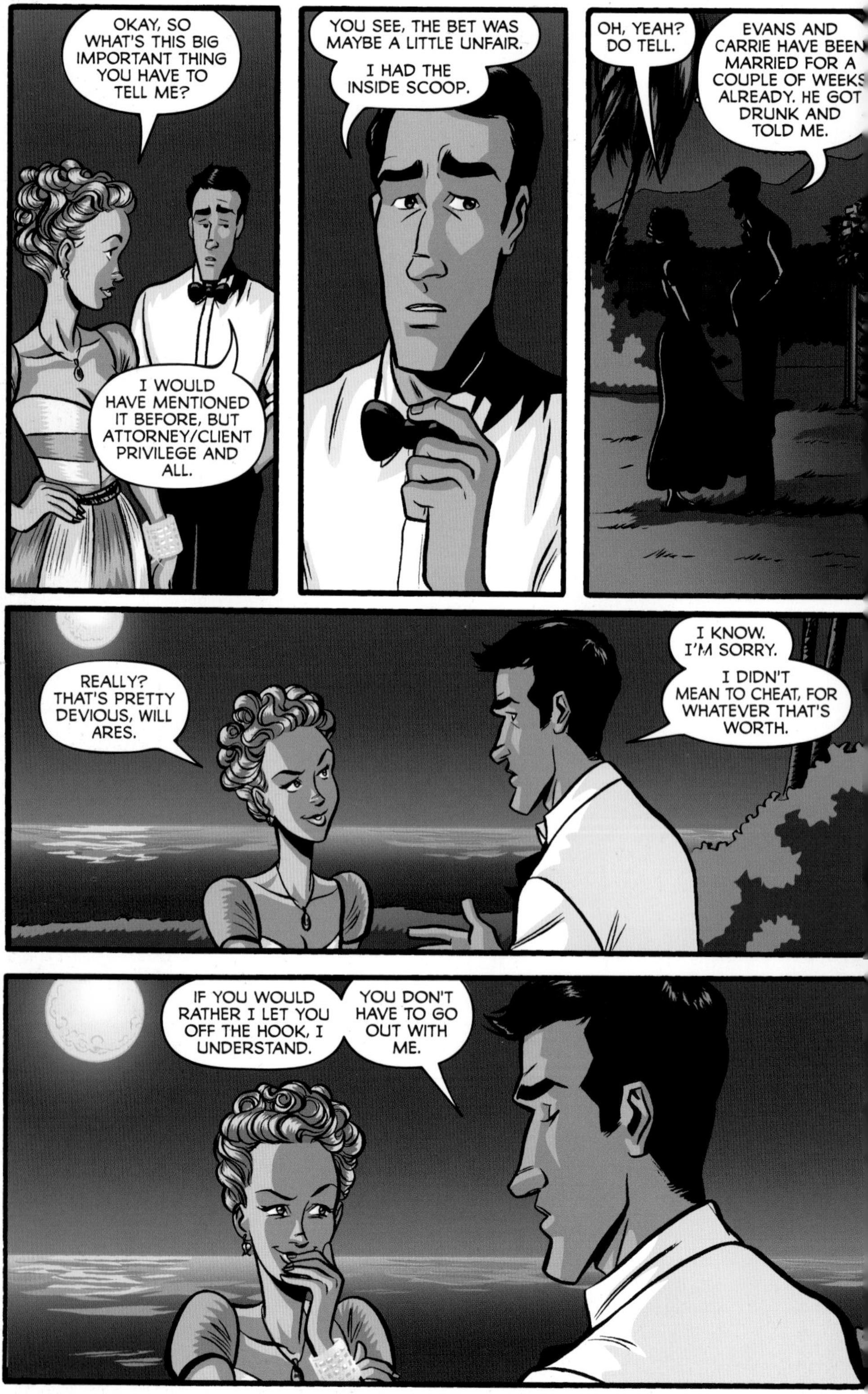
OKAY, SO WHAT'S THIS BIG IMPORTANT THING YOU HAVE TO TELL ME?
I WOULD HAVE MENTIONED IT BEFORE, BUT ATTORNEY/CLIENT PRIVILEGE AND ALL.
YOU SEE, THE BET WAS MAYBE A LITTLE UNFAIR.
I HAD THE INSIDE SCOOP.
OH, YEAH? DO TELL.
EVANS AND CARRIE HAVE BEEN MARRIED FOR A COUPLE OF WEEKS ALREADY. HE GOT DRUNK AND TOLD ME.
REALLY? THAT'S PRETTY DEVIOUS, WILL ARES.
I KNOW. I'M SORRY.
I DIDN'T MEAN TO CHEAT, FOR WHATEVER THAT'S WORTH.
IF YOU WOULD RATHER I LET YOU OFF THE HOOK, I UNDERSTAND.
YOU DON'T HAVE TO GO OUT WITH ME.

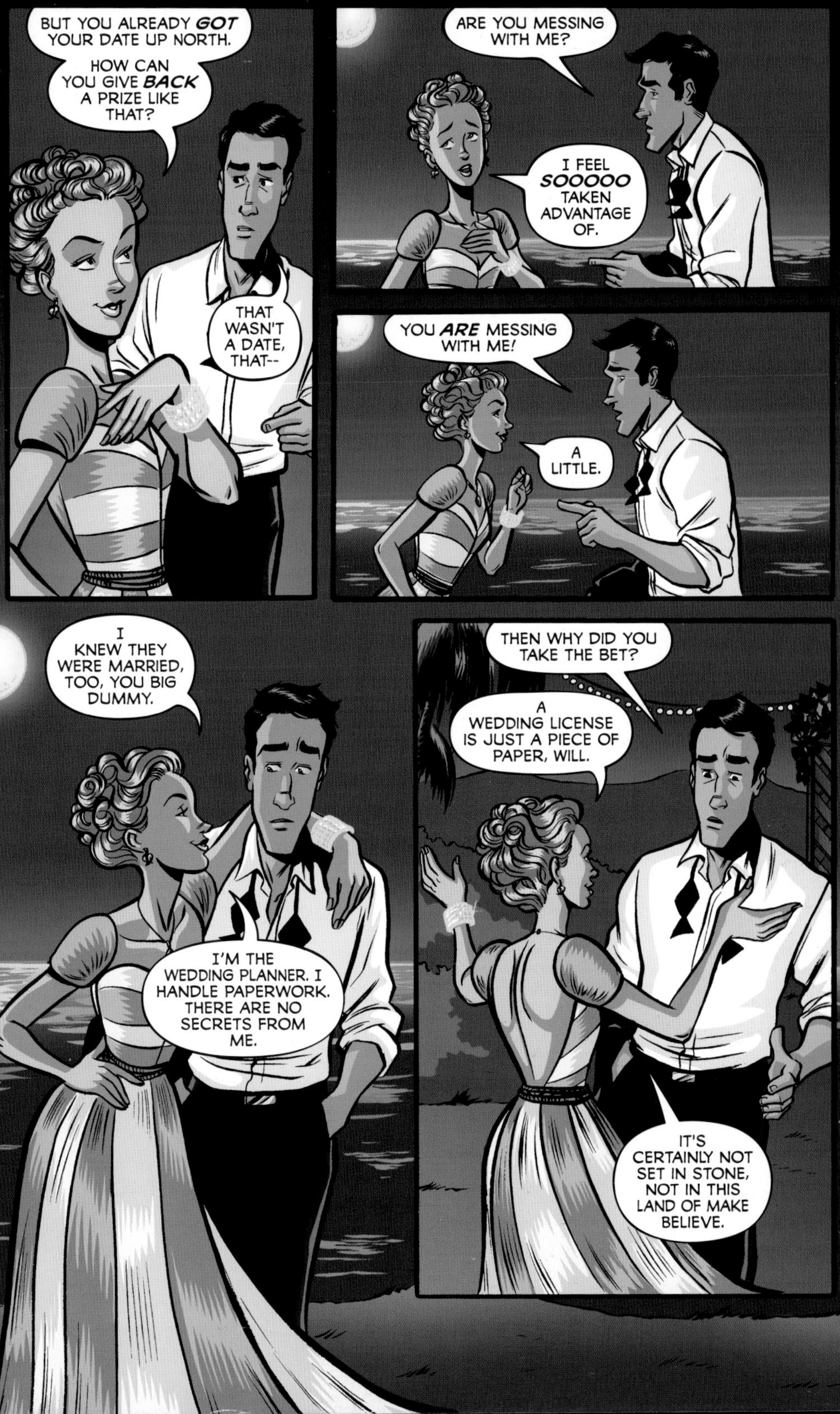
BUT YOU ALREADY GOT YOUR DATE UP NORTH.
HOW CAN YOU GIVE BACK A PRIZE LIKE THAT?
THAT WASN'T A DATE, THAT--
ARE YOU MESSING WITH ME?
I FEEL SOOOOO TAKEN ADVANTAGE OF.
YOU ARE MESSING WITH ME!
A LITTLE.
I KNEW THEY WERE MARRIED, TOO, YOU BIG DUMMY.
I'M THE WEDDING PLANNER. I HANDLE PAPERWORK. THERE ARE NO SECRETS FROM ME.
THEN WHY DID YOU TAKE THE BET?
A WEDDING LICENSE IS JUST A PIECE OF PAPER, WILL.
IT'S CERTAINLY NOT SET IN STONE, NOT IN THIS LAND OF MAKE BELIEVE.

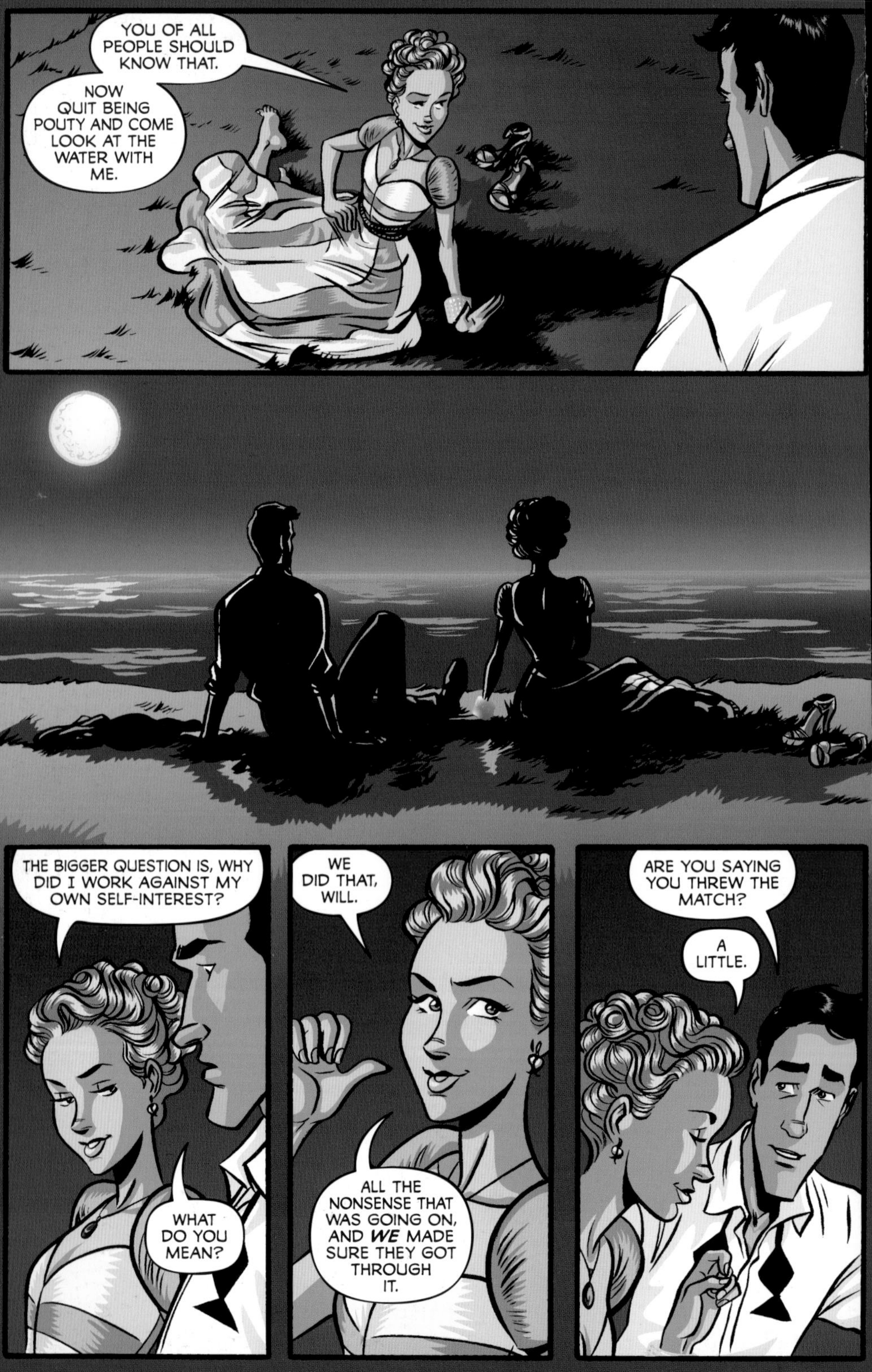
YOU OF ALL PEOPLE SHOULD KNOW THAT.
NOW QUIT BEING POUTY AND COME LOOK AT THE WATER WITH ME.
THE BIGGER QUESTION IS, WHY DID I WORK AGAINST MY OWN SELF-INTEREST?
WHAT DO YOU MEAN?
WE DID THAT, WILL.
ALL THE NONSENSE THAT WAS GOING ON, AND WE MADE SURE THEY GOT THROUGH IT.
ARE YOU SAYING YOU THREW THE MATCH?
A LITTLE.

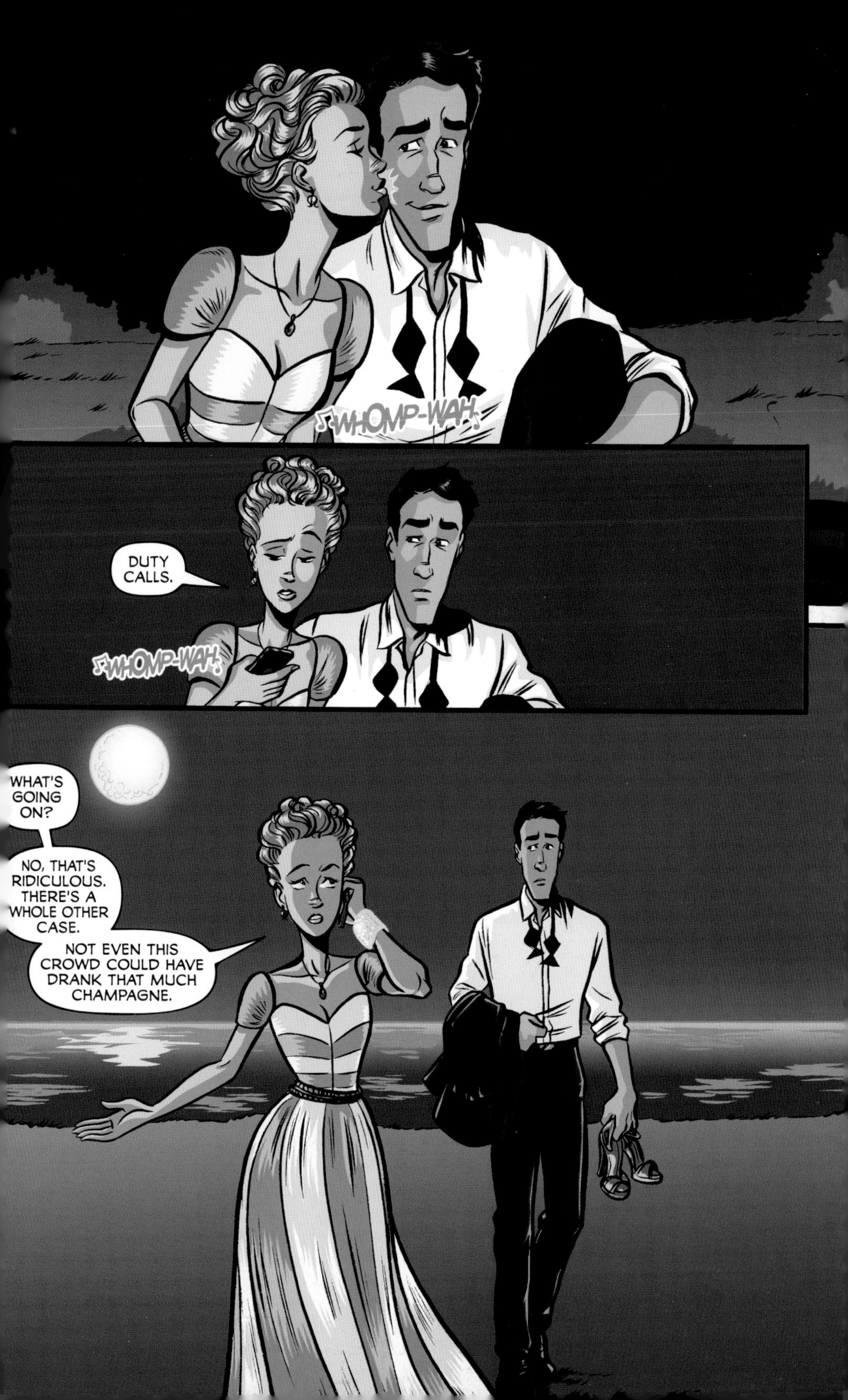
WHOMP-WAH
DUTY CALLS.
WHOMP-WAH
WHAT'S GOING ON?
NO, THAT'S RIDICULOUS. THERE'S A WHOLE OTHER CASE.
NOT EVEN THIS CROWD COULD HAVE DRANK THAT MUCH CHAMPAGNE.

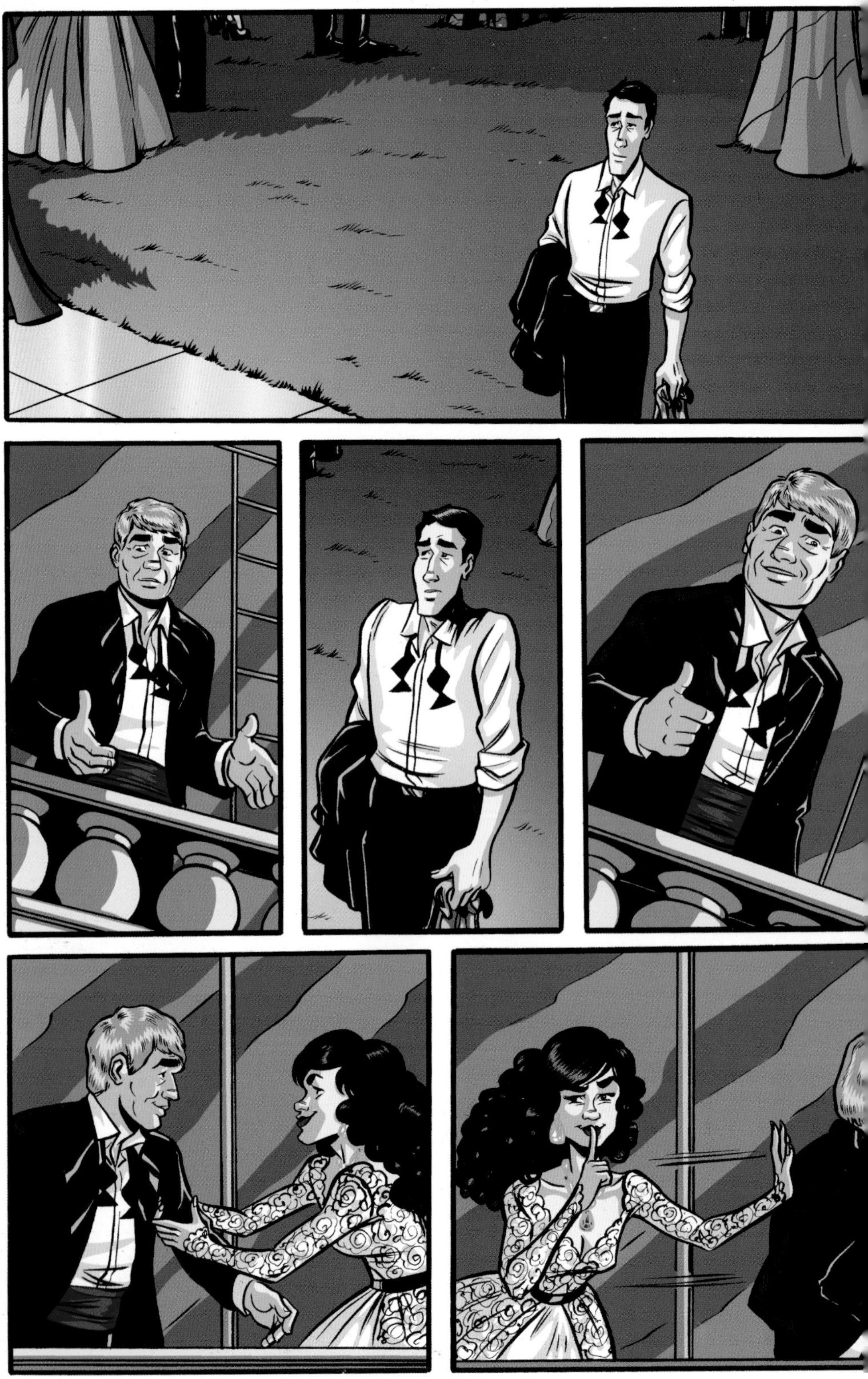

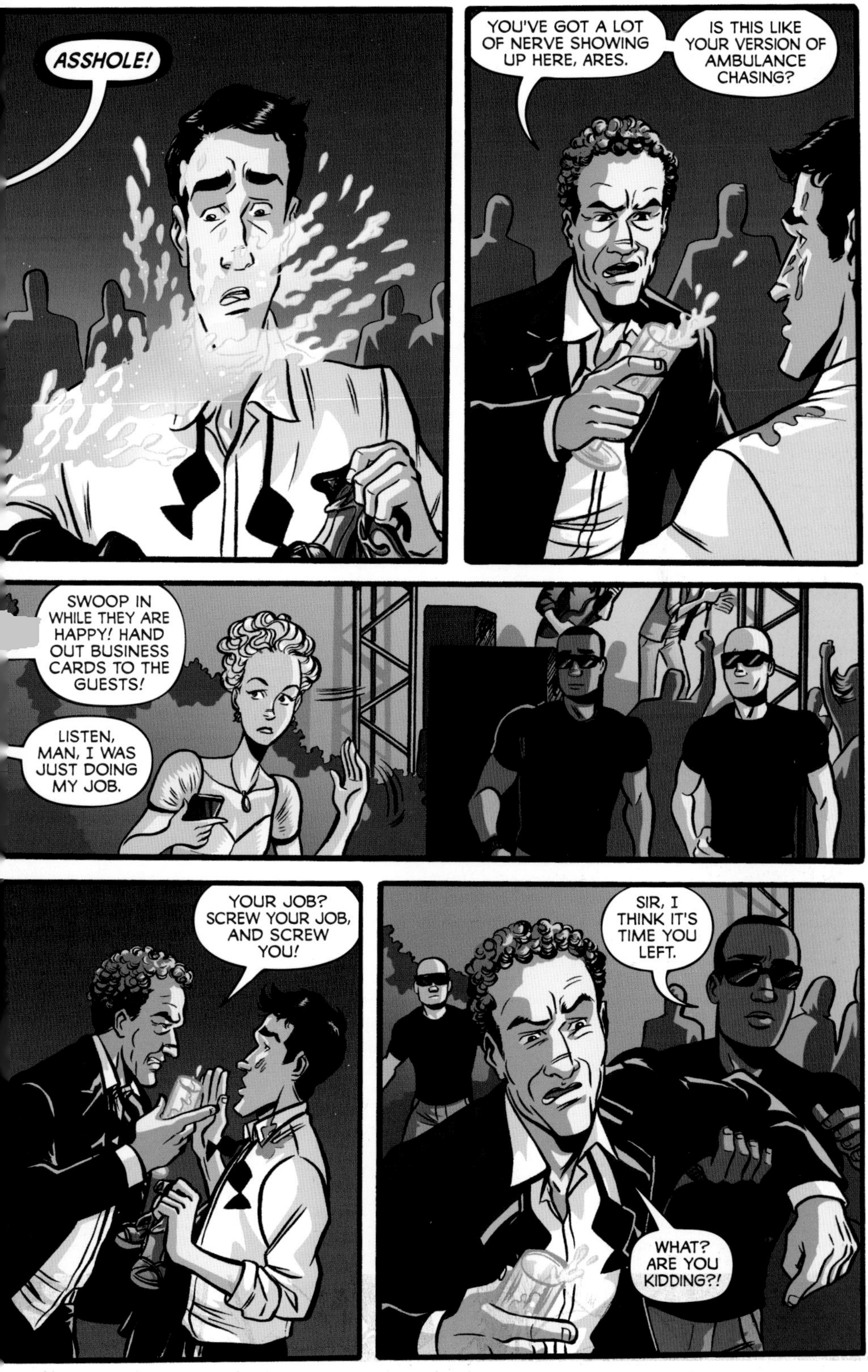

ASSHOLE!
YOU'VE GOT A LOT OF NERVE SHOWING UP HERE, ARES.
IS THIS LIKE YOUR VERSION OF AMBULANCE CHASING?
SWOOP IN WHILE THEY ARE HAPPY! HAND OUT BUSINESS CARDS TO THE GUESTS!
LISTEN, MAN, I WAS JUST DOING MY JOB.
YOUR JOB? SCREW YOUR JOB, AND SCREW YOU!
SIR, I THINK IT'S TIME YOU LEFT.
WHAT? ARE YOU KIDDING?!

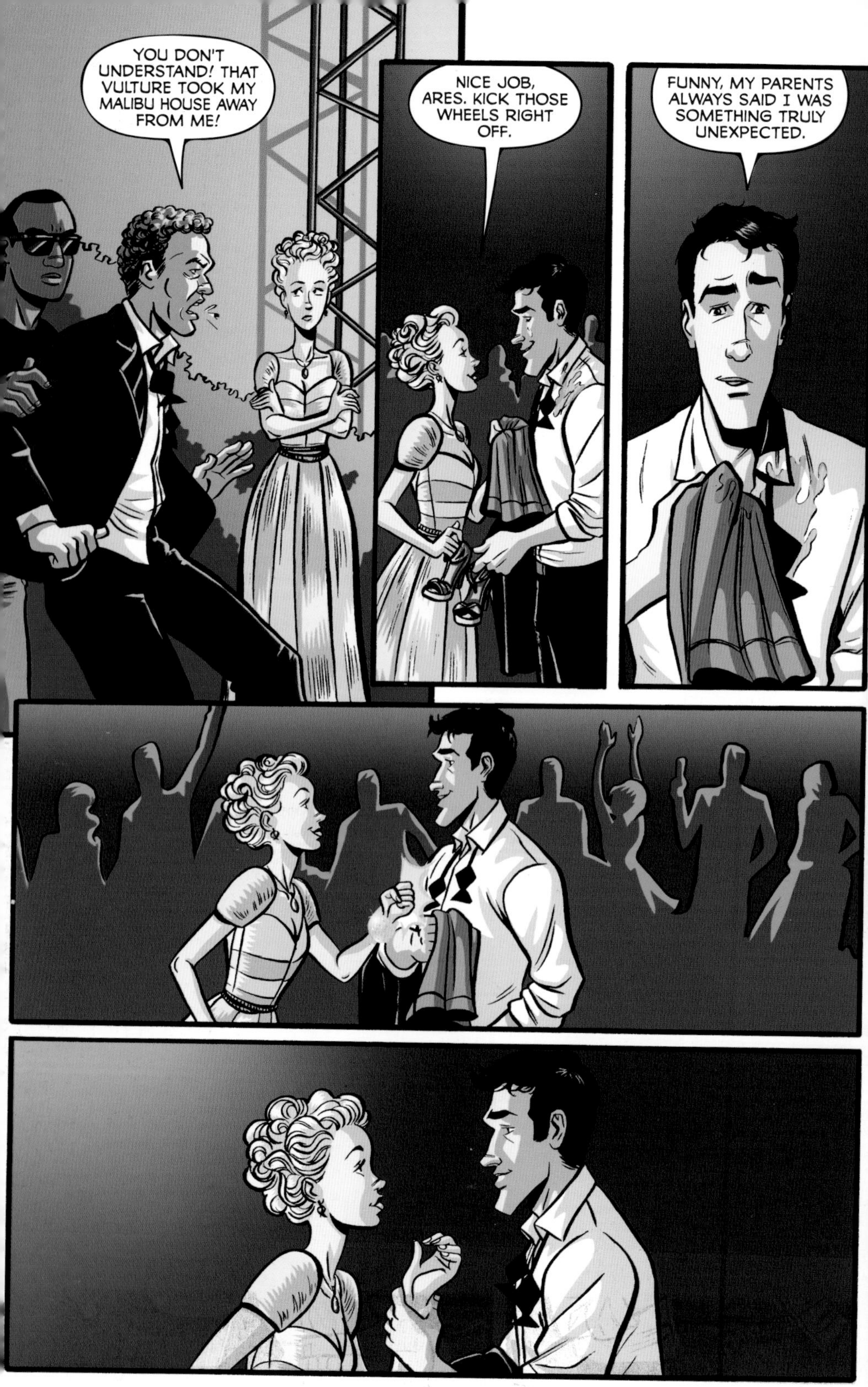
YOU DON'T UNDERSTAND! THAT VULTURE TOOK MY MALIBU HOUSE AWAY FROM ME!
NICE JOB, ARES. KICK THOSE WHEELS RIGHT OFF.
FUNNY, MY PARENTS ALWAYS SAID I WAS SOMETHING TRULY UNEXPECTED.

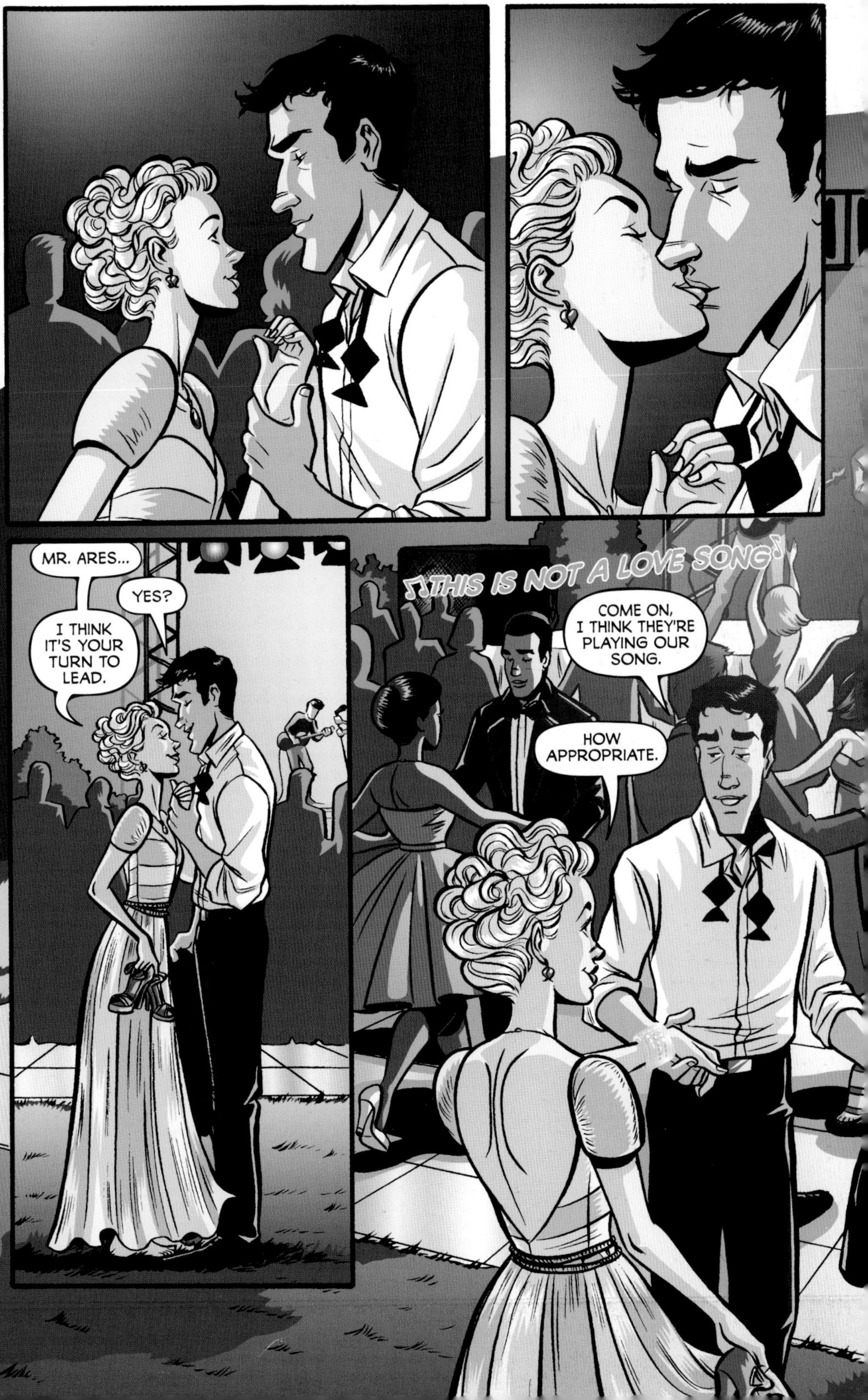
MR. ARES...
YES?
I THINK IT'S YOUR TURN TO LEAD.
♫THIS IS NOT A LOVE SONG♫
COME ON, I THINK THEY'RE PLAYING OUR SONG.
HOW APPROPRIATE.

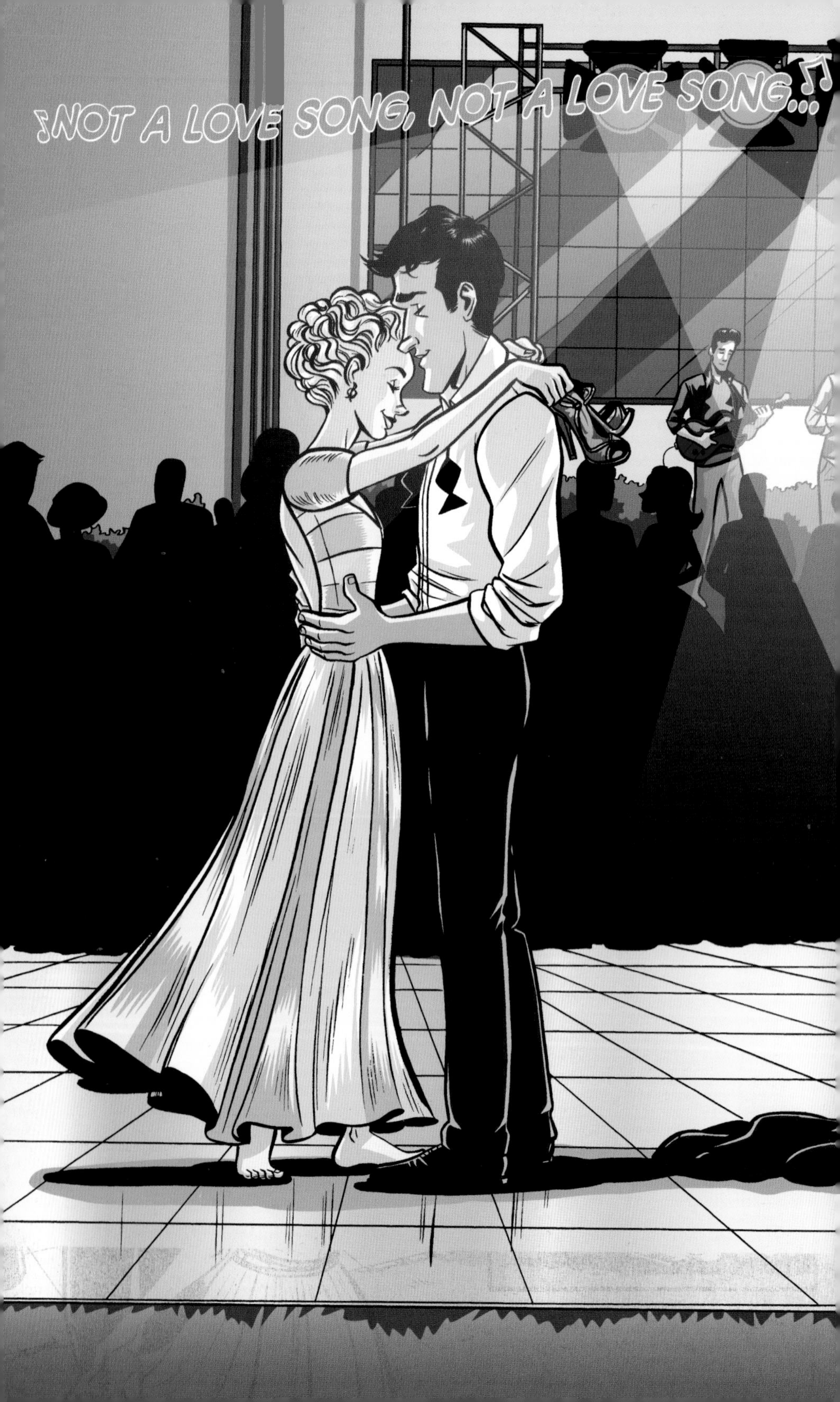
NOT A LOVE SONG, NOT A LOVE SONG...

# CHAPTER TWELVE

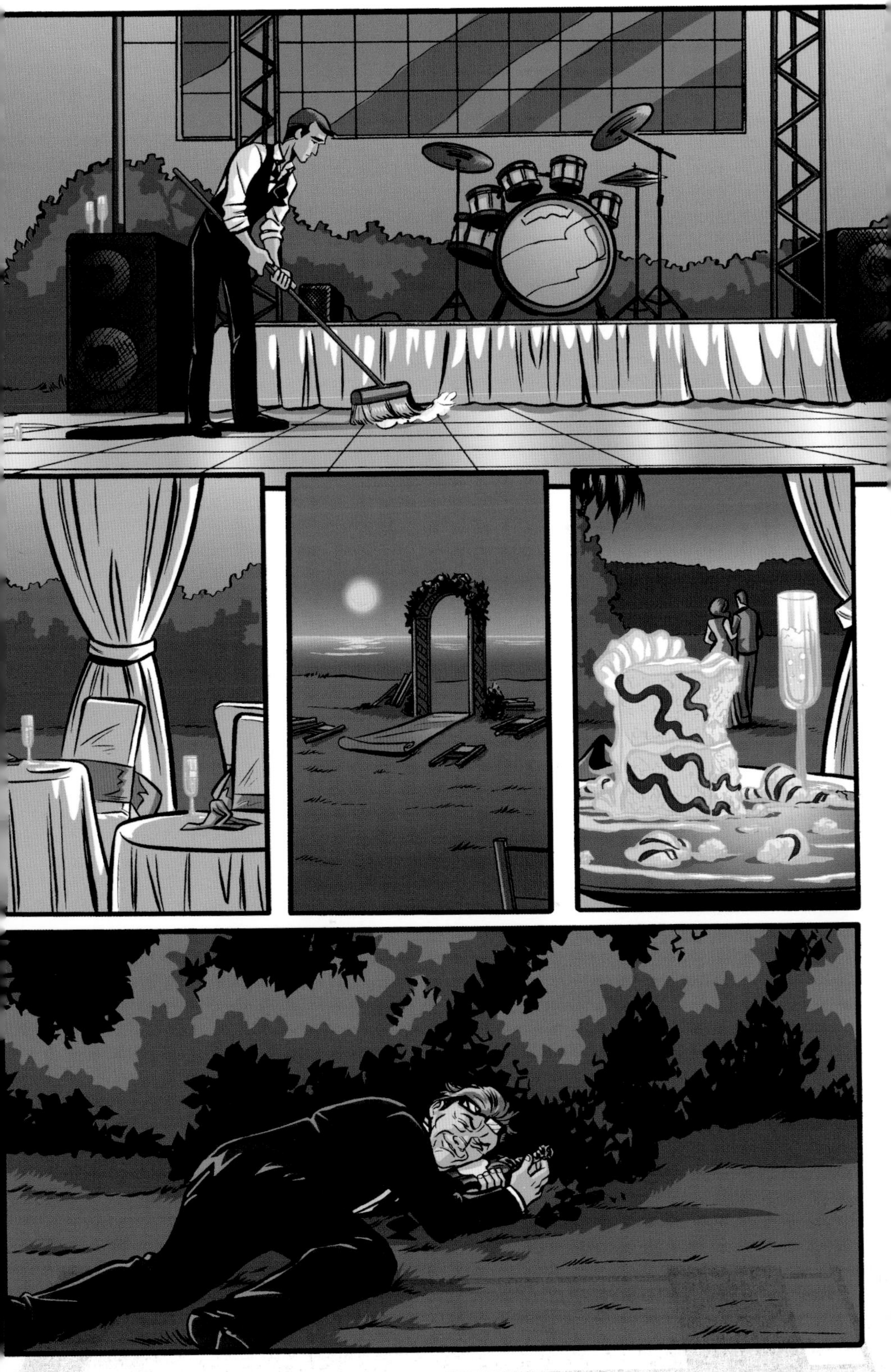

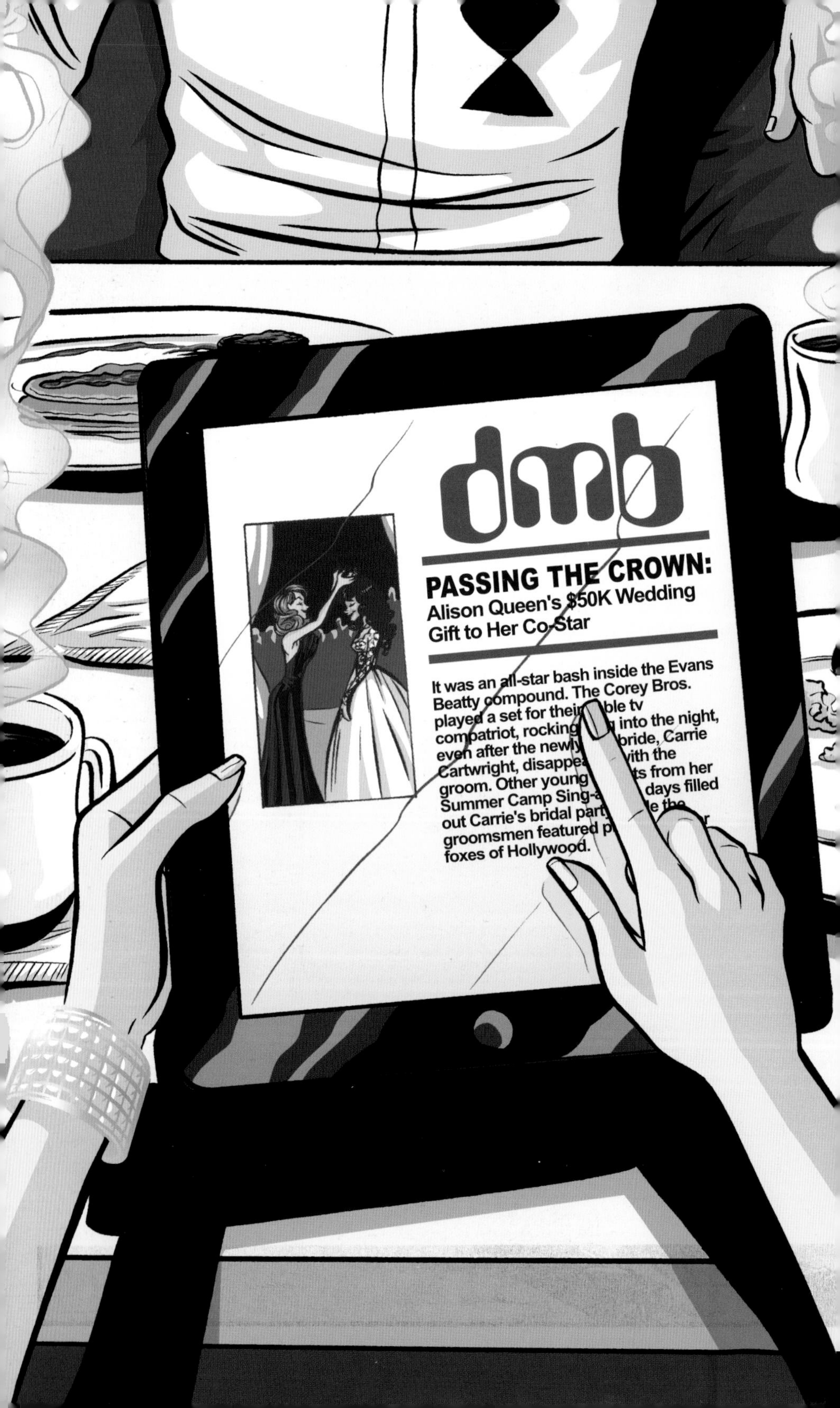
dmb
PASSING THE CROWN:
Alison Queen's $50K Wedding
Gift to Her Co-Star
It was an all-star bash inside the Evans
Beatty compound. The Corey Bros.
played a set for their ble tv
compatriot, rocking into the night,
even after the newly bride, Carrie
Cartwright, disappea with the
groom. Other young ts from her
Summer Camp Sing-a days filled
out Carrie's bridal party
groomsmen featured p
foxes of Hollywood.

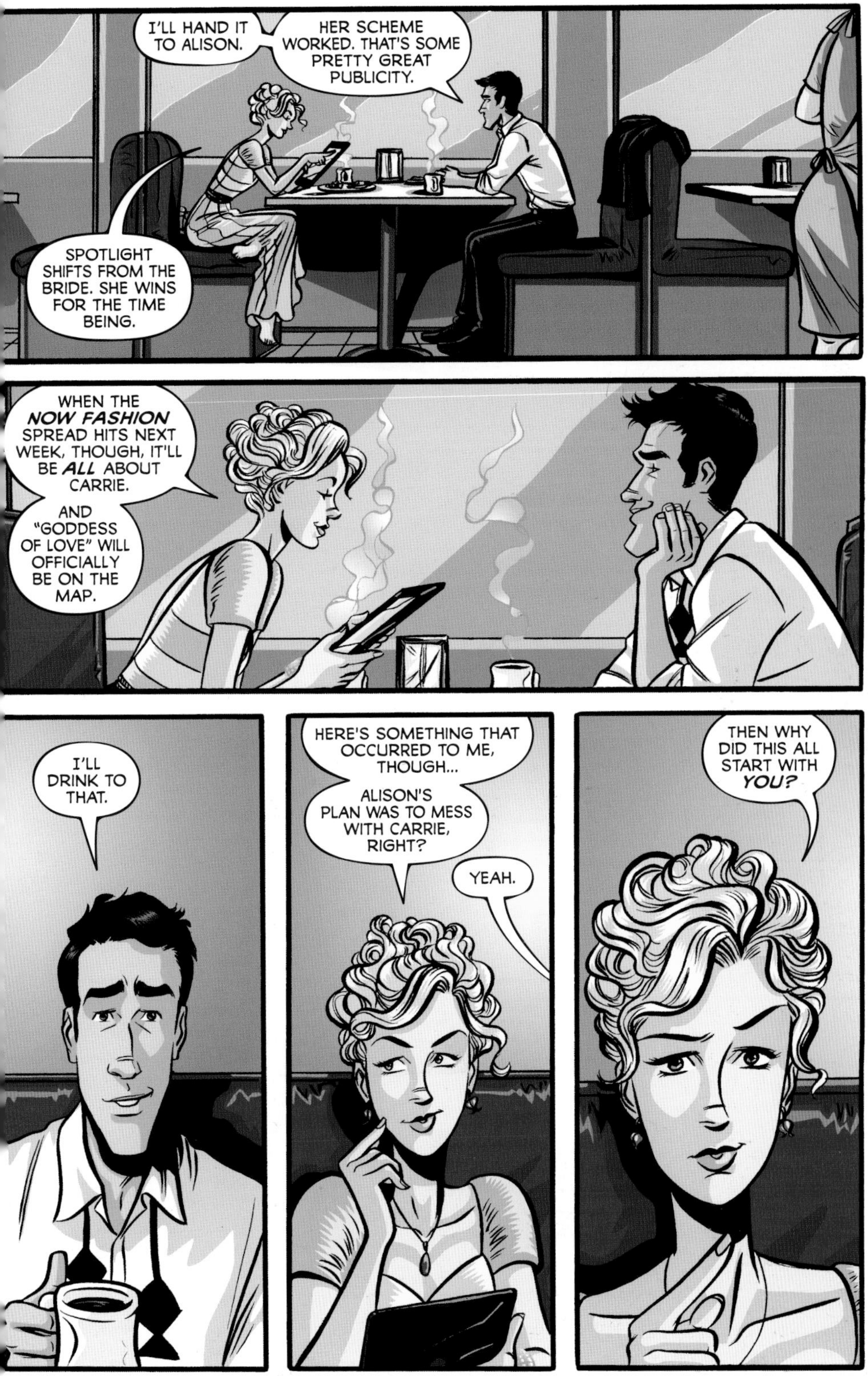
I'LL HAND IT TO ALISON.
HER SCHEME WORKED. THAT'S SOME PRETTY GREAT PUBLICITY.
SPOTLIGHT SHIFTS FROM THE BRIDE. SHE WINS FOR THE TIME BEING.
WHEN THE *NOW FASHION* SPREAD HITS NEXT WEEK, THOUGH, IT'LL BE *ALL* ABOUT CARRIE.
AND "GODDESS OF LOVE" WILL OFFICIALLY BE ON THE MAP.
I'LL DRINK TO THAT.
HERE'S SOMETHING THAT OCCURRED TO ME, THOUGH...
ALISON'S PLAN WAS TO MESS WITH CARRIE, RIGHT?
YEAH.
THEN WHY DID THIS ALL START WITH *YOU?*

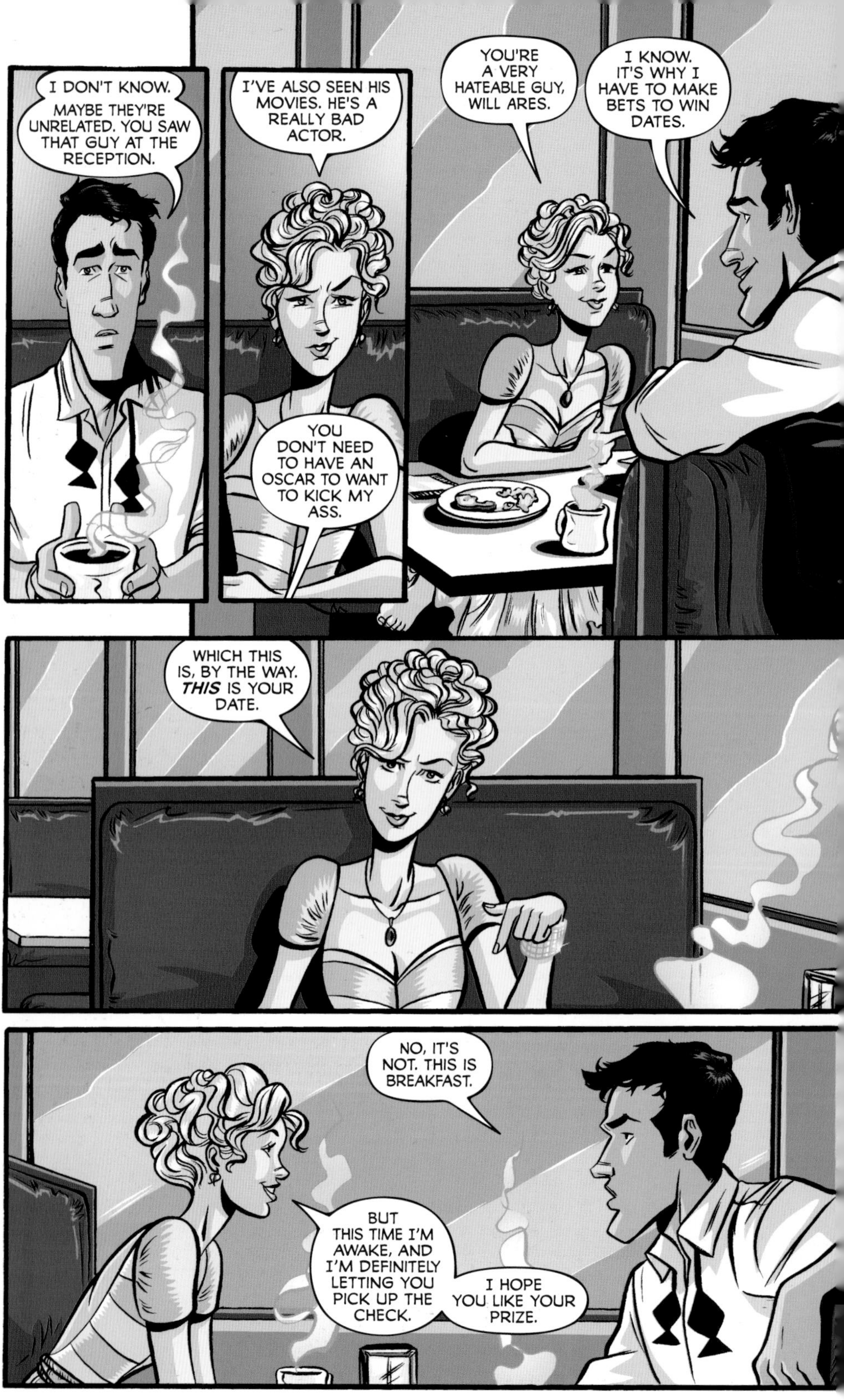
I DON'T KNOW.
MAYBE THEY'RE UNRELATED. YOU SAW THAT GUY AT THE RECEPTION.
I'VE ALSO SEEN HIS MOVIES. HE'S A REALLY BAD ACTOR.
YOU DON'T NEED TO HAVE AN OSCAR TO WANT TO KICK MY ASS.
YOU'RE A VERY HATEABLE GUY, WILL ARES.
I KNOW. IT'S WHY I HAVE TO MAKE BETS TO WIN DATES.
WHICH THIS IS, BY THE WAY. *THIS* IS YOUR DATE.
NO, IT'S NOT. THIS IS BREAKFAST.
BUT THIS TIME I'M AWAKE, AND I'M DEFINITELY LETTING YOU PICK UP THE CHECK.
I HOPE YOU LIKE YOUR PRIZE.

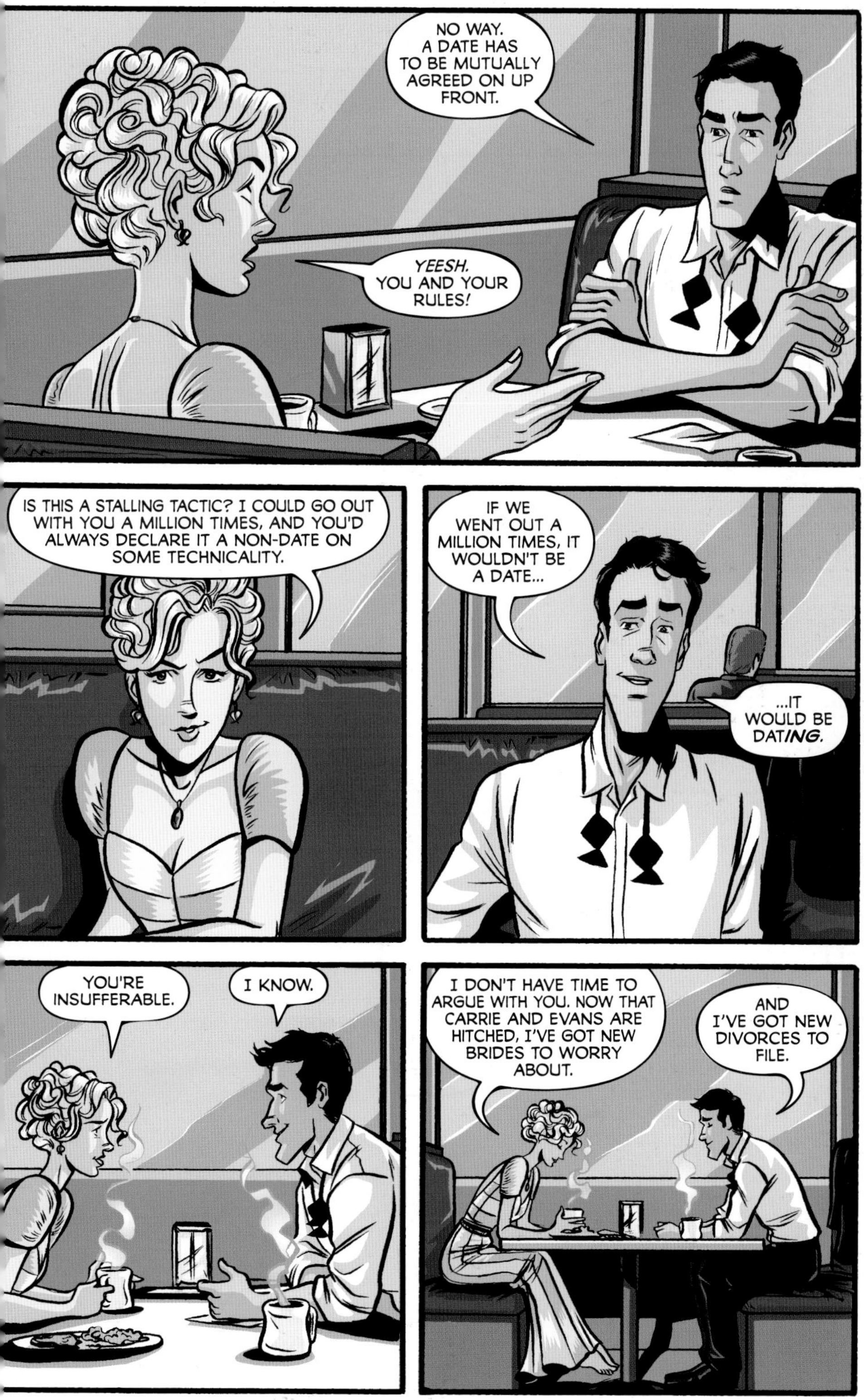
NO WAY. A DATE HAS TO BE MUTUALLY AGREED ON UP FRONT.
YEESH. YOU AND YOUR RULES!
IS THIS A STALLING TACTIC? I COULD GO OUT WITH YOU A MILLION TIMES, AND YOU'D ALWAYS DECLARE IT A NON-DATE ON SOME TECHNICALITY.
IF WE WENT OUT A MILLION TIMES, IT WOULDN'T BE A DATE...
...IT WOULD BE DATING.
YOU'RE INSUFFERABLE.
I KNOW.
I DON'T HAVE TIME TO ARGUE WITH YOU. NOW THAT CARRIE AND EVANS ARE HITCHED, I'VE GOT NEW BRIDES TO WORRY ABOUT.
AND I'VE GOT NEW DIVORCES TO FILE.

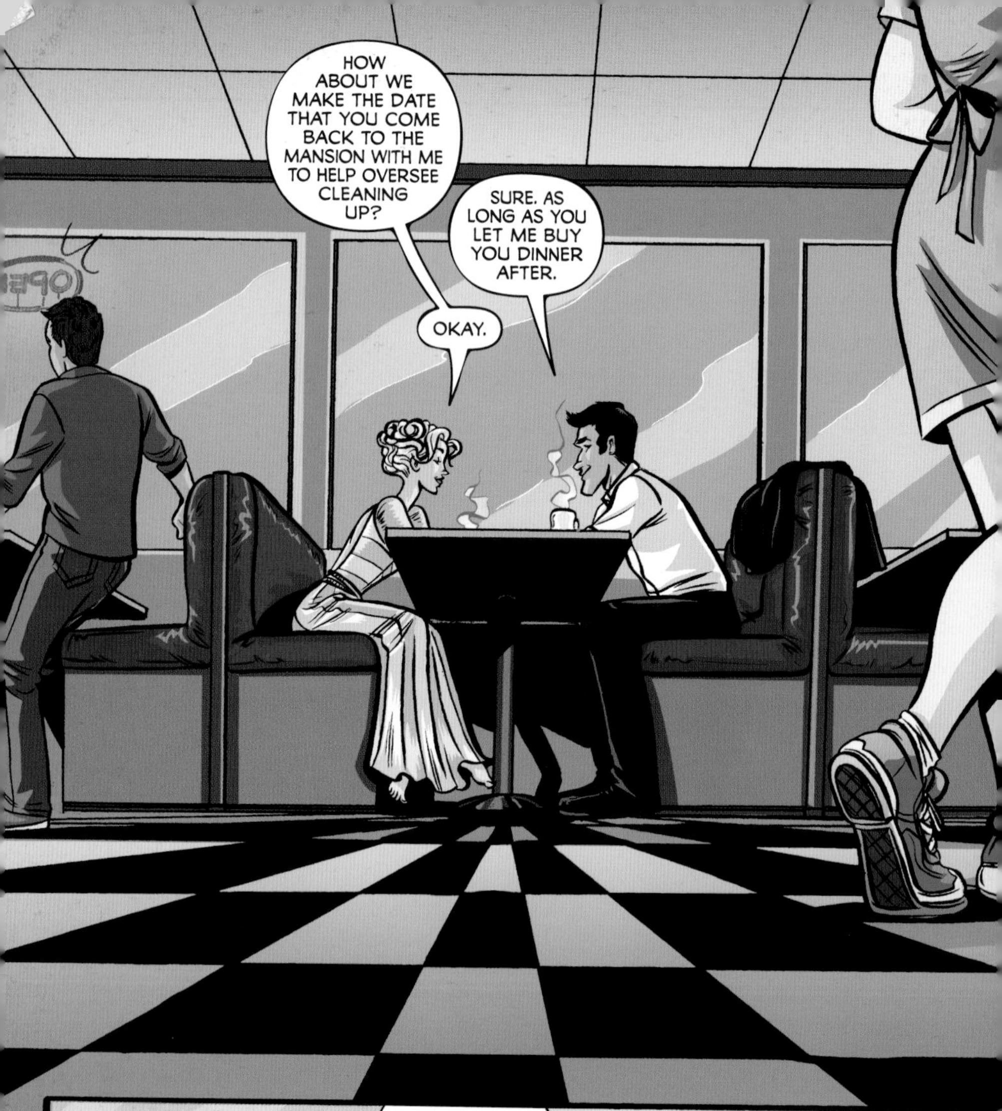
HOW ABOUT WE MAKE THE DATE THAT YOU COME BACK TO THE MANSION WITH ME TO HELP OVERSEE CLEANING UP?
SURE. AS LONG AS YOU LET ME BUY YOU DINNER AFTER.
OKAY.

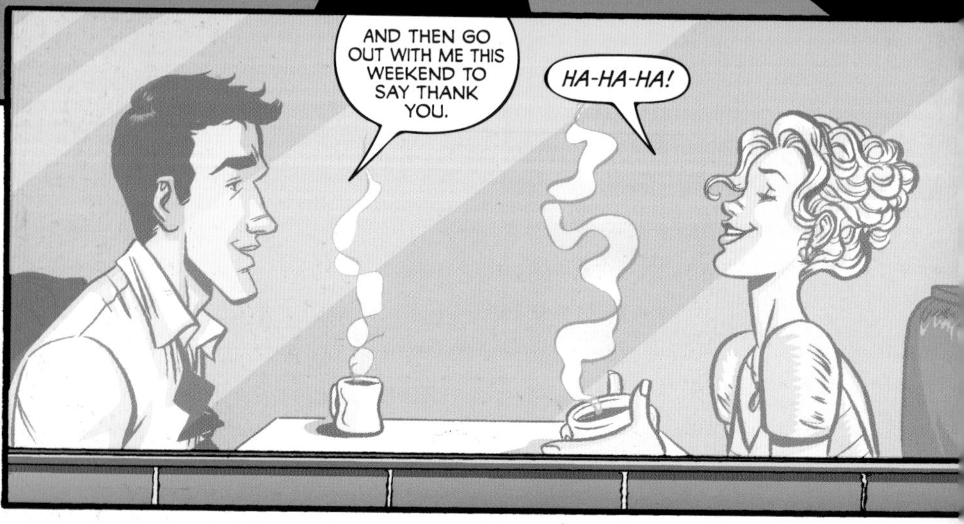
AND THEN GO OUT WITH ME THIS WEEKEND TO SAY THANK YOU.
HA-HA-HA!

THE FOLLOWING **PREVIEW** HAS BEEN APPROVED FOR

## ALL AUDIENCES

BY THE FILM & MOVIE PRODUCTION ASSOCIATION

confessions123.com                    buzzingoverbombshell.blogspot.com

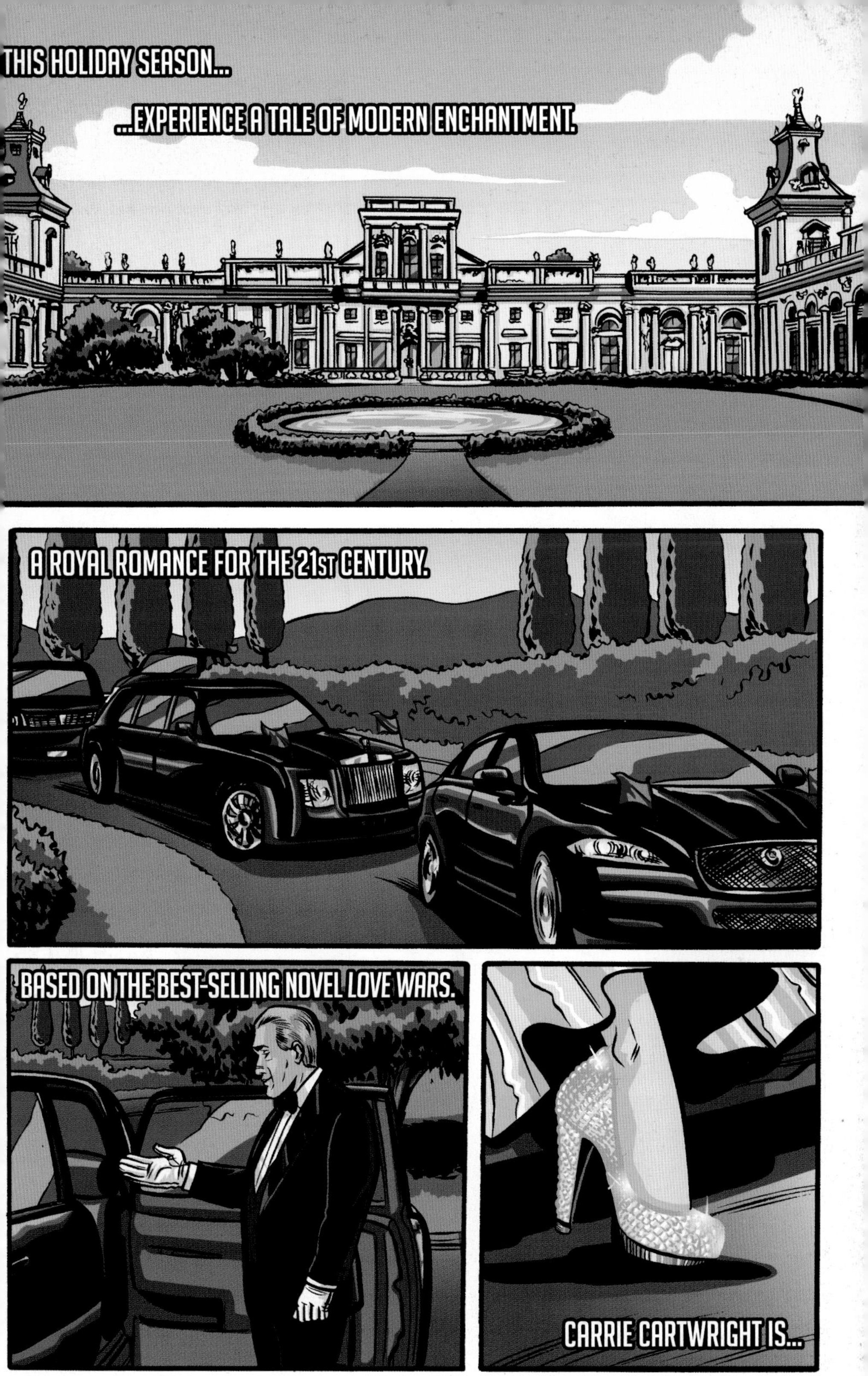

THIS HOLIDAY SEASON...
...EXPERIENCE A TALE OF MODERN ENCHANTMENT.
A ROYAL ROMANCE FOR THE 21ST CENTURY.
BASED ON THE BEST-SELLING NOVEL *LOVE WARS.*
CARRIE CARTWRIGHT IS...

# CROWN PRINCESS

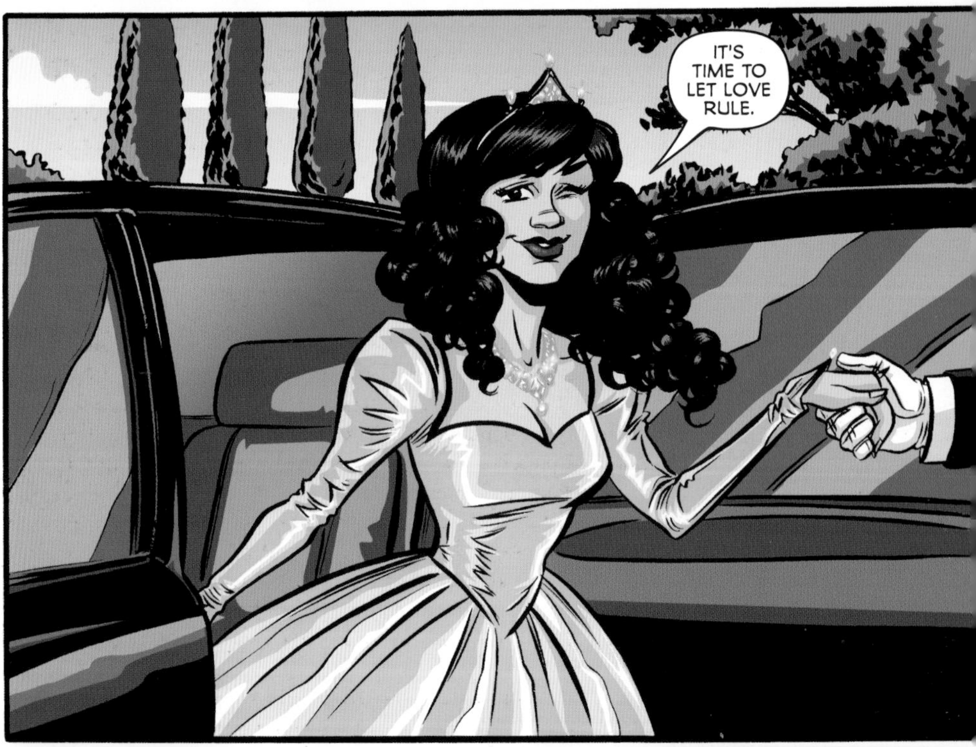
IT'S TIME TO LET LOVE RULE.

# AFTERWORD

*"This is Hollywood...where the wildest dreams sometimes come true...
but where the streets are paved with broken hearts..."*
—"The Curse of Beauty!" Hollywood Romances #52 (April 1970)

The first time that I picked up a romance comic, I was completely and utterly *smitten*. The art, the stories, the raw emotions; I simply fell head over heels in love with all of it. As I flipped through the pages, the beautifully illustrated stories of love lost and flames renewed tugged at my heartstrings. Flowing hair, bell-bottoms, and the colorful characters appealed to the nostalgic side of me, while the stories of dating and marriage customs, race relations, and social justice appealed to the historian in me. This infatuation led me to create *Sequential Crush*, the only place on the Web dedicated to the romance comic books of the 1960s and 1970s. For over five years now it has been my pleasure and distinct honor to bring the stories, artists, and history of the romance comics to a modern audience.

When Jamie S. Rich approached me about writing the afterword for *Ares & Aphrodite: Love Wars*, I was excited to say the least. In today's pantheon of mainstream comic books that center primarily on superhero characters, stories focusing on the romantic side of life told in sequential form are sorely needed. Back in 2009 when I started *Sequential Crush*, it was my hope to preserve the genre for future generations, *and* to demonstrate that comic books without superheroes are worthy of attention. Many times over the years, readers have written to me inquiring, "Where are the romance comics of today?" While romance stories and plots are popular in the Manga medium, there remains little romantic fare for those who wish for a more "Western" style. Having gone from being one of the most popular genres in comic books of the mid-century, it is almost hard to believe that from the mid-1970s on, romance would all but disappear.

You might be surprised to hear that it once dominated the newsstands. First created in 1947 by the legendary team of Jack Kirby and Joe Simon (yes, believe it or not, the very same dynamic duo that created the epitome of the superhero—Captain America!), romance comics with titles such as *Young Love*, *Romantic Adventures*, and *Campus Loves* were widely read. Romance comic books were ubiquitous—for every comic book that was on the newsstand between 1949 and mid-1950, approximately one out of four was of the romance variety. Their importance on the landscape of American popular culture can't be denied. From bobby sox wearing high-schoolers of the 1950s to Roy Lichtenstein's pop art swipes, romance comics held, and continue to hold, special allure. Clearly, the genre and its conventions still do for the creative team behind *Ares & Aphrodite*.

With a delicate touch and a swooning glance, *Ares & Aphrodite* plays on many of the themes so central to the romance comics, but with a modern twist. Heartbreak, jealousy, inner-strength, doubt; all a part of the original romance comics, and all still ever-present and relatable to the modern audience when it comes to love and dating today. Even the title itself, *Ares & Aphrodite*, is a play on two of the most timeless elements of any romance story—love and war. The original romance comics excelled in creating tension between potential lovers, and you better believe that this story does, too. Though leading lady Gigi sheds nary a tear as her romance comic ancestors once did, she embodies the main qualities that make the romance comics of yesteryear so appealing on a human level—Gigi has insecurities and vulnerabilities. Will Ares does too, for that matter. It is these imperfections that have us rooting for these characters, and what makes their eventual romance so triumphant.

The Hollywood setting that *Ares & Aphrodite* occupies is one that is familiar to many a vintage romance comic book. Perhaps the most well-known of these Hollywood stories being the Jim Steranko-illustrated "My Heart Broke in Hollywood" from *Our Love Story* #5 (June 1970). When you think about it, Hollywood is the perfect place for a romantic tale. Stories set in Tinseltown are full of glamour, beauty, wealthy and powerful directors, doe-eyed ingénues waiting for their turn in the spotlight, and most importantly for a romance story: *heartbreak*. This setting was *so* alluring that Charlton comics even had an entire title dedicated to the movie industry called *Hollywood Romances* that ran from 1966 through 1971. Occupations and the daily ins and outs of the characters' respective jobs were very important in the pages of romance stories. They were so important that often in romance comics, it is these jobs that cause the main characters to meet, just as Will and Gigi do. Though many stories from the 1940s through the 1970s focused on the careers available for women at the time, such as secretary, flight attendant, and nurse; actresses, models, dancers and other showbiz types were common. What makes *Ares & Aphrodite* unique in the tradition of the Hollywood-set romances, is the fact that it focuses on the "little people," the folks behind the people on camera. And as so many of us know, oftentimes the people on the periphery are far more interesting than those directly in the spotlight.

Though admittedly, I have been reluctant to embrace new romance comics, I am delighted that Jamie asked me to be a part of *Ares & Aphrodite*. I'm extremely excited for the future of the genre. It is my hope that new readers to the romance genre will pick this up and feel a connection to the story, just as I did so many years ago when I fell in love with the romance comics from the 1960s and '70s. Though the "golden age" of romance comics may be over, it is high time for a new era to be ushered in. I am confident that *Ares & Aphrodite* will not only stand the test of time, but will be one of the modern romance tales that leads the way for a true resurgence in the genre. After all, how can the beat of a heart or the thrill of new love…be anything but timeless?

—*Jacque Nodell, 2014*
*www.sequentialcrush.com*

# BONUS MATERIAL

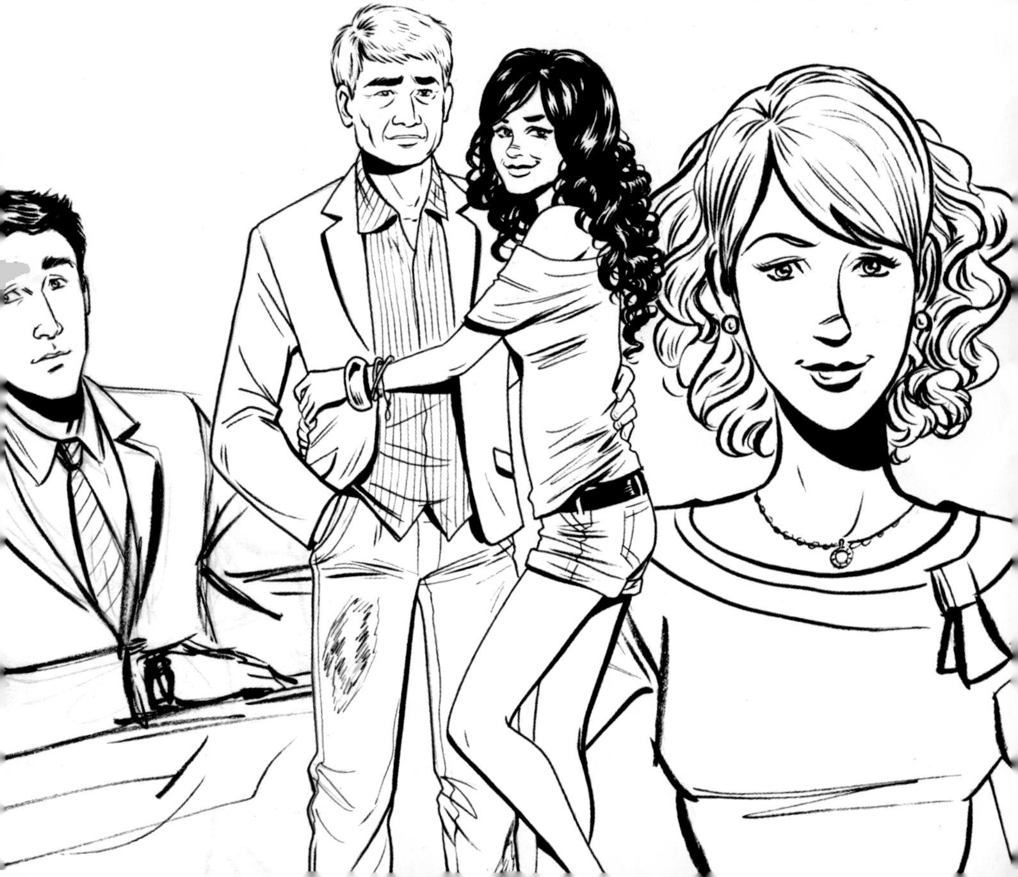

*the following pages show the art process for page 7 of*

# ARES&APHRODITE

*(page 13 in the book)*

# PAGE 7

PANEL 1

Outside the house, the pair separate, heading to their respective cars.

I am thinking in contrast to Will's car, Gigi's should be more sensible. Maybe more round.

Or maybe larger. Like an SUV.

[As per our e-mail, don't forget to make this house have a large driveway, maybe circular, so that at different times, Gigi and Will can talk around their cars.

Also, I liked your idea of her having a Mini or a modern Bug.]

PANEL 2

Los Angeles traffic. Perhaps an aerial shot of the freeway, the wall to wall cars, etc. Gigi's car is amongst them. We have split from Will and gone with her.

PANEL 3

Gigi sits in her car, bored, waiting to move.

> RADIO
> ...is another Carmageddon upon us? It's bumper-to-bumper, like a long metal serpent winding along the highways...

PANEL 4

Gigi pulling up on the street in front of her shop.

We see the name of the store painted on the window, wedding gowns behind the glass.

> WINDOW
> (logo)
> GODDESS OF LOVE NUPTIALS
> (smaller)
> Weddings by Gigi Averelle

# THUMBNAILS

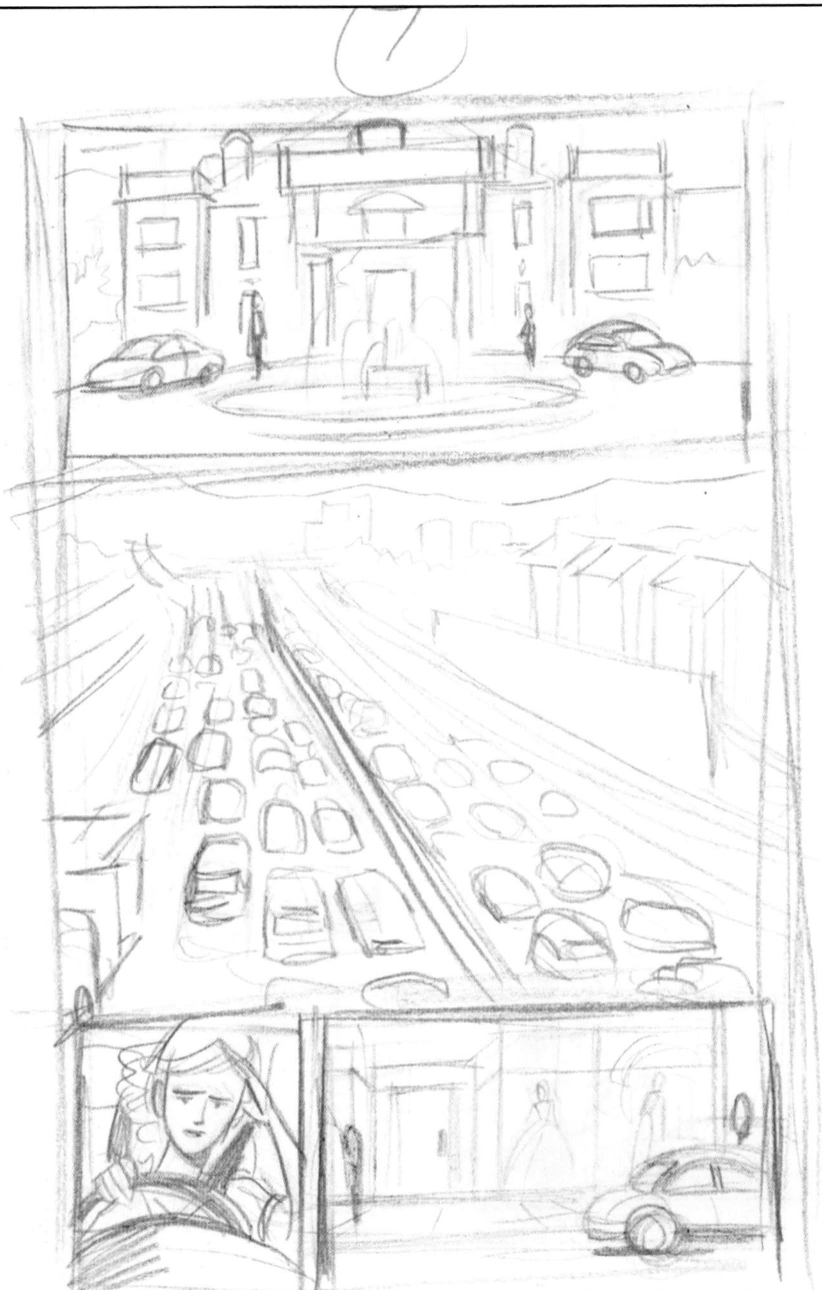

# PENCILS

CANSON
COMIC BOOK ART BOARD
TITLE A&A
ISSUE # 1 PAGE# 7 DATE
CREATED BY
EXTEND ALL BLEED ART TO SOLID OUTER LINE

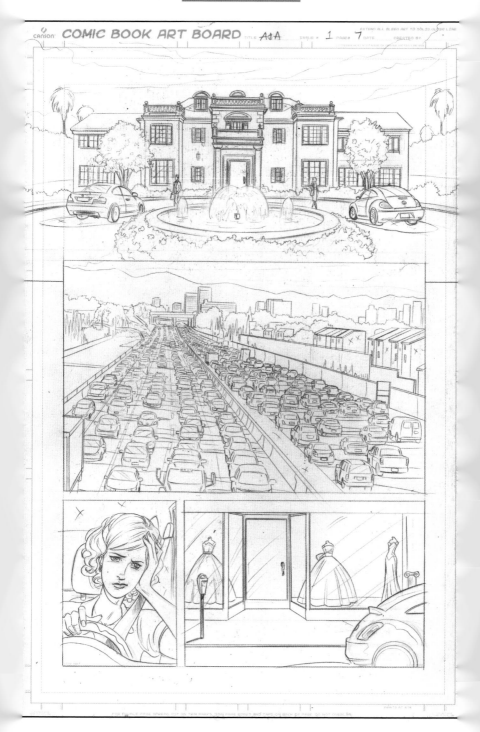

# INKS

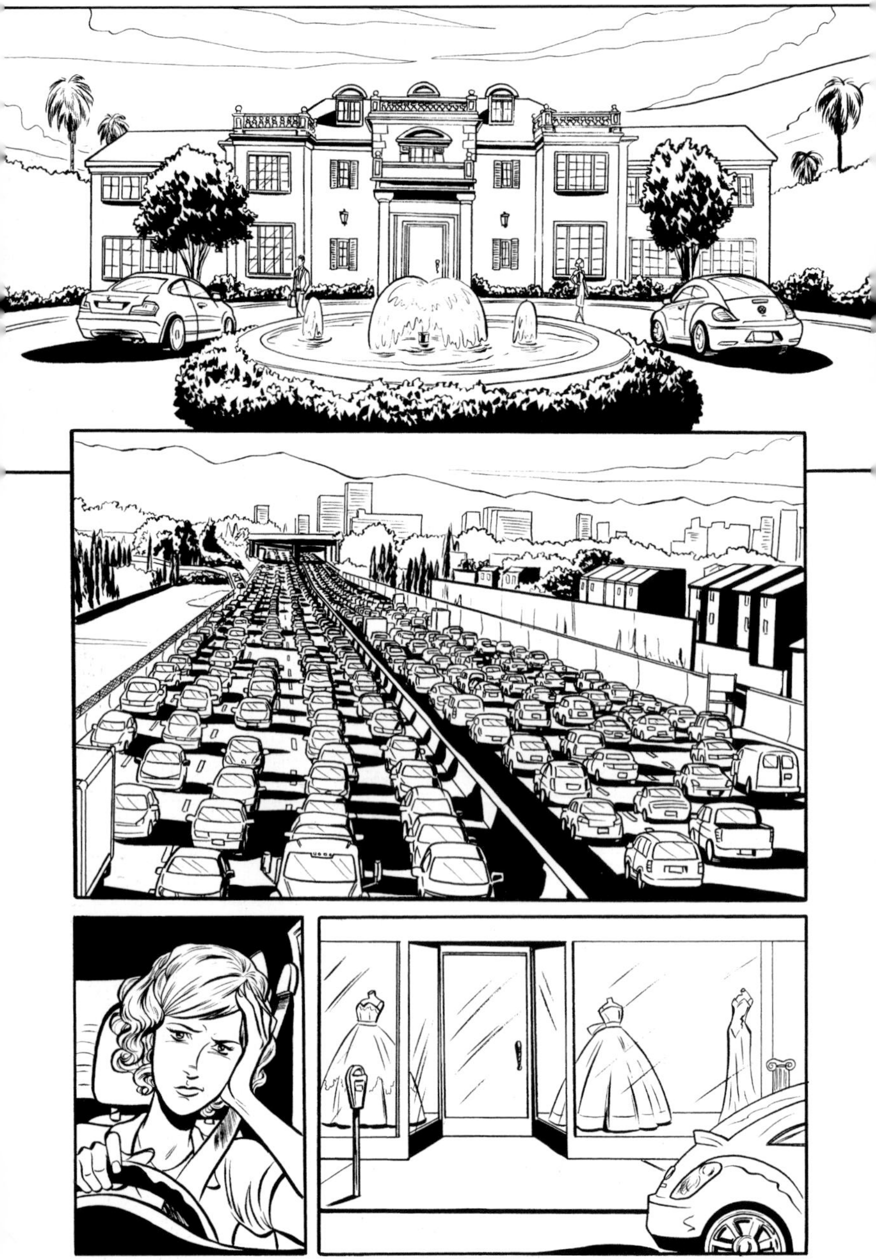

# COLORS

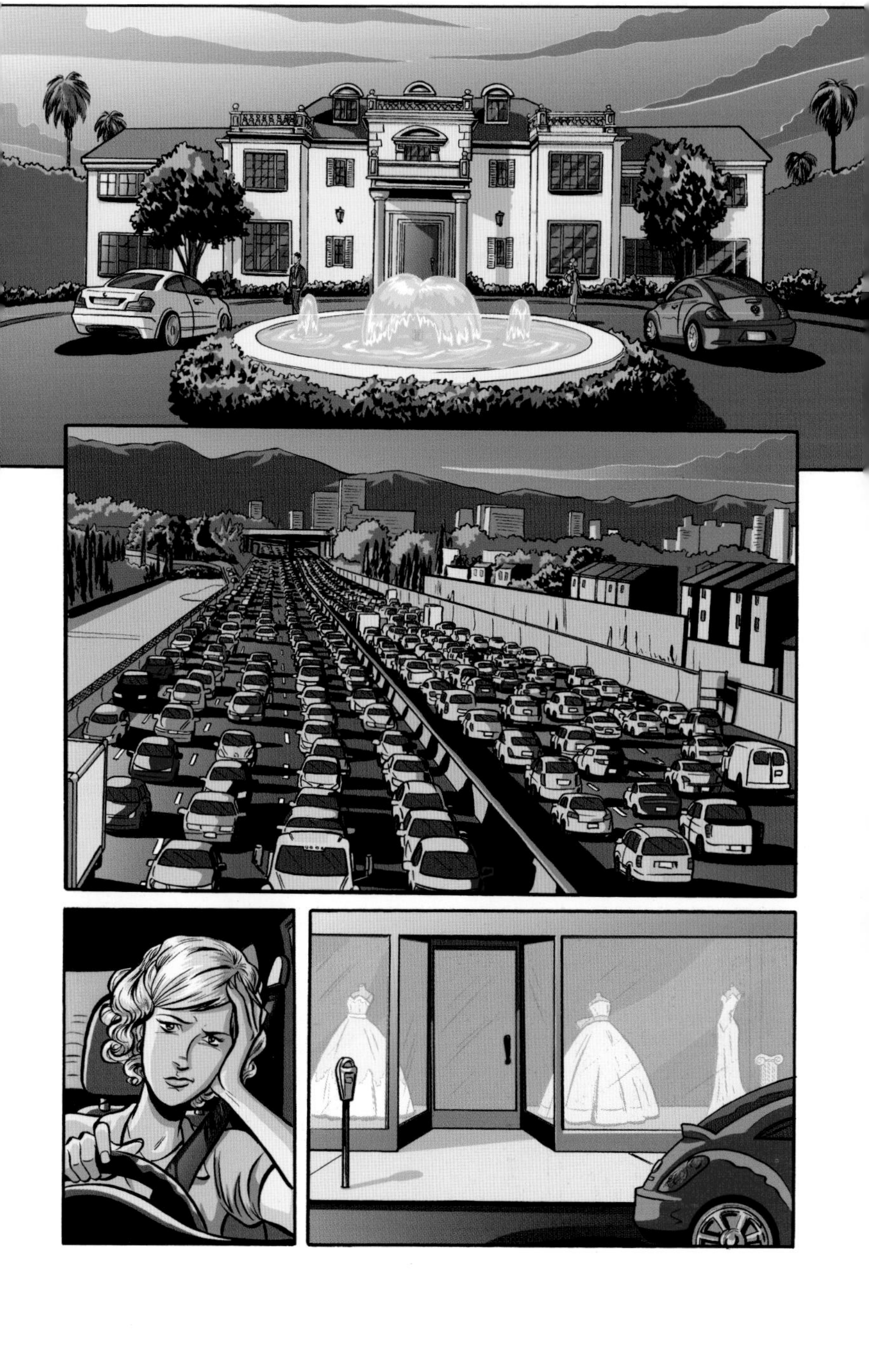

# TWO WHEELS, TWO FEET

The story "Two Wheels, Two Feet" has had a long gestation period for something so short. I originally wrote it in 2007 for an anthology that never happened. When Megan and I started talking about working with each other in 2009, I handed her the script to see if she wanted to draw it as a trial run. She did…and then nothing happened with it.

Not until 2011, when Mike Norton asked if I wanted to do something for the Valentine's Day issue of *Double Feature*, a digital anthology he and Tim Seeley put together under their own Four Star Studios banner. It was like fate…or something. We owe a huge thanks to those dudes.

By the way, bridges in Portland, OR really do have those clearly demarcated lanes for pedestrians and bicyclists. Stay on your side of the line!

*—Jamie*

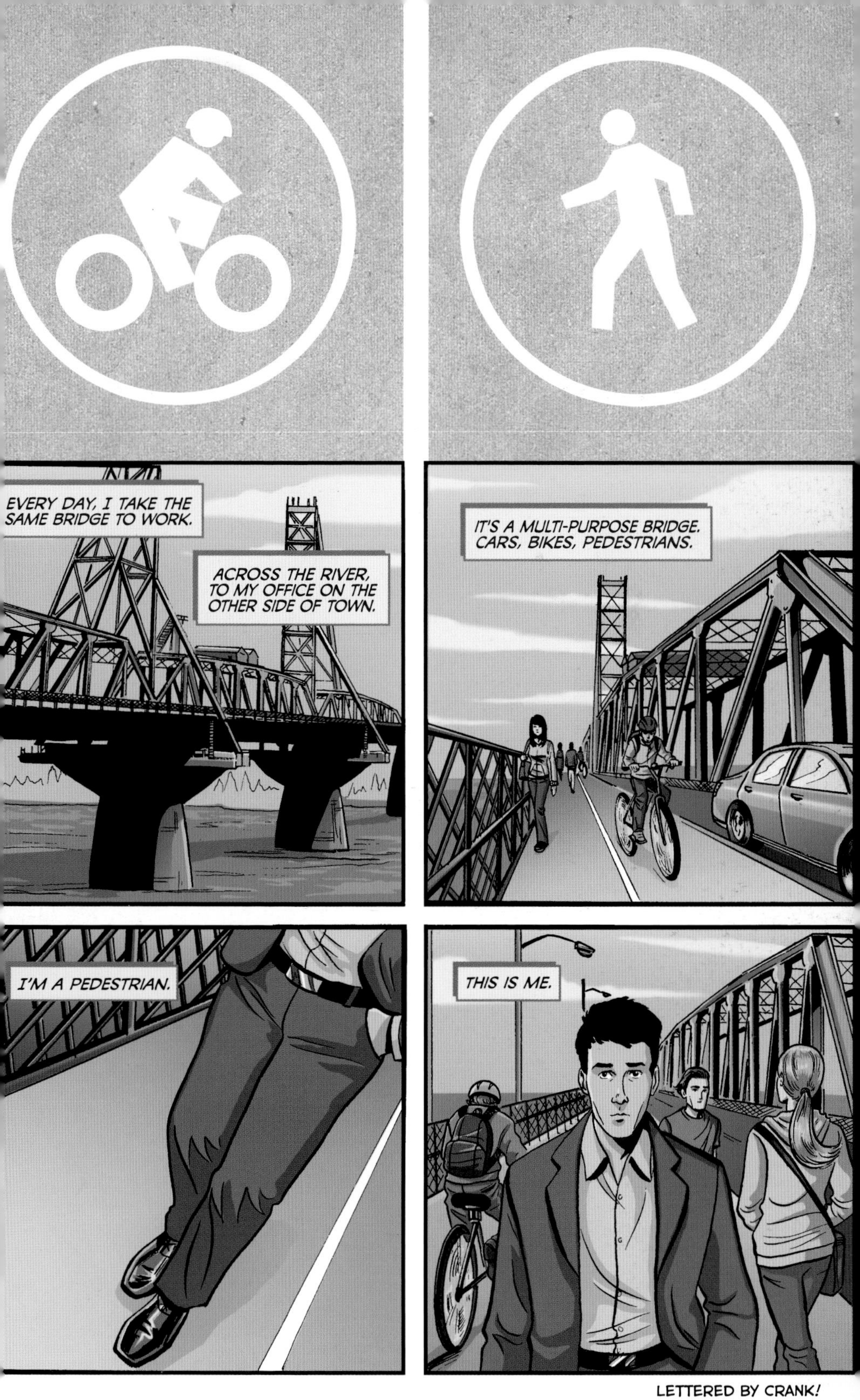
EVERY DAY, I TAKE THE SAME BRIDGE TO WORK.
ACROSS THE RIVER, TO MY OFFICE ON THE OTHER SIDE OF TOWN.
IT'S A MULTI-PURPOSE BRIDGE. CARS, BIKES, PEDESTRIANS.
I'M A PEDESTRIAN.
THIS IS ME.

LETTERED BY CRANK!

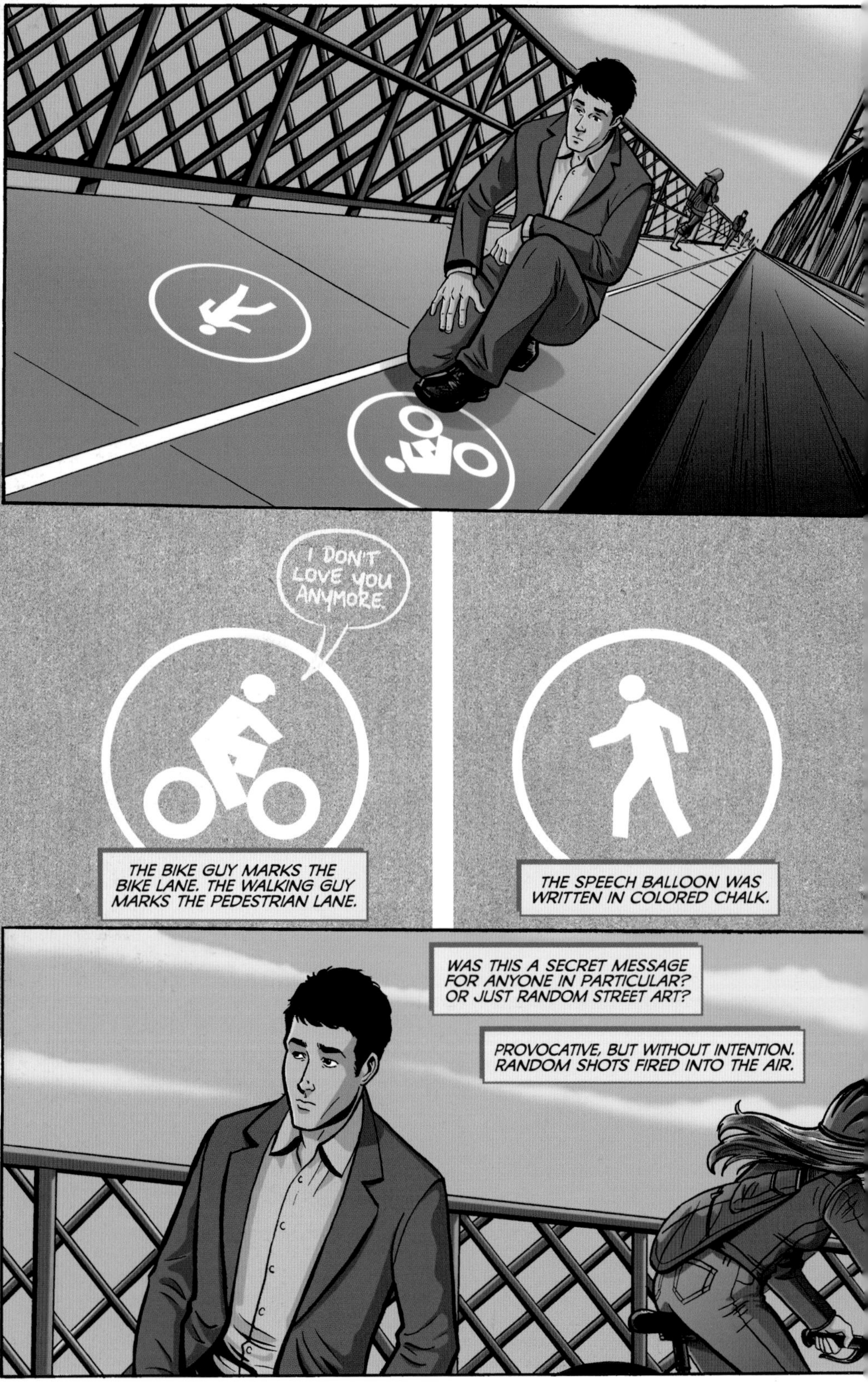
I DON'T LOVE YOU ANYMORE.
THE BIKE GUY MARKS THE BIKE LANE. THE WALKING GUY MARKS THE PEDESTRIAN LANE.
THE SPEECH BALLOON WAS WRITTEN IN COLORED CHALK.
WAS THIS A SECRET MESSAGE FOR ANYONE IN PARTICULAR? OR JUST RANDOM STREET ART?
PROVOCATIVE, BUT WITHOUT INTENTION. RANDOM SHOTS FIRED INTO THE AIR.

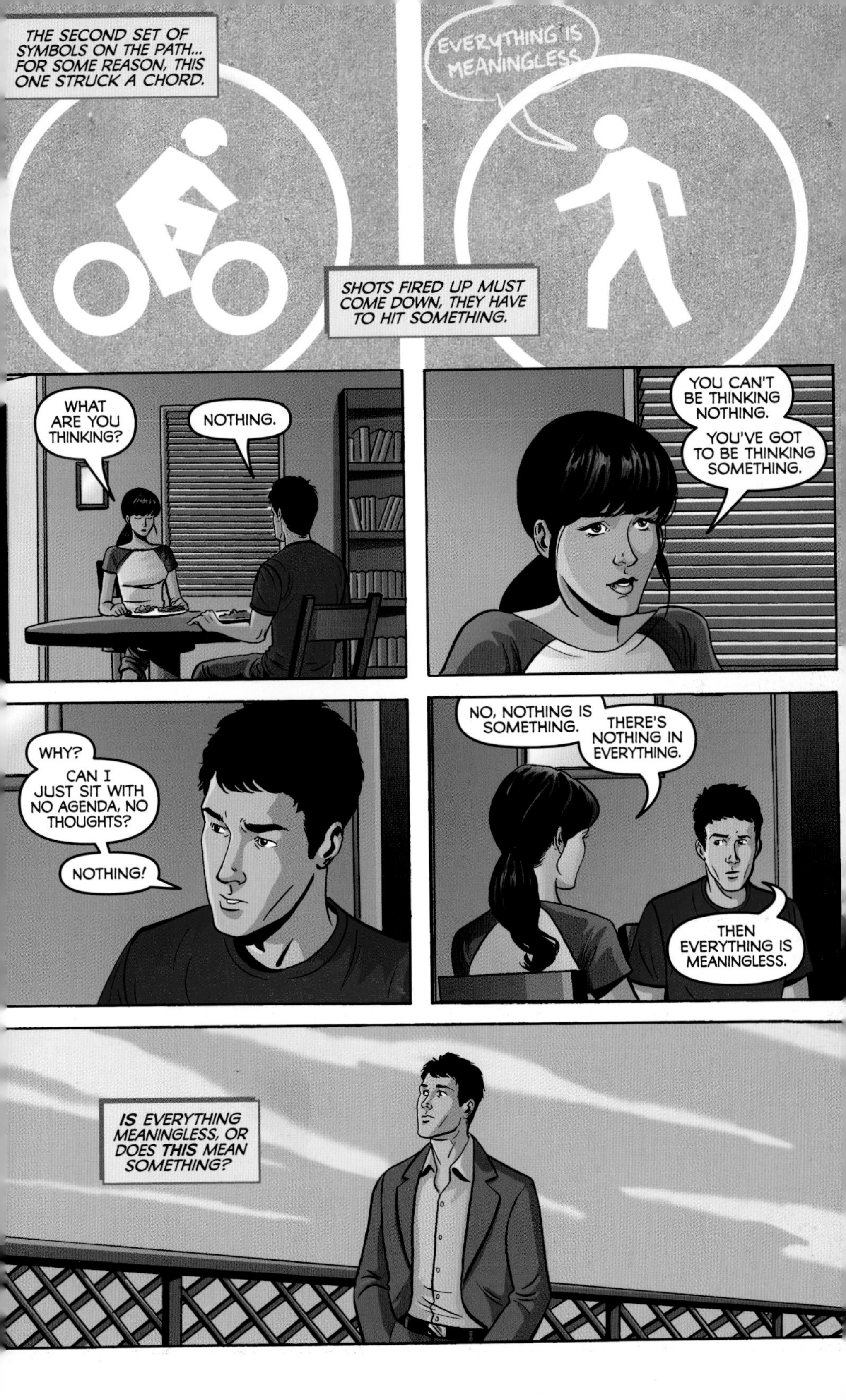
THE SECOND SET OF SYMBOLS ON THE PATH... FOR SOME REASON, THIS ONE STRUCK A CHORD.
EVERYTHING IS MEANINGLESS
SHOTS FIRED UP MUST COME DOWN, THEY HAVE TO HIT SOMETHING.
WHAT ARE YOU THINKING?
NOTHING.
YOU CAN'T BE THINKING NOTHING.
YOU'VE GOT TO BE THINKING SOMETHING.
WHY?
CAN I JUST SIT WITH NO AGENDA, NO THOUGHTS?
NOTHING!
NO, NOTHING IS SOMETHING.
THERE'S NOTHING IN EVERYTHING.
THEN EVERYTHING IS MEANINGLESS.
IS EVERYTHING MEANINGLESS, OR DOES THIS MEAN SOMETHING?

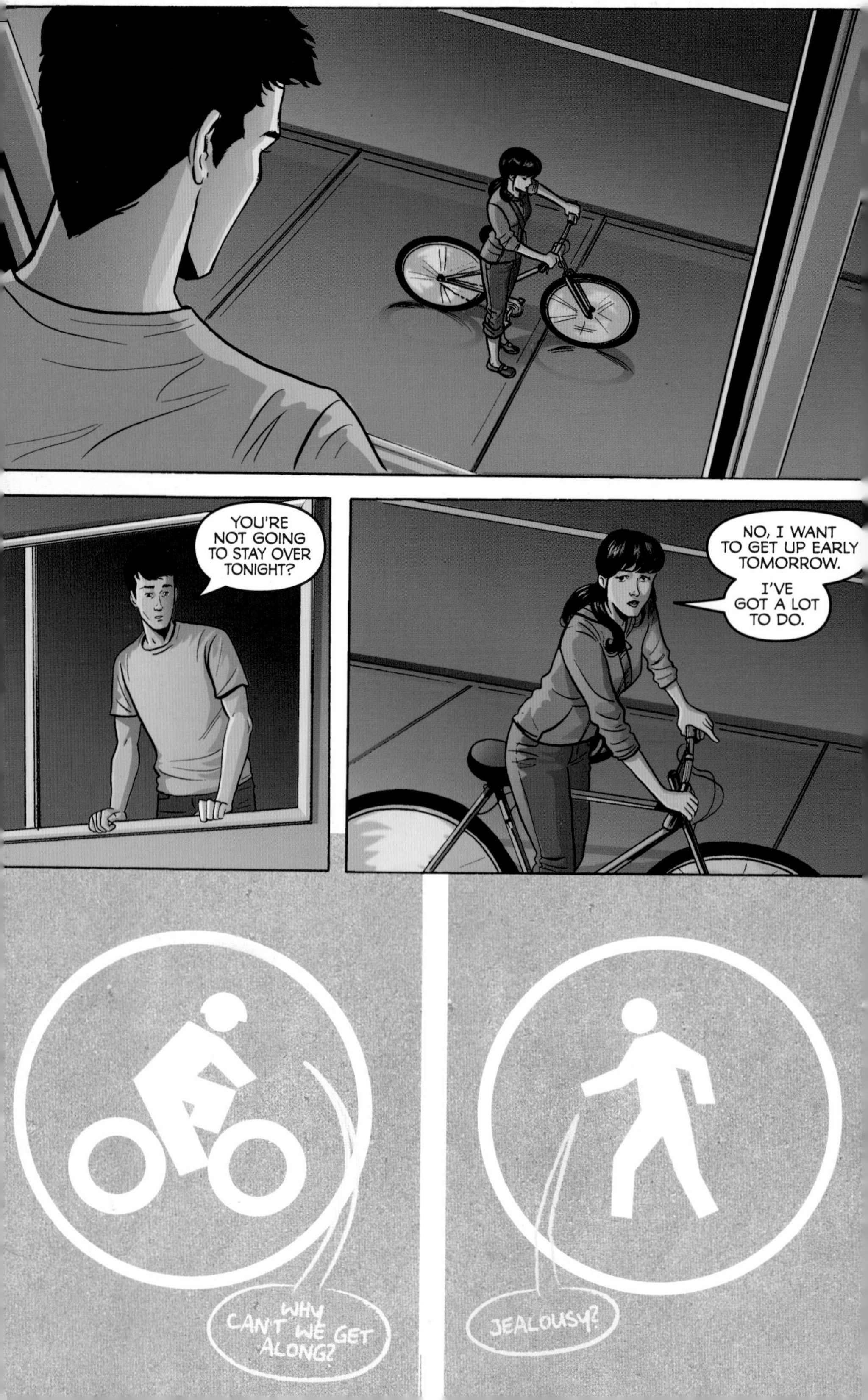
YOU'RE NOT GOING TO STAY OVER TONIGHT?
NO, I WANT TO GET UP EARLY TOMORROW.
I'VE GOT A LOT TO DO.
WHY CAN'T WE GET ALONG?
JEALOUSY?

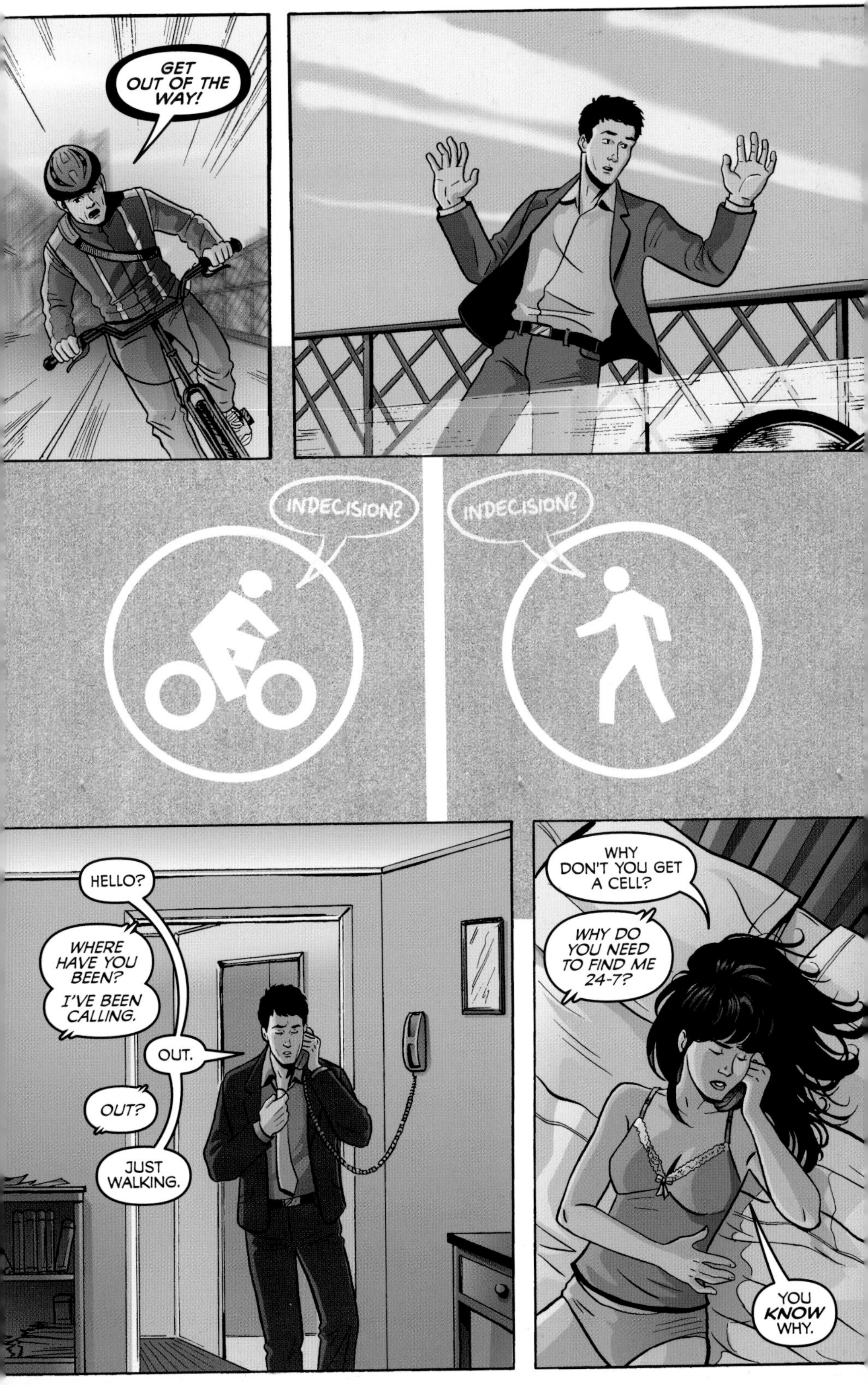
GET OUT OF THE WAY!
INDECISION?
INDECISION?
HELLO?
WHERE HAVE YOU BEEN?
I'VE BEEN CALLING.
OUT.
OUT?
JUST WALKING.
WHY DON'T YOU GET A CELL?
WHY DO YOU NEED TO FIND ME 24-7?
YOU KNOW WHY.

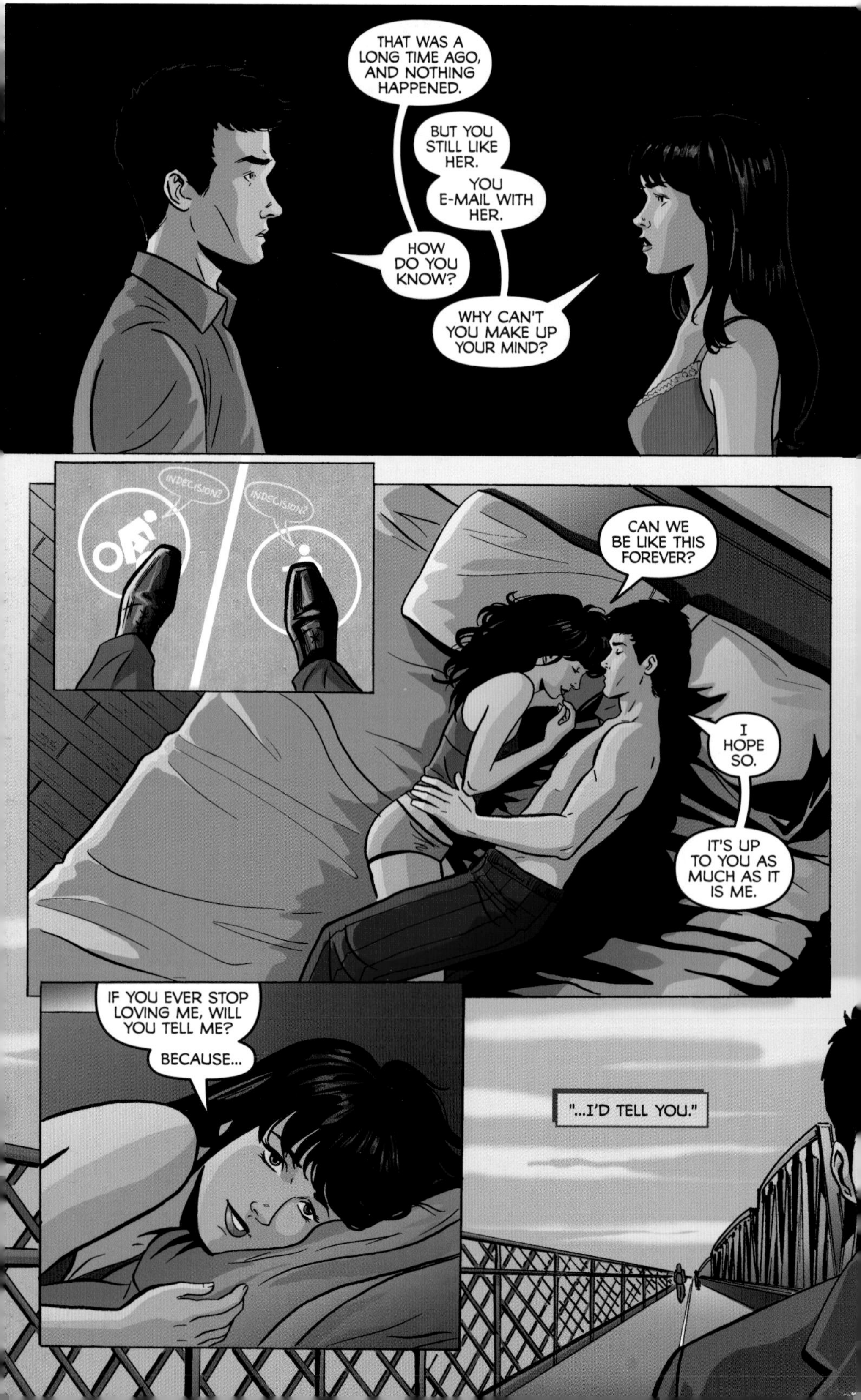
THAT WAS A LONG TIME AGO, AND NOTHING HAPPENED.
BUT YOU STILL LIKE HER.
YOU E-MAIL WITH HER.
HOW DO YOU KNOW?
WHY CAN'T YOU MAKE UP YOUR MIND?
INDECISION?
INDECISION?
CAN WE BE LIKE THIS FOREVER?
I HOPE SO.
IT'S UP TO YOU AS MUCH AS IT IS ME.
IF YOU EVER STOP LOVING ME, WILL YOU TELL ME?
BECAUSE...
"...I'D TELL YOU."

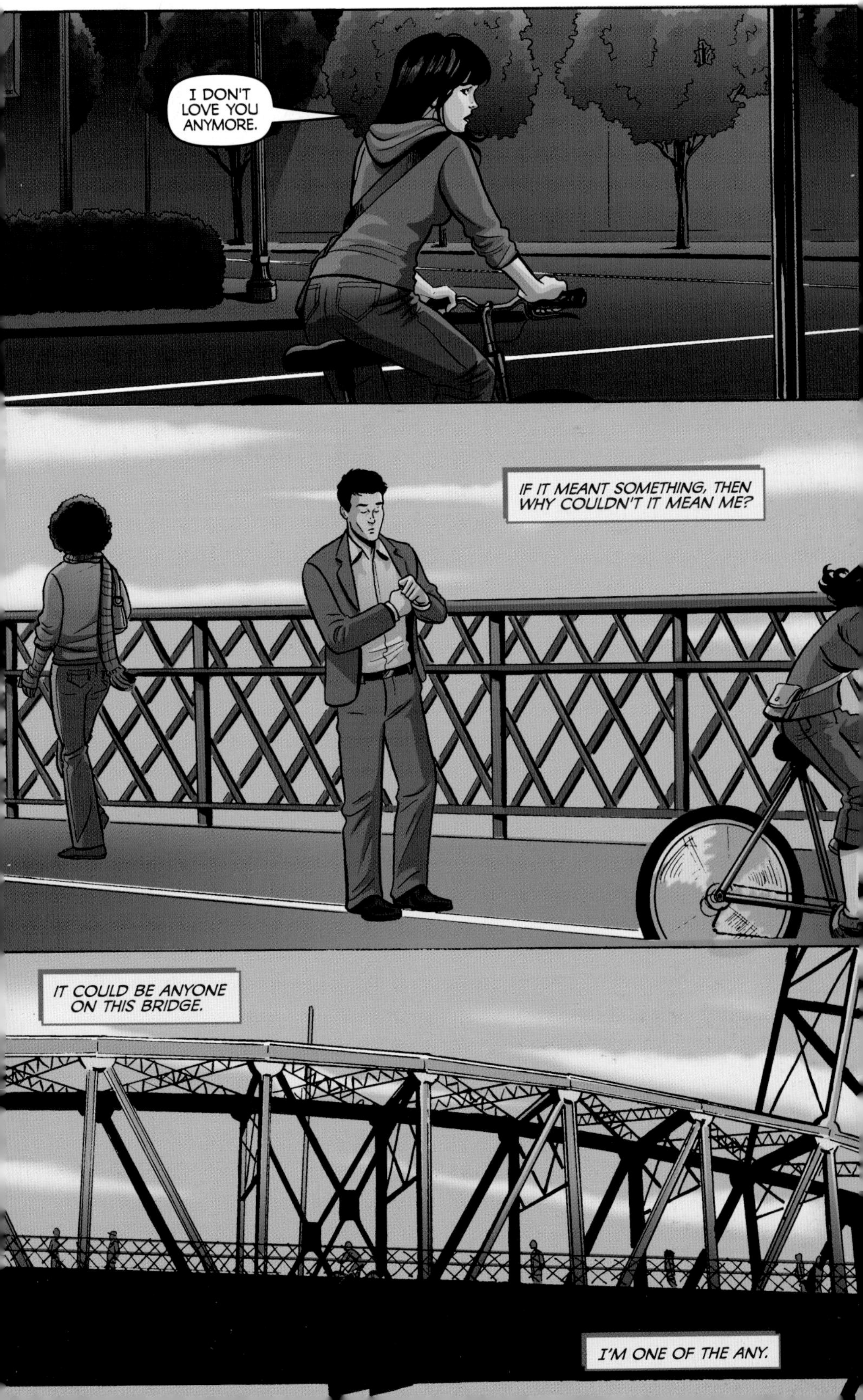
I DON'T LOVE YOU ANYMORE.
IF IT MEANT SOMETHING, THEN WHY COULDN'T IT MEAN ME?
IT COULD BE ANYONE ON THIS BRIDGE.
I'M ONE OF THE ANY.

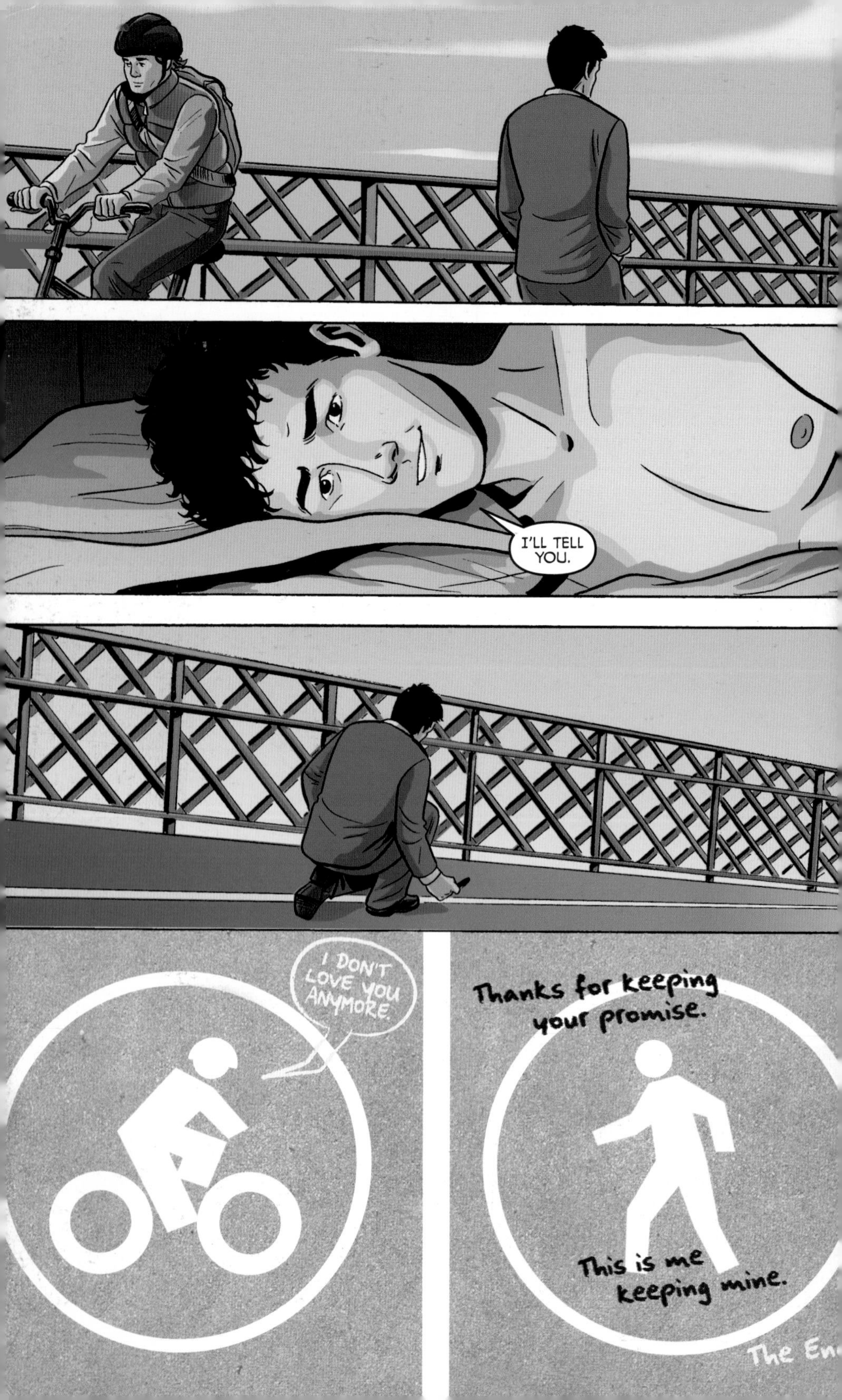
I'LL TELL YOU.
I DON'T LOVE YOU ANYMORE.
Thanks for keeping your promise.
This is me keeping mine.
The En

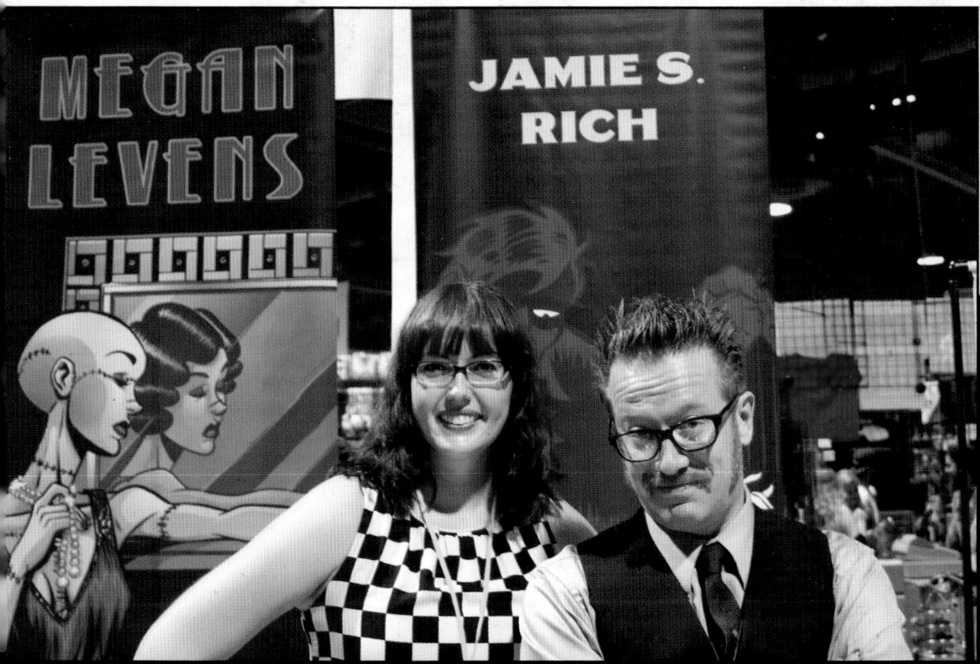
MEGAN
LEVENS
JAMIE S.
RICH

*Jamie S. Rich* is an author whose venues include Oni Press, Image Comics, DVDTalk.com, and various dive bars around Portland, OR. He is best known for his collaborations with artist Joëlle Jones on the graphic novels *12 Reasons Why I Love Her*, *You Have Killed Me*, and, most recently, *Lady Killer*. He published his first prose novel, *Cut My Hair*, in 2000, and his first superhero comic book, *It Girl and the Atomics*, in 2012. In between, he has worked on multiple projects in both mediums, including his most recent graphic novels, *A Boy and a Girl*, drawn by Natalie Nourigat, and *Archer Coe and the Thousand Natural Shocks* with Dan Christensen. He previously collaborated with Megan Levens on the horror comic *Madame Frankenstein*. Currently, Rich reviews film for the Oregonian and blogs at confessions123.com.

Born and raised in rural Missouri, *Megan Levens* began her art career as soon as she was old enough to draw on the walls. Fortunately, her parents never liked that wallpaper design very much anyway. After graduating from the Savannah College of Art and Design's sequential art program, Megan moved to Los Angeles to begin a career in advertising illustration, which helped support the pursuit of her lifelong dream to draw comics. *Madame Frankenstein* (Image Comics) was her first published comics work, and second collaboration with writer Jamie S. Rich, after the Oni Press romance *Ares & Aphrodite: Love Wars*. She also recently worked on the *Buffy the Vampire Slayer* comic books for Dark Horse.

Photo by Aron Tiongco
Follow on Instagram @LoveAndComics

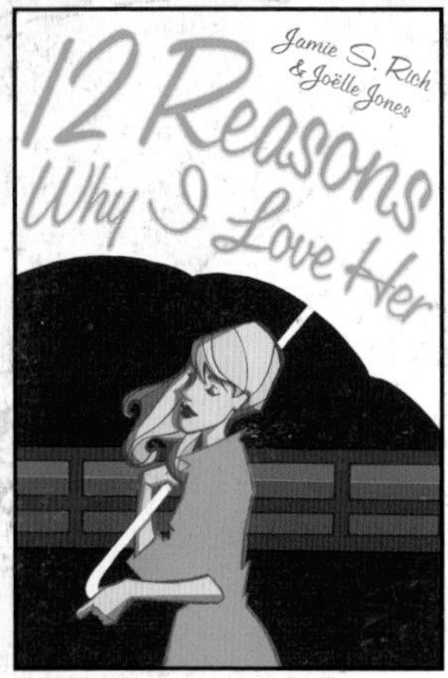
Jamie S. Rich
& Joëlle Jones
12 Reasons
Why I Love Her

**12 REASONS WHY I LOVE HER**
By Jamie S. Rich & Joëlle Jones
152 pages, Softcover, B&W interior
ISBN 978-1-932664-51-5

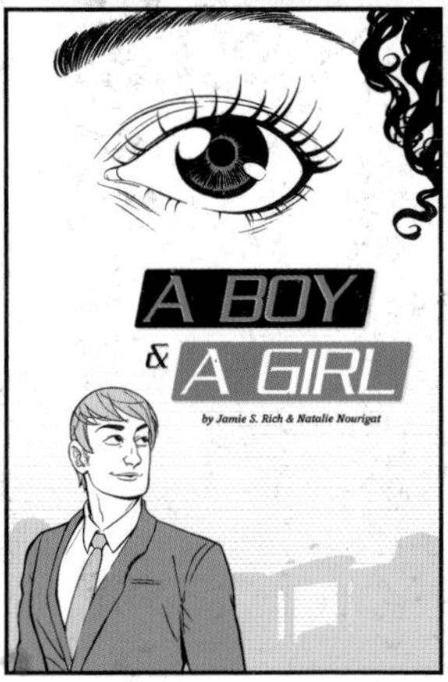
A BOY
& A GIRL
by Jamie S. Rich & Natalie Nourigat

**A BOY AND A GIRL**
By Jamie S. Rich & Natalie Nourigat
176 pages, Softcover, 2-Color interior
ISBN 978-1-62010-089-9

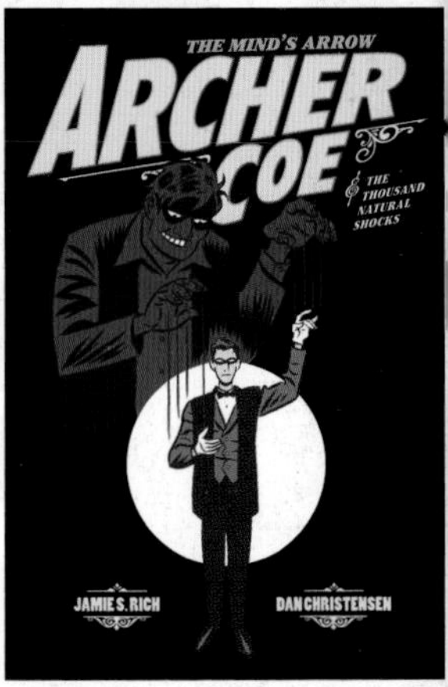
THE MIND'S ARROW
ARCHER
COE
THE THOUSAND NATURAL SHOCKS
JAMIE S. RICH
DAN CHRISTENSEN

**ARCHER COE & THE THOUSAND NATURAL SHOCKS**
By Jamie S. Rich & Dan Christensen
160 pages, Softcover, B&W interior
ISBN 978-1-62010-121-6

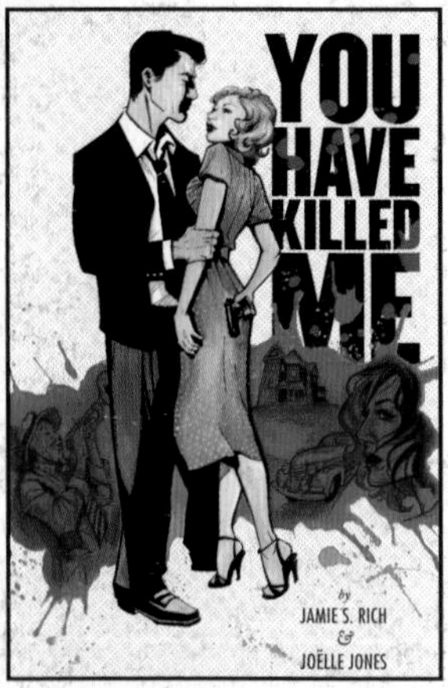
YOU
HAVE
KILLED
ME
by
JAMIE S. RICH
&
JOËLLE JONES

**YOU HAVE KILLED ME**
By Jamie S. Rich & Joëlle Jones
192 pages, Hardcover, B&W interior
ISBN 978-1-932664-88-1

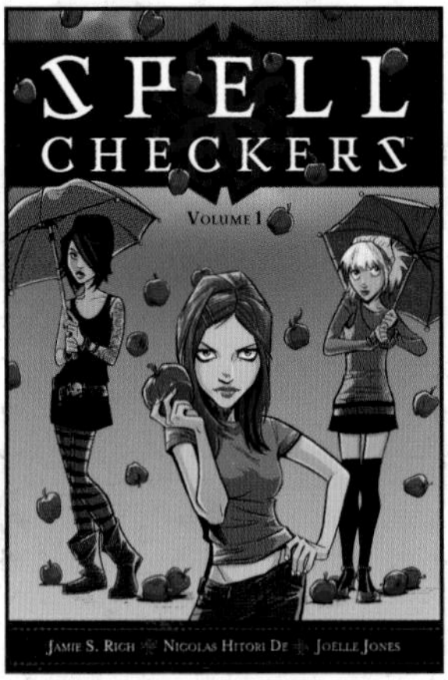
SPELL
CHECKERS
VOLUME 1
JAMIE S. RICH
NICOLAS HITORI DE
JOËLLE JONES

**SPELL CHECKERS, VOL. ONE**
By Jamie S. Rich, Nicolas Hitori De, Joëlle Jones
152 pages, Softcover, B&W interior
ISBN 978-1-934964-32-3

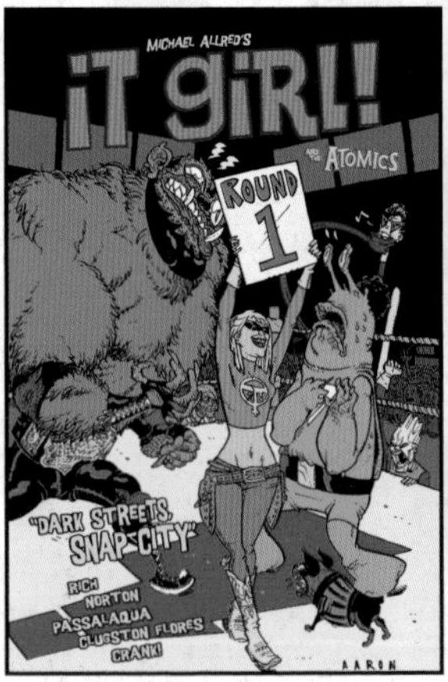
MICHAEL ALLRED'S
iT GiRL!
AND THE ATOMICS
ROUND 1
"DARK STREETS SNAP CITY"
RICH
NORTON
PASSALAQUA
CLUGSTON FLORES
CRANK!

**IT GIRL & THE ATOMICS, VOL. ONE**
By Jamie S. Rich, Mike Norton,
& Chynna Clugston Flores
168 pages, Softcover, Full Color interior
ISBN 978-1-607067-25-2

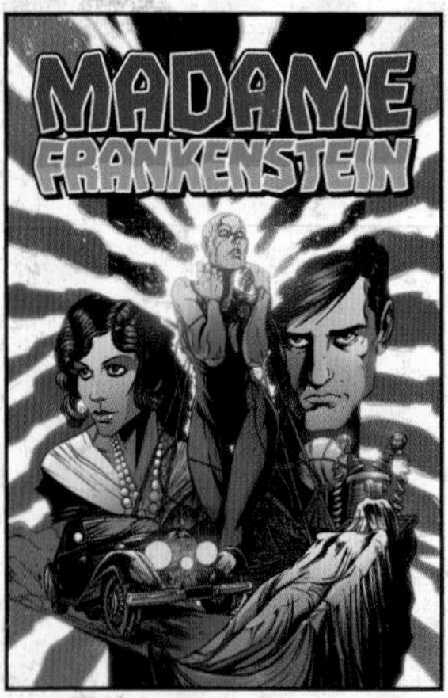
MADAME
FRANKENSTEIN

**MADAME FRANKENSTEIN**
by Megan Levens & Jamie S. Rich
192 pages, Softcover, B&W interior
ISBN 978-1632151-97-1

# MORE FROM JAMIE S. RICH AND MEGAN LEVENS